HUMAN DEVELOPM
SOUTH ASIA 2010/2011

Food Security in South Asia

Published for

The Mahbub ul Haq Human Development Centre
Lahore, Pakistan

OXFORD

UNIVERSITY PRESS

OXFORD
UNIVERSITY PRESS

No. 38, Sector 15, Korangi Industrial Area, PO Box 8214,
Karachi-74900, Pakistan

Oxford University Press is a department of the University of Oxford.
It furthers the University's objective of excellence in research, scholarship,
and education by publishing worldwide in

Oxford New York

Auckland Cape Town Dar es Salaam Hong Kong Karachi
Kuala Lumpur Madrid Melbourne Mexico City Nairobi
New Delhi Shanghai Taipei Toronto

With offices in

Argentina Austria Brazil Chile Czech Republic France Greece
Guatemala Hungary Italy Japan Poland Portugal Singapore
South Korea Switzerland Turkey Ukraine Vietnam

Oxford is a registered trademark of Oxford University Press
in the UK and in certain other countries

Published in Pakistan by Oxford University Press, Karachi

ISBN 978-0-19-906296-6

Typeset in Adobe Garamond Pro
Printed in Pakistan by
New Sketch Graphics, Karachi.
Published by
Ameena Saiyid, Oxford University Press
No. 38, Sector 15, Korangi Industrial Area, PO Box 8214,
Karachi-74900, Pakistan.

AOA	Agreement on Agriculture
APL	Above poverty line
BADC	Bangladesh Agricultural Development Corporation
BBS	Bangladesh Bureau of Statistics
BISP	Benazir Income Support Programme
BMI	Body Mass Index
BPL	Below poverty line
BRAC	Bangladesh Rural Advancement Committee
BRRI	Bangladesh Rice Research Institute
BTK	Bangladeshi taka
CAP	Common Agricultural Policy
CBI	Community-based infrastructure
CED	Chronic energy deficiency
DALYs	Disability-adjusted life years
DCIM	Direct Calorie Intake Method
EU	European Union
FAO	Food and Agriculture Organization of the United Nations
FSP	Food Support Programme
GDP	Gross domestic product
GHI	Global Hunger Index
GLOFs	Glacial lake outburst floods
GNP	Gross national product
HYV	High-yielding varieties
ICM	Integrated coastal management
ICZM	Integrated Coastal Zone Management
IFPRI	International Food Policy Research Institute
ILO	International Labour Organization
INR	Indian rupee
IPRs	Intellectual property rights
IRI	International Research Institute for Climate and Society

LDCF	Least Developed Countries Fund
KPK	Khyber Pakhtunkhwa
MCPAs	Marine and coastal protected areas
MDGs	Millennium Development Goals
MFF	Mangroves for the Future
MGNREGA	Mahatma Gandhi National Rural Employment Guarantee Act
MOA	Memorandum of Agreement
NAPA	National Adaptation Programme of Action
NGOs	Non-governmental organizations
OECD	Organization for Economic Cooperation and Development
PASSCO	Pakistan Storage and Supply Corporation
PFDS	Public Food Distribution System
PKR	Pakistani rupee
PPP	Purchasing power parity
PSMA	Pakistan Sugar Mills Association
R&D	Research and development
SCs	Scheduled Castes
SEWA	Self-Employed Women's Association
SPI	Sensitive Price Index
STs	Scheduled Tribes
TCB	Trading Corporation of Bangladesh
TCP	Trading Corporation of Pakistan
TPDS	Targeted Public Distribution System
TRIPS	Trade-Related Intellectual Property Rights
TNCs	Transnational corporations
UN	United Nations
US	United States of America
WFP	World Food Programme
WPI	Wholesale Price Index
WTO	World Trade Organization

Foreword

This has been an eventful year for Mahbub ul Haq Human Development Centre (MHHDC). This is the year the Centre moved to Lahore to establish its new home within the campus of the Lahore University of Management Sciences (LUMS). I am so grateful to that visionary Pakistani, Syed Babar Ali, the founder of LUMS and now a benefactor of MHHDC. This shift to LUMS has been a dream come true to me as I always wanted to be a part of a great academic community. My thanks go to Syed Babar Ali, the Board of Governors of LUMS, the Vice Chancellor of LUMS, and to all faculty members, teachers and students. We are grateful to be here, to be a part of your community.

This report on *Food Security in South Asia* has been done over a period of two years, 2010–2011. This is not only due to the fact that the Centre was in the midst of a major shift to its new location, it is also because of the diminution of our staff capacity. During the year 2010 we lost a number of our staff members to other organizations. However, the remaining staff and our collaborators in the region showed a tremendous amount of stamina to do the work and complete the report. I am so grateful to them.

The report focuses on the imperative of ensuring food security for all in South Asia. The human development model asserts that socio-economic justice is the corner stone of sustaining economic growth and building social cohesion. Economic growth that is not linked to peoples' lives cannot be sustained either socially or politically.

The report presents critical analyses of all dimensions of food security—food availability, access, and absorption—and argues that if the current trend of rising poverty and hunger is not addressed by governments and other policy makers, the ethical foundation of these societies would disintegrate. The report further argues that the global and regional institutions of governance must implement the many policies and goals that they have devised over the years.

The report contains seven chapters, in addition to the Overview. Chapter 1 analyses the conceptual framework of food security. Chapter 2 critically analyses the food security situation in India. Chapter 3 describes the food security issues in Pakistan and presents some options for policy makers. Chapter 4 explores the very interesting case of Bangladesh where despite a very difficult economic and climatic condition, the food security of the majority is being addressed by adopting a number of policy tools. Chapter 5 analyses the critical role played by women of South Asia in food production, access and absorption. Chapter 6 looks at the environmental impact of climate change on food security. Finally, chapter 7 briefly analyses the results of global commitments to food security.

I would like to put on record my very grateful thanks to the Royal Norwegian Embassy for supporting the preparation of this report. Without Norway's consistent support, it would not have been possible for the Centre to do this work. I would also like to acknowledge the contribution of the United Nations Development Programme (UNDP) Asia-Pacific Regional Centre, Bangkok.

Human Development in South Asia 2010/2011 has been prepared under the direction of Khadija Haq, President of the MHHDC. The outline of this report was developed with the help of Sartaj Aziz and M. Syeduzzaman, both prominent scholars in food and agriculture. I must first offer my grateful thanks to them for their contributions. Research was conducted by a small team consisting of Nazam Maqbool and Umer Malik, with contributions from Abeer Masood, Seeme Mallick and Shazra Murad. I would like to convey my deep gratitude to Dr Smita Gupta of the Indian Institute of Human Development for contributing an excellent paper for this report. Dr Quazi Shahabuddin and Dr Uttam Kumar Deb, formerly of the Centre for Policy Dialogue in Dhaka, wrote the country paper for Bangladesh. We could not have got a better team to write about this topic. This is the kind of South Asian collaboration that keeps this Centre both alive and relevant for South Asia.

Khadija Haq

Lahore
18 May 2011

Team for the preparation of the 2010/2011 Report

Coordinator and Principal Author: Khadija Haq

Core team:

Nazam Maqbool
Umer Malik

Consultants:

Abeer Masood
Seeme Mallick
Shazra Murad
Smita Gupta (India)
Uttam Kumar Deb (Bangladesh)
Quazi Shahabuddin (Bangladesh)

Acknowledgements

The preparation of this report owes a great deal to many individuals and organizations. The financial support for the report was provided by the Royal Norwegian Embassy, and UNDP Asia-Pacific Regional Centre, in particular the UNDP Regional Centre in Colombo.

We would also like to thank the United Nations Information Centre (Pakistan), and the librarians of the ILO, World Bank and PIDE libraries in Islamabad for their kind assistance.

We are always thankful to the Oxford University Press, Pakistan for the professional manner in which they handle the publication of our report. We wish to thank particularly Ameena Saiyid for her commitment to this project.

About Mahbub ul Haq Human Development Centre

Under the umbrella of Foundation for Human Development in Pakistan, Mahbub ul Haq Human Development Centre was set up in November 1995 in Islamabad, Pakistan by the late Dr Mahbub ul Haq, founder and chief architect of the United Nations Development Programme (UNDP) Human Development Reports. With a special focus on South Asia, the Centre is a policy research institute and think tank, committed to the promotion of the human development paradigm as a powerful tool for informing people-centred development policy, nationally and regionally.

The Centre organizes professional research, policy studies and seminars on issues of economic and social development as they affect people's well-being. Believing in the shared histories of the people of this region and in their shared destinies, Dr Haq was convinced of the need for cooperation among the seven countries of the region. His vision extended to a comparative analysis of the region with the outside world, providing a yardstick for the progress achieved by South Asia in terms of socio-economic development. The Centre's research work is presented annually through a report titled, *Human Development in South Asia.*

Continuing Mahbub ul Haq's legacy, the Centre provides a unique perspective in three ways: first, by analysing the process of human development, the analytical work of the Centre puts people at the centre of economic, political and social policies; second, the South Asia regional focus of the Centre enables a rich examination of issues of regional importance; and third, the Centre's comparative analysis provides a yardstick for the progress and setbacks of South Asia vis-à-vis the rest of the world.

The current activities of the Centre include: preparation of annual reports on *Human Development in South Asia*; preparation of *Pakistan National Human Development Report 2011: Human Security in Pakistan*; publication of a collection of unpublished papers of Mahbub ul Haq; preparation of policy papers and research reports on poverty reduction strategies; organization of seminars and conferences on global and regional human development issues, South Asian cooperation, peace in the region and women's empowerment.

Mahbub ul Haq Human Development Centre
Lahore University of Management Sciences
Opposite Sector U, DHA, Lahore Cantt, 54792.
Tel: 042-35608000 ext. 4435 Fax: 92-42-35748713
e-mail: hdc@comsats.net.pk website: www.mhhdc.org

Contents

Chapter 6

Impact of Climate Change on Food Security in South Asia   117

Chapter 7

Global Commitments to Food Security   127

Boxes

Tables

Figures

Overview

'Oh God that bread should be so dear
And flesh and blood so cheap.'
— Thomas Hood*

Since 2008, the world has been experiencing a food crisis when the majority of the developing nations in the world have been failing to meet the challenge of adequate food requirements for all their people. For the vast majority of the South Asians food insecurity has become the most urgent concern. The region's food insecurity has been worsening starting with the global food, fuel and financial crises, and these challenges got exacerbated by a number of the region's domestic challenges such as, declining availability of food, runaway food inflation, violent conflicts, high levels of job loss, and the adverse effects of climate change on food security. Each of the three large countries of South Asia that are the focus of this report has been experiencing increased hunger, malnutrition and poverty. And this is the scenario when the economic growth in the region, particularly in the largest country India, has been consistently high over the decade, when a new class of consumers with sophisticated taste in food and lifestyle has risen in the region, and when resources are available in each country to ensure food security for all its people including the poor and the marginalized. So this is not a report about scarcity of food. This is about the inability of policy makers to address the plight of the poor. And it is also an exploration of the possibility to overcome the constraints to food security through a people-centred development philosophy.

Strong economic growth is a prerequisite for improvement of human development as it provides the required resources for improving the provision of social services as well as income-earning opportunities. However, the benefits of economic growth have to be equitably distributed through progressive public policy initiatives to achieve maximum welfare gains for all people, irrespective of class, caste or gender. This was the message of the founder of the Centre, Mahbub ul Haq, and the focus of the Centre's annual Human Development Reports. Thus the theme of this report, Food Security in South Asia, is also based on the belief that an equitable GDP growth is not only good for the economy it is also good for the country as a whole, as it improves the availability of and access to food, thus improving the well-being of all people—poor and rich alike.

Food insecurity is caused by a variety of economic, political, social and environmental factors. Food availability is dependent on domestic production, imports, stocks and aid. Access is determined by income, purchasing power, assets distribution, demography, market infrastructure, and social safety net programmes. The absorption of food suffers from inadequate health and sanitation facilities, as well as poor child feeding practices, eating habits and nutritional knowledge. Fluctuating world prices, conflicts and variations in the weather hurt the stability of food production, access and utilization.

Access to adequate supplies of food seems to be a bigger problem in South Asia than the availability of food. This is reflected in the alarming number of people who remain undernourished despite increases in per capita availability of food in the region. Economic indicators such as income, employment and prices determine food security through their influence on access to food.

*As quoted by Barbara Ward in Foreword to Sartaj Aziz (ed.), *Hunger, Politics and Markets: The Real Issues in the Food Crisis.* New York: New York University Press.

Government policies have a critical role to play in ensuring food security. These policies include the maintenance of buffer stocks, support prices, land reforms, and management of the food distribution system.

Agricultural liberalization in South Asia has been associated with increased volatility in both prices and production at the national level. Trade policies affect food security through their effect on incomes, expenditures, employment and government revenues.

Education levels and gender inequalities play a significant role in creating food insecurity within households. Research suggests that higher education levels lead to better health and nutrition outcome. Education also increases farm and non-farm productivity and improves food utilization.

Conflicts have caused food insecurity in various parts of South Asia. In the northern parts of Pakistan terrorist attacks led to food shortages, rising food prices and deteriorating incomes, all of which contributed to a marked increase in individual food insecurity in the region. In Nepal Maoist insurgency was responsible for deteriorating food insecurity across several parts of the country.

As a result of climate change, the glacier melt in the Himalayas threatens the long-term availability of water supplies and more frequent and extreme flooding. Rising temperatures and changing precipitation patterns will increase the frequency of droughts. Sea level rise, storm surges and cyclones can lead to salinization of freshwaters, damaging fisheries and reducing drinking water supplies.

The important point that emerges from this report is that without an explicit commitment to food security, economic growth is neither sustainable nor just. The imperative of promoting an equitable and sustainable economic growth has been a continuing message in all our previous reports. Yet poverty has persisted, the number of hungry people has increased and human insecurity endangered in this region. The deprivation of a huge absolute number of people has created the potential for social turmoil which, if not addressed now, could cause severe damage to the integrity of the region.

The report focuses on analysing food security in all its dimensions—availability, access, absorption and stability—as well as the policies and programmes of South Asian governments to address this challenge. Based on the analysis, the report comes up with six broad findings:

First, high economic growth is a necessary but not a sufficient condition for food security. To ensure food security for all people at all times, special efforts must be made through the adoption of the strategy of pro-poor growth.

Second, all dimensions of food security have to be included in policies for food security. Food must be available for all; accessible to all with adequate purchasing power, marketing and distribution; and there must be adequate facilities for healthcare, water and sanitation for the deprived.

Third, supportive government policies are essential in all countries, especially those that suffer from disadvantages due to geographical location and/or natural calamities.

Fourth, women whose labour is as critical as that of men in all aspects of food production, distribution and access, do not get equal recognition in their national income accounts. Women have the least access to means of production, receive the lowest wages and know least about how to improve the productivity of land with modern inputs and technology. Migration by rural men to urban areas, or overseas, to escape poverty has increased the number of women who have to carry the full burden of earning income and managing households for their families; and yet there have been very few strategies and facilities to enable women to do so.

Fifth, lack of transparency and accountability in implementing safety net programmes are hampering effectiveness of these programmes to reach those who need them most.

Sixth, global commitments to protect the vulnerable peoples and nations from food security crisis through various goals and initiatives have remained mostly on paper. An effective food security reserve at the regional or global level to buffer the countries from cyclical volatility, a sensitive trade regime to protect the small farmers of developing countries, or a global regulatory authority to regulate the working of the multinational corporations—these are all dreams never to be fulfilled. Each country will have to look after its own.

The path of economic reforms that has resulted in high economic growth in some regions and sectors in India has been accompanied by failure on the food security front, in terms of food security in all aspects—production, availability, distribution, affordability, absorption and nutrition—which makes India one of the most undernourished countries in the world.

The high economic growth rate of the past few years has been accompanied by a failure in rural development, employment generation, and poor investment in and delivery of public services. In recent years Indian agriculture is facing an unprecedented crisis pushing rural India towards impoverishment, food shortages and hunger.

- The growth rate of both productivity and production in agriculture has declined.
- Poverty has increased in rural areas, though it is also alarming in urban areas.
- Unemployment has grown faster than population.
- There has been continual rise in food prices. Food inflation has been double digit for prolonged periods.
- Rise in fuel prices has exacerbated the situation.
- One in every four rural households does not have access to safe drinking water or sanitation facilities.

- Seven to ten per cent of urban households also do not have access to safe drinking water.

India is witnessing the paradox of high economic growth and low food security, in terms of nutrition levels, consumption of food grains as well as per capita availability of food grains.

- Seventy six per cent of Indians suffer from inadequate food consumption.
- More than half of India's women and three-quarters of children are anaemic, with incidence among pregnant women an even higher 59 per cent.
- According to the *Economic Survey of India*, food grain production in India has declined by 11 per cent from 208 kg per annum per capita in 1996–97 to 186 kg in 2009–10.
- Unemployment among agricultural labour households grew from 9.5 per cent in 1993–94 to 15.3 per cent in 2004–05.
- The Global Hunger Index of 2010 shows that endemic hunger continues to affect a large section of the Indian people, placing India in the category of 'alarming'.

Immediately after Independence, agricultural development became the cornerstone of national policy of India. Food security, in the sense of national self-sufficiency in domestic production as well as protection of deficit areas and people through food distribution, was seen as the foundation of a self-reliant economic growth strategy. The importance of agriculture was recognized in fighting inflation, and the early national five-year plans reflected this. The country made significant advances in agricultural production, including food, production, due to active state support through public investment in infrastructure like power, electrification, irrigation; the Green Revolution technological strategy; price policy based on minimum support price and procurement operations for some crops; expansion in agricultural credit and extension services, etc. Land reforms were seen as an intervention to promote equity. The home market was protected through tariff and non-tariff restrictions on the import and export of agricultural commodities. These helped achieve agricultural growth and self-sufficiency.

Over the years as a response to the fragility of food security in India, various regimes have formulated policies to increase availability, and improve access. These policies have changed over time, with a shift from import-based availability to large irrigation led 'grow more food' strategy; from land reforms in terms of tenancy reforms and distribution of surplus land, towards self-reliance in food production through Green Revolution; from an emphasis on crop diversification to high value crops based on regional comparative advantage in spices, horticulture, floriculture, etc. Access has been addressed by generating wage employment in public works with cash or food payment, by distributing subsidized food and food grain through public procurement initially to the entire population, and later to a target group.

After the droughts in the 1960s, India knew what to do to ensure food security to its people. In the mid-1960s, the country put in place a sound matrix of policies for food security, through production, procurement, storage and distribution. Problems notwithstanding, the outcome was positive from the point of view of national availability and price stabilization of cereals. However, this was dismantled with liberalization since the primary aim was to cut the food subsidy rather than provide full-fledged food security. This has compromised food security, with inflation compounding the problem.

In recent years the Targeted Public Distribution System (TPDS) has led to a high incidence of exclusion of the more vulnerable groups and a sizable section of even those who the government defines as income poor. The *National Sample Survey 2004–05* demonstrates that a large proportion of agricultural labour and other manual labour households, households belonging to the Scheduled Castes and Tribes, households with little or no land, and households in the lowest expenditure classes, are excluded from the TPDS today.

As India became more affluent in the last two decades in terms of national income, the cereal consumption of the rural population continued to be low and falling. The inequality across expenditure groups remains high with the lowest 10 per cent of the population consuming roughly 60 to 73 per cent the quantity consumed by the highest. This is clearly a reflection of their distress in terms of dwindling incomes and employment, increasing burden of other expenses (such as healthcare, schools, fuel, light and transport) and the inability of the TPDS to intervene effectively. The food expenditure of the poor has been squeezed due to the privatization of other services pushing up the costs of non-food requirements. Rising prices of cereal has also meant that there is inadequate access of the poorer sections of the population to foods such as pulses, vegetables, oil, fruits, and meat products which provide essential proteins, fats, and micronutrients. Lack of access to safe drinking water and toilets within easy distance too results in poor absorption of whatever is consumed. The inadequate spread and reach of government infrastructure and services has only compounded these problems. Thus the Millennium Development Goal (MDG) to halve hunger by 2015 does not look possible. This is happening at a time when there is excess stockholding in the government system (at about three times the norm).

The Government of India needs to take a number of steps such as: a) increase food production; b) disperse growth to the drylands; c) improve land use policies; d) ensure remunerative and assured employment; e) universalize and expand public food distribution and other safety net programmes; f) control inflation; g) improve healthcare, water and sanitation; and h) increase public investment on agriculture, employment generation, and public food distribution.

The worsening food security situation in Pakistan has more to do with socio-economic access than production. Unprecedented inflation has taken food out of reach of people. This combined with the destruction caused by flood affected food availability, deteriorated food security situation further.

Pakistan has never developed a comprehensive food security strategy that included all dimensions of food security as defined by the Food and Agriculture Organization of the United Nations (FAO). Over the years, food security situation has deteriorated.

- Though food production has been increasing, the growth has been volatile, with increase in one year followed by a collapse in the next. In contrast, wheat utilization has constantly been rising as a result of population growth, implying worsening food security situation.
- Overall agriculture growth rates have declined owing to declining productivity and limited water availability. This has been due to restricted crop diversification, unequal distribution of land, poor agricultural research and development, and declining credit availability especially to small and subsistence farmers.
- Growth in income per capita has been overtaken by inflation, reducing the real purchasing power of people.
- Unemployment has gradually increased over the years. The employed labour force also has a significant share of unpaid family workers and workers of informal sector characterized by low wages and long working hours.
- Limited access to safe drinking water and weak sanitation facilities, especially in rural areas and urban slums, has resulted in poor food absorption and utilization.

The report underlines inflation as one of the major causes of Pakistan's food insecurity. Food price inflation has outpaced non-food prices, and within food the prices of essential items like wheat, flour, rice and pulses have risen significantly. The poorest has suffered disproportionately more as compared to the richest as prices of food commodities that constitute the consumption basket of the poor have risen more than those of the rich. Inflation also has disproportionately affected certain segments of the society: fixed income groups, landless daily wage workers in agriculture sector and domestic workers—the income of these groups has not kept pace with inflation. The impact of this price inflation has also varied according to geographic location. Food consumption of households that produce their own food has not been affected as much as those who buy food. Thus food insecurity is more prevalent in urban areas compared to rural areas. Even in rural areas those people who derive their livelihoods from non-farm sources also face food insecurity.

Poor food security situation has exacerbated poverty, widened inequality and deteriorated human development. Households have adopted various coping mechanism to mitigate the impact of food security: they have reduced expenditure on education, health and nutrition, adversely affecting human development. Households have even resorted to selling their productive assets like animals, livestock and land to meet their current needs at the expense of long-term loss of future income. Others have preferred to reduce quality over quantity and resorted to shifting to less nutritious and cheaper food. The deteriorating food quality and reduced quantity have resulted in undernourishment. Child nutrition has also deteriorated leading to stunting and wasting. Anaemia and micronutrient deficiencies amongst pregnant women are highly prevalent. This has translated into high maternal and child mortality.

In addition to inflation, the report highlights poor governance as major factor undermining food security: it includes absence of rule of law, violent conflicts, lack of transparency and accountability, endemic corruption and weak public administration. Excessive involvement of political interests with public policy and functioning of the food markets is identified as a major cause of poor governance that increases food security.

The flood of 2010 have worsened the already poor food security situation. The flood has caused unprecedented disaster to agriculture, destroying standing and stored crops, livestock and property. The destruction to infrastructure like roads, bridges, and markets severely damaged the food distribution network.

As an immediate relief for those suffering from food insecurity the government needs to provide social safety nets. However a balance must be struck between social protection needs and financial costs. The Benazir Income Support Programme needs to be strictly targeted with enhanced coordination between the implementing agencies to avoid duplication of beneficiaries. In the long-run a pro-poor growth strategy that leads to adequate employment and livelihood opportunities for all is essential to guarantee food security for all.

Bangladesh has serious food security concerns on all fronts, in availability, access and utilization of food. Food insecurity in Bangladesh largely originates from natural calamities like floods, cyclones or draughts that are beyond human control. The country however is making serious efforts to address these concerns and to avert food insecurity for its vulnerable population.

Food availability in Bangladesh has improved since the late 1990s largely due to acceleration in growth of production, increased trade and the success the country achieved in reducing population growth. Production of rice and wheat has increased significantly over the years due to adoption of high-yielding varieties. The production of cereals has become more resilient to natural disasters because of change in seasonal composition of production.

Bangladesh possesses substantial biological and physical resources for fish production and the fisheries industry has seen rapid growth in recent years compared to sluggish growth in the 1970s and 1980s. The country has ensured that its domestic shortfall is met by imports. The imports of all food items, specifically rice and wheat, have increased substantially over the years. The rapidly rising imports however is an important concern as imports are becoming a major drain on the limited foreign exchange earnings of the country.

With regards to access to food, per capita income growth has accelerated since the 1990s though followed by increased income inequality and growing rural-urban divide. Diversification of labour to rural non-farm activities and migration of labour from rural to urban areas has also increased real wages and thus the affordability of food. The incidence of poverty determining both the economic and physical accessibility of food as measured by poverty headcount ratio and in terms of population with less than minimum calorie intake has declined over the years. However, the food price increase in 2007 and 2008 had reduced these gains and had negative impact on real income, food availability, consumption, food security and poverty in Bangladesh. It impoverished 2.5 million people and left 6.8 million undernourished. Households were forced to cut their food consumption, and reduce non-food expenditure like expenses on education and health.

Bangladesh also suffers from climate change and natural disasters like flood, cyclones and droughts that directly affect food security through crop damage and asset loss and indirectly through loss of employment opportunities, increase in health expenditure and also increase in necessary food expenditure. It also affects water quality and quantity worsening production of both food crops and fishery.

The government however is aware of the food security concerns of its people and has taken initiatives to augment availability and enhance access to food. It has extended the agriculture research system to develop and diffuse improved crop varieties. The technological progress has been supported by both public and private investment for irrigation, flood control and drainage, and has also resulted in effective water management. Government has also undertaken initiatives to enhance procurement and distribution of agricultural inputs and outputs through the expansion of agricultural markets.

Measures for enhancing access to food incorporate providing assistance to the poor through social safety net programmes, both food and cash-based, and converting price subsidies to targeted food distribution. The public expenditure on various targeted programmes for the poor has doubled over the 15 year period. The government recently has adopted market-based measures such as, establishing new wholesale markets and reducing the number of market intermediaries; and non-market based measures such as, credit for agriculture and for import of food commodities, subsidizing fuel and fertilizers, increased coverage of safety net programmes, food for work programmes and employment generation schemes.

Despite impressive gains in increasing domestic food grain production, problems for food and nutrition security remains. Bangladesh is yet to achieve comprehensive food security that resolves the problem of inadequate food intake and chronic malnutrition among those who are poor and vulnerable. To meet these challenges, an integrated strategy is needed encompassing major aspects of comprehensive food security to ensure adequate food supply through increased production and imports, access to food through public distribution and expanded safety net programmes, and improved food utilization and nutrition.

Despite their significant contributions to production, access and utilization of food, both at household and national levels, women's key role as food producers and providers is often overlooked and undervalued.

Women in South Asia are active participants in agricultural work and participate in many tasks related to crop production and also contribute to post-harvest food processing. The share of female agricultural workers, as a percentage of total economically active women, in South Asia has remained quite high over the years. Their role has further increased due to increasing trend of migration amongst rural males to urban areas making women the head of the household. Yet almost 59 per cent of the total female labour force in South Asia is classified as contributing family workers who are largely unpaid for working on family farms. Wages in the agriculture sector is lowest compared to other sectors, and this impacts on women workers far more as more than two-thirds of all employed women in South Asia are associated with agriculture. Women also have limited access to land, credit, and other inputs and extension services.

As consumers women are the most malnourished. Most women in the region do not afford a diet that is nutritionally adequate, thus exposing women to risks of poor health, especially reproductive health. South Asian women constitute the highest percentage of women suffering from acute energy deficiency. Rural women in South Asia continue to struggle with dual responsibility of economic production and domestic labour, and many are exposed to poverty, illiteracy, high health risks and inadequate access to health and sanitation services. Maternal mortality is still very high in the region. It seems the region as a whole is not yet on track to achieve the targets set by the MDGs.

To realizing the role of women as vital to ensure food security for their households, there is a need to support policies that promote women's economic opportunities through public works programmes; improve women's nutritional health support through food transfers; and reduce poverty through direct cash transfer. Above all, women need the protection of the law in order to be able to engage in all activities that could improve the food security of families and nation.

The disruption of global weather patterns has serious consequences for South Asia. With climate change, the monsoon rain system has been disrupted resulting in untimely rains or floods. Climate change related warming is melting the glaciers of Hindukush, Karakorum and Himalaya on an accelerated rate creating water scarcity concerns for future.

The natural ecosystems that agriculture depends on are severely affected by climate change. Agriculture in South Asia is reliant on the monsoon rain system which recently has become highly variable and unpredictable, resulting in frequency and severity of floods and droughts. The situation has worsened due to global warming and the recent trend indicates that South Asia is very likely to get warmer during this century. The immediate impact of this is the frequent occurrences of floods due to rapid melting of snow. This would imply a drop in river flows and decreased water availability for agriculture. The socio-economic impact of this is uncertainty in agricultural productivity, declining yields and production that exacerbate inflation and poverty and hence increase the number of people at risk of hunger and food insecurity.

Increased desertification is another environmental challenge that poses significant threat to food security in dry-lands of South Asia. Human activities and climate change persistently degrade the dryland ecosystem and convert it into desert. Water scarcity in drylands limits the production of crops, forage and wood, thereby affecting food security, triggering internal and international migration and resource-based conflicts.

Global warming also increased the risk of sea and river flooding in coastal and delta areas, affecting sea and inland fish farming. The deteriorating coastal environment threatens the food supply and livelihoods of the vulnerable coastal communities and millions of fishermen, fish farmers and coastal inhabitants. These communities, already living in precarious conditions because of poverty and underdevelopment, would experience less stable livelihoods due to changes in the availability and quality of fish.

Climate change would worsen the living conditions of millions of farmers, and fishery dependent communities in South Asia. Their economic, food, health and physical security is likely to suffer through higher incidences of crop damage and the loss of livestock from floods and droughts. Poorer people stand to suffer most, as they have the least capacity to withstand the effects of climate change. Thus it is extremely important to adopt mitigation strategies to limit the impact of climate change on livelihood and food security of people.

For adaptation to climatic change, there is a need for an environmentally sustainable agricultural system in South Asia. Innovative technologies are needed to improve agricultural productivity, particularly the technologies geared towards adapting to increasing climatic variation such as, new crop varieties that are drought and frost resistant, and irrigation technologies based on water efficiency in agriculture as a means to adapt to water shortages in the future. Extensive agriculture research is thus the need of time to adapt to climate change to minimize food security concerns.

Farmers should focus on crop rotation and change in crop varieties, along with re-adjusting the timing of planting and harvesting. They should aim for minimum disturbance of soil composition and increase the proportion of leguminous crops to boost soil nitrogen. Farmers would also have to implement various other adaptation measures. These include switching cropping pattern or switching from crops to livestock. Under certain climatic conditions, livestock species may provide more flexibility to some farmers and could help offset losses in crop income. The farm to market infrastructure and transport system will also need to be in sync with these changing crops and livestock breeds.

Meanwhile, disaster preparedness for devastation caused by floods, storms and cyclones needs to be accelerated in climatically vulnerable areas. Since the challenges posed by climate change are more pronounced there is a need of South Asia region-wide coordinated effort to mitigate the adverse effects of climate change on food and human security.

Since 1945 when the FAO was established, there have been many proposals, strategies and institutional innovations to fight poverty and hunger in developing countries. Yet poverty has persisted, number of hungry people in the world increased, and the world has faced food crisis several times, most recently since 2008.

The World Food Summit set the goal of halving the number of undernourished people in the world between 1990–92 and 2015. This goal was reinforced in the World Food Summits of 2002 and 2009 and the MDGs of the United Nations (UN). But in 2009 more than a billion people in the world suffered from hunger.

High food prices in international trade have affected the food security of consumers as well as producers in developing countries. In 2008 in Bangladesh an additional 7.5 million people became food insecure. The increase of global food prices was transmitted into domestic retail prices adversely affecting the purchasing power of all people but hurting the poor most.

The implementation of the World Trade Organization (WTO) Agreement on Agriculture hurt the farmers in poor countries as a result of huge subsidies provided by rich countries to their farmers. These subsidies eroded the production base of developing-country agriculture, made the poor farmers exposed to volatile world markets, and increased food insecurity of small farmers and agricultural workers.

Food security of developing countries has deteriorated further in recent years, despite global institutions and commitments. Despite being an agrarian economy, South Asia has the largest number of undernourished people in the world.

To improve global food security, international institutions of governance should ensure that their political, economic and trade policies do not negatively affect the food security of developing countries. A balanced conclusion of Doha Round of trade negotiations is urgent now to allow developing countries to use various safeguard mechanisms in case of price and output volatility. There is also a need to improve the working of the international supervisory machinery to prevent the negative impact of transnational corporations on food security of poor people and poor nations.

Chapter 1

Food Security and Human Development:
A Conceptual Framework

The evolving concept of food security

The term food security originated in the mid-1970s and attracted much global attention during the World Food Conference of 1974. Since then there has been considerable debate on the subject and several revisions to operational definitions of the term.[1] Developments in the discourse on the subject reflect both a greater understanding of the multi-dimensional challenges to food security, as well as changing perceptions on the importance of food security as a means to an end rather than a goal in and of itself over the years.

The definition of food security coined in the 1970s was primarily concerned with food supplies, as according to the Food and Agriculture Organization of the United Nations (FAO), it was the 'Availability at all times of adequate world food supplies of basic foodstuffs to sustain a steady expansion of food consumption and to offset fluctuations in production and prices.' The food crisis of 1973–75, which had come about through a series of bad weather events around the world and rapid increases in the price of petroleum, had given rise to the problems of food insecurity, famine, and hunger.[2] It thus led to deep interest in ensuring the stable availability of adequate food supplies, together with relatively steady prices at the national and global levels.

In 1983, the FAO revised this definition to incorporate the demand side of the issue, highlighting access to food at household and individual levels in addition to national and global levels, 'Ensuring that all people at all times have both physical and economic access to the basic food that they need.' The realization that availability alone could not ensure the adequate consumption of food had

dawned. There was an increasing interest in the link between poverty reduction and food security. A number of factors contributed to the dialogue in this period, including the era of structural adjustment in the 1980s, where poverty reduction and basic needs often took a backseat to debt management and macroeconomic stability, and the fact that the Green Revolution had not led to rapid improvements in poverty and malnutrition levels everywhere. Here, Amartya Sen's theory of famine highlighted the impact of personal entitlements to food access.[3] A few years later in 1986, the World Bank also highlighted the temporal dynamics of food security by introducing the distinction between chronic and transitory food insecurity.[4] The former is associated with factors such as low incomes and structural poverty, while the latter is often caused by events such as economic crises, conflicts, or natural disasters.

The 1990s saw further deliberations on the concept of food security and its widespread acceptance of the issue as a socio-political construct, as well as a moral and humanitarian matter. The importance of essential micronutrients, food composition, safe water, hygiene, sanitation, intra-household allocations, and effective livelihood strategies to reduce vulnerabilities and manage risks, was highlighted. Food security became a context specific concept that had to include people's food preferences. It also changed from an end in itself to a group of intermediating actions that could help promote a healthy and active way of life. The World Food Summit in 1996 defined it as, 'Food security, at the individual, household, national, regional and global levels is achieved when all people, at all times, have physical and economic access to sufficient, safe and nutritious food to meet their dietary needs and food preferences for an

Food security is achieved when all people, at all times, have physical and economic access to sufficient, safe and nutritious food to meet their dietary needs

active and healthy life.' In 2001, the FAO report, *The State of Food Insecurity 2001* refined this definition further, 'Food security is a situation that exists when all people, at all times, have physical, social and economic access to sufficient, safe and nutritious food that meets their dietary needs and food preferences for an active and healthy life.'[5] Food insecurity refers to a situation where people have inadequate physical, social or economic access to food as defined above.[6] For the purpose of this report, the term food security will refer to the 2001 definition, which comprises four dimensions: availability, access, utilization and stability.

The importance of food security is reflected in the many global commitments made towards improving it. In 1996, leaders from 186 countries met at the World Food Summit and made a commitment to halve the number of undernourished people from about 800 to 400 million by 2015. At the United Nations (UN) Millennium Summit in the year 2000, the international community also made the commitment to halve the proportion of undernourished between 1990 and 2015 (under Goal 1, target 1C). However, progress towards these goals remains unsatisfactory. While the number of undernourished declined during the 1970s and 1980s, it has been increasing since the mid-1990s.[7] The food, fuel and economic crises of 2006–09 have worsened the situation. The FAO estimated that there were 1.02 billion people undernourished in 2009, and this number only declined to 925 million in 2010. This is not only higher than the number of undernourished people before the crises but also higher than that which existed at the time that hunger reduction targets were set at the World Food Summit in 1996. The proportion of undernourished did decline between 1990–92 and 2010 from 20 to 16 per cent but the decline has been too slow to meet the target set under the Millennium Development Goals (MDGs).[8]

In South Asia, the present day obstacles to achieving food security arise from a complex interplay of the domestic and global economy, political situation, social norms, natural environment, and household characteristics. Food availability is dependent on domestic production, imports, stocks, and aid. Access is constrained by incomes, purchasing power, distribution of assets, demographic factors, transport, market infrastructure, social security entitlements, and distribution programmes. The absorption and utilization of food suffers from inadequate health and sanitation facilities, as well as poor child feeding practices, eating habits and nutritional knowledge. Fluctuating prices, conflicts, and variations in the weather hurt the stability of food production, access, and utilization. The impact of food insecurity can be seen in the form of rising economic insecurities, deteriorating health outcomes, poor cognitive development, and conflicts and unrest.

The following sections of this chapter define the concepts of food availability, access, utilization, and stability, analyse the factors that cause food insecurity in South Asia and then discuss the impact of food insecurity on human development. Understanding these challenges and outcomes is essential as a first step towards designing effective interventions to improve individual food security in the region.

Dimensions of food security

Food security comprises four equally important dimensions: availability, access, utilization, and stability. Food security and the objective of ensuring healthy and active lifestyles cannot be realized if performance and achievements are poor along any of these dimensions.

Availability

Food availability refers to the supply side of food security and the availability of an adequate amount of food of suitable quality for consumption. Aggregate food availability is a function of domestic food

The number of undernourished declined during the 1970s and 1980s, it has been increasing since the mid-1990s

production, net food imports (imports minus exports), food aid, and built-up stocks of food (excluding any losses due to storage and handling). Domestic production is dependent upon agricultural conditions such as irrigation, climate, soil quality, availability of water and the length of the growing period, as well as government policies such as agricultural support prices.[9] However, not every country can grow all the food it requires and many import a significant proportion of foodstuffs, the extent of which is limited by total foreign exchange earnings.

Per capita availability of food has increased in most South Asian countries over time. As shown in table 1.1, per capita dietary energy supply (DES) exceeds the minimum dietary energy requirement (MDER) across the region.[10] However, per capita DES remains much lower in South Asia than in many other developing countries, including neighbours Iran and China, where DES was 3,040 and 2,970 kcal/person/day, against an MDER of 1,830 and 1,900 kcal/person/day, respectively, in 2005–07.[11]

Access

Access to food is dependent on economic, legal, political and social structures that allow control over resources which can be used to acquire foods for a nutritious diet.[12] Income and employment levels, the prevailing market price of food products and control over land and other inputs needed to grow food affect the diversity of food eaten and the frequency of consumption. Well-developed market infrastructure, distribution systems, and transport facilities are also essential. The absence of such facilities prevents the food that is available from reaching various segments of the population, such as urban populations dependent on food supplies from rural areas, people living in remote areas, etc. On the other hand, panic buying and/or the hoarding of food by traders (for example, because of expectations that food prices will rise due to shortages in international markets, conflicts or disasters

expected in the future) reduce access to food.

Social safety nets and food distribution programmes, including government-sponsored and privately-supported subsidies for food, low cost rations, food aid packages, and other schemes, are essential to ensure access to food for the poor. Finally, cultural mores such as gender norms and power relations also affect access. For example, in most parts of South Asia, men are given preferential treatment and access to family resources over women. Thus, in the event of food shortages, it is usually women who suffer the most, as they curtail their consumption to first feed the men and children in their families. They are also often unregistered, without the requisite identification papers required to qualify for public subsidies.

Access to adequate supplies of food is arguably a bigger problem in South Asia than the availability of food. This is reflected in the alarming proportion and number of people who remain undernourished despite increases in the per capita availability of food in the region and dietary energy supplies greater than the MDER (table 1.1).[13] While some countries such as Sri Lanka and Bangladesh have made progress in terms of reducing the proportion of the population that is

Access to adequate supplies of food is arguably a bigger problem in South Asia than the availability of food

Table 1.1 Food needs and supply, 1990–2007

Country	Time period	Minimum dietary energy requirement (MDER) (kcal/person/day)	Dietary energy supply (DES) (kcal/person/day)
Bangladesh	1990–92	1,690	1,960
	2005–07	1,760	2,250
India	1990–92	1,740	2,300
	2005–07	1,780	2,300
Maldives	1990–92	1,660	2,400
	2005–07	1,790	2,680
Nepal	1990–92	1,690	2,190
	2005–07	1,720	2,350
Pakistan	1990–92	1,690	2,210
	2005–07	1,730	2,250
Sri Lanka	1990–92	1,770	2,170
	2005–07	1,810	2,390

Source: FAO 2011b.

Table 1.2   Food Deprivation Indicators, 1990–2007

Country	Time period	Proportion undernourished (%)	Number undernourished (millions)	Food deficit of undernourished population (kcal/person/day)
India	1990–92	20	172.4	290
	2005–07	21	237.7	260
Pakistan	1990–92	25	29.6	270
	2005–07	26	43.4	280
Bangladesh	1990–92	38	44.4	310
	2005–07	27	41.7	290
Nepal	1990–92	21	4.2	240
	2005–07	16	4.5	190
Sri Lanka	1990–92	28	4.8	260
	2005–07	19	3.8	250
Maldives	1990–92	9	0.0191	170
	2005–07	7	0.0198	80

Source: FAO 2011b.

In South Asia, food utilization remains a tremendous challenge because of the under provision of key services

undernourished since 1990–92, others have seen a deterioration of the same (table 1.2). In Pakistan, for example, between 1990–92 and 2005–07, the proportion of undernourished increased from 25 to 26 per cent, while the number of undernourished increased from 29.6 to 43.4 million. India saw an increase in the number of undernourished from 172.4 to 237.7 million in the same period.

Utilization

Food utilization attracted much attention as an essential component of food security in the 1990s. Earlier discussions had focused on the quantity of food consumed, revolving around the need for an adequate intake of calories and protein.[14] However, later there was the recognition that food security could not be ensured without essential micronutrients such as vitamin A, iron and iodine, as well as access to non-food inputs such as education, clean water, environmental hygiene, sanitation facilities and healthcare.

These inputs allow people to meet their physiological needs by making the most of the food they eat through the effective absorption of various nutrients. They are crucial for good physical and mental health, as well as cognitive achievement.

For example, poor education, especially the poor education of primary caretakers (usually women), can lead to lack of information on healthy eating practices, culinary habits and food selection and preparation. Inadequate access to clean drinking water, environmental hygiene, sanitation facilities and healthcare can lead to the widespread prevalence of diseases such as diarrhoea and typhoid, which prevent the absorption of food eaten into the body.

In South Asia, food utilization remains a tremendous challenge because of the under provision of key services and infrastructure. As illustrated in table 1.3, less than a third of the populations of

Table 1.3   Percentage of population with access to safe water and sanitation in South Asia, 2008

	Access to safe water	Access to adequate sanitation
India	88	31
Pakistan	90	45
Bangladesh	80	53
Nepal	88	31
Sri Lanka	90	91
Bhutan	92	65
Maldives	91	98

Source: World Bank 2011d.

Nepal and India have access to adequate sanitation.

Stability

This aspect is reflected in the definition of food security by the phrase, '. . . at all times. . . .' It refers to the continuous stability of the other three dimensions over time. To be food secure, individuals and households must be free from the risk of running out of food through challenges to availability and access. They must also live in conditions that allow for the effective absorption and utilization of the food they consume at all times.

Stability can be threatened by cyclical events that cause seasonal food insecurity, such as changes in the climate, cropping patterns, the demand and supply of work opportunities, the prevalence of specific diseases during certain times of the year, etc.[15] Food security can also be disrupted by unexpected domestic, regional or global political, climatic or economic events. For example, in the past few years, civil war in various parts of Sri Lanka and Nepal, the recent floods in Pakistan and the global food, fuel and financial crises have hurt the food security of millions of people across South Asia. The exposure of people to the risks posed by cyclical and unexpected events must be minimized to ensure their food security.

Causes of food insecurity

Food security is affected by a range of factors, economic, political, natural, and man-made in nature. The following include some of the most important determinants of food insecurity in South Asia.

Economic conditions

Economic indicators such as income, employment and prices are often the greatest determinants of food security through their influence on access to food. This influence is even greater when government sponsored safety nets are weak. In 2008, gross national income per capita (at purchasing power parity) across South Asia was a low US$2,695.[16] As a region, this was the second lowest in the world, higher only than Sub-Saharan Africa. Consequently, as illustrated in table 1.4, food expenditures comprise a large proportion of the total basket of household expenditures. For poor and rural families, this proportion can be as high as over 60 per cent.

During the food crisis of 2007–08, prices peaked in mid-2008, and fell thereafter, but the FAO cereal index in February 2010 was still 60 per cent higher than in 2005.[17] Given the high proportion of expenditure on food in South Asia, not surprisingly, such increases in prices are devastating for food security. Food prices had risen because of a combination of demand and supply factors. On the demand side, higher incomes, particularly in Asia, had led to rise in the demand for foodstuffs, especially meat, which in turn led to high demand for cereal as animal feed. Population growth, the demand for biofuels, and speculation, also led to increases in demand. On the supply side, a series of weather related shocks, low stocks, falling investment in agriculture, declining agricultural productivity, rising energy prices, and export restrictions combined to reduce supplies. Later, the financial crisis led to falling employment, a slowdown in investment, credit and aid, and falling or stagnant remittances throughout the world.[18] As a combined effect of these crises, almost one in six people across the globe were under-nourished in 2009.

Economic indicators such as income, employment and prices are often the greatest determinants of food security

Table 1.4		Share of food expenditure to total household expenditure		
				(%)
		National	Rural	Urban
India	2004	49.50	54.00	41.60
Pakistan	2004	47.60	53.60	39.60
Bangladesh	2005	53.81	58.50	45.20
Nepal	2003	59.00	62.90	39.10
Sri Lanka	2002	44.50	46.20	35.90
Bhutan	2007	39.20	44.80	32.50
Maldives	2003	29.90	...	...

Source: FAO 2011b.

Agricultural productivity

Beginning in the late 1960s, the Green Revolution brought unprecedented growth in agricultural productivity in South Asia through a combination of breeding and agronomic practices. This growth did not come without its set of drawbacks. The Green Revolution is largely responsible for a loss of biodiversity and over reliance on a few varieties of crops. It was heavily dependent on large supplies of water and thus exacerbated inequality between heavy rainfall and irrigated lands versus non-irrigated, low rainfall areas. It also led to falling levels of groundwater as more water was pumped for irrigation than was replenished every year. Irrigation practices also led to building up of salt in water. Moreover, the excessive use of pesticides and fertilizers polluted waterways and killed useful insects, fauna and wildlife.

Nevertheless, between 1970 and 1995, per capita calorie availability increased by 30 per cent in Asia, despite a 60 per cent increase in the population.[19] However, growth rates of productivity have slowed down over time. In India, for example, agricultural growth rates declined from 3.5 per cent between 1981–82 and 1996–97 to around 2.0 per cent between 1997–98 and 2004–05.

Today, South Asia requires a second Green Revolution, one that not only ensures food security but also creates sustainable livelihoods for the poor and takes into account environmental impacts. The challenges in increasing agricultural productivity are much higher now than they were 40 years ago. The new Green Revolution will have to focus on dryland areas, cope with the risks of global trading systems and associated price volatility, climate change, declining soil fertility, waterlogging and smaller farm sizes. Special efforts will be needed to overcome the deficits in credit, infrastructure, research and extension services, education and skills, and well-functioning markets.[20] Better land management practices are needed and can be promoted by a number of policies, including the promotion of phosphate and potassium and discouragement of nitrogen fertilizers in countries such as India and Pakistan, where the use of nitrogen is well over optimal levels.[21] Water conservation, storage and management also need to be made a top priority. Investments in these areas can help enhance agricultural productivity over the next few decades.

Government policies

Government policies have a large role to play in ensuring or worsening food security across a country through their impact on production, access, distribution and stability of food supplies. Examples of the above are abundant in South Asia. In Pakistan, for example, wheat shortages were experienced in the western parts of the country in 2008 and the early months of 2009 because of a ban on the movement of wheat from surplus to deficit areas.[22] The ban was responsible for huge differentials in prices among different regions.

In India, a Public Distribution System (PDS) was initiated in the aftermath of the food shortages of the 1960s and was replaced by a Targeted Public Distribution System (TPDS) in June 1997, to ensure access to adequate food for families below the poverty line. However, the TPDS has been fraught with problems, including high exclusion errors, leakages, and the non-viability of fair price shops.[23] In Sri Lanka, the government bound tariffs on agricultural goods at 50 per cent as of 1 January 1995, and then removed quantitative restrictions on all agricultural products other than wheat and wheat flour. After 1990, the government's monopoly on rice imports was also eliminated and private traders were allowed to import rice.[24] The government has also initiated welfare programmes, such as mid-day meals for over 1.5 million school children, to reduce malnutrition and improve access to food.[25]

Over the years, other policies have also had significant impacts on food security in South Asia. These include the maintenance

Government policies have a large role to play in ensuring or worsening food security

of buffer stocks, support prices, land reforms, monitoring and management of the food produce supply chain, promotion of urban and industrial growth at the expense of rural and agricultural development through exchange rate maintenance and import/export duties and exemptions, etc. The country case studies in chapters 2, 3, and 4 discuss several of these policies in more detail.

Global trading system and international agreements

Apart from national policies, global trading regimes and international agreements signed by domestic governments also have a significant impact on individual food security. Trade policies affect food security through their effect on incomes, expenditures, employment and government revenues. Agricultural liberalization has been associated with increased volatility in both prices and production at the national level.

In the past few decades, several South Asian countries have shifted from a strategy of self-sufficiency, where enough food is produced domestically to meet domestic consumption requirements, to self-reliance, where food sources can be determined by international trade patterns. The results of this shift have often been mixed. A prime example is provided by the case of Bangladesh.[26]

Gradual liberalization of the rice trade and agricultural input markets helped Bangladesh reduce volatility of supplies and increase domestic production of cereals between 1978 and 1990. Consequently, broader liberalization in the 1990s allowed private imports of wheat and rice, which helped stabilize wheat and rice prices, eliminated the need for large government stocks and allowed the closure of major ration channels. By the end of the decade, price floors and ceilings were no longer defended by public purchases and sales and over 85 per cent of public sector distribution was targeted towards poor households. Private imports would increase in years where domestic production fell

and would decrease when domestic surpluses would lead to prices below international levels. The benefits of these policies were made strongly evident in 1998, when floods destroyed over 20 per cent of the monsoon rice crop. Following the floods, Bangladesh adopted a trade-oriented stabilization strategy, where moderate purchases were made by the government to supply public distribution channels, but zero tariffs and other measures were adopted to encourage private sector imports. The opening up of private food grain exports from India in 1994 also worked in Bangladesh's favour as it could substitute rice imports from Thailand with cheaper imports from India (because of low transport costs and faster delivery).

International agreements often have serious implications for the food security of developing countries. One such agreement is the Trade-Related Aspects of Intellectual Property Rights (TRIPS), which came into effect with the establishment of the World Trade Organization (WTO) in 1995. Developing countries were given until January 2000 to become TRIPS compliant. The Agreement was created to protect intellectual property rights through patents, copyrights, etc., most of which usually last for a period of 20 years.

Article 27.3(b) of TRIPS allows the patenting of life forms and requires WTO members to protect new plant varieties (plants that have been improved by breeding to make them stable, distinct, and uniform) through patents, plant breeders' rights, etc. Prior to this Agreement, life forms and their components were not considered patentable. While the Agreement allows farmers some privileges, such as reusing their own crop for seed purposes, it does not allow them to exchange or sell such seeds. This can be disastrous for countries such as India, where 70 per cent of seed supply comes from farmers' sales of reproduced seeds.[27] Furthermore, transnational corporations (TNCs) have engaged in a race to patent plant varieties and genes that are tolerant

International agreements often have serious implications for the food security of developing countries

to extreme climatic conditions and could be essential for adapting to climate change.

Social factors

Social factors such as education levels and gender inequalities play a significant role in creating food insecurity. Research suggests that higher education levels lead to better health and nutrition outcomes by increasing farm and non-farm productivity and improving food utilization. A study by the World Bank estimates that farmers with primary education were on average, nine per cent more productive than those with no education. Mothers' education is particularly important, as for each year of formal schooling received by a mother, the odds of her child being stunted decrease by 4 to 5 per cent.[28]

Women are also important as food producers and constitute a significant part of the agricultural workforce in South Asia, comprising about 30 per cent of the total in India and Pakistan and over 50 per cent in Bangladesh. However, differential access to essential inputs and credit account for significant differences in agricultural productivity between men and women. Estimates suggest that the yield gap between male and female farmers is about 20 to 30 per cent and most of this difference is because of differences in resource use, such as fertilizers, improved seeds, mechanical tools, etc. If this yield gap were eliminated, agricultural productivity in developing countries would increase by 2.5 to 4.0 per cent and the number of undernourished people worldwide would decline by 12 to 17 per cent.[29]

Conflicts

Conflicts have both immediate and long-lasting impact on food security. It hurts the availability of food supplies as it restricts access to land and other essential inputs required for farming and leads to outmigration and internal displacement of farmers and landowners. When conflicts occur in prime agricultural lands, they can lead to escalating food insecurity beyond the conflict zone to the entire country. Conflicts also witness the erosion of food supplies through theft, seizure and confiscation of stocks by militants. Access to food is impeded as food imports into markets and distribution of food supplies by government, non-governmental agencies, and other actors are interrupted.[30] Furthermore, the destruction of community infrastructure such as sewage and sanitation facilities, and the spread of diseases during wars hurt the effective absorption of what little food is available and consumed. Landmines and environmental damages during conflicts can also render valuable lands unfit for future agricultural production.

Various parts of South Asia have witnessed repeated periods of food insecurity due to conflicts. In Pakistan, the militancy in Khyber Pakhtunkhwa has led to food shortages, rising food prices and deteriorating incomes, all of which contributes to a marked increase in individual food insecurity in the region. In Nepal, the Maoist insurgency was responsible for deteriorating food insecurity across several parts of the country. In the districts of Mugu and Jajarkot, the World Food Programme had to cease its 'work for food' programme after Maoists looted stores, affecting some 15,000 people who worked on a road in exchange for food. In other parts of the country, transportation blockades restricted access to fertilizers and seeds, and Maoists seized village food supplies.[31] The food insecurity wrought by such conflicts can lead to long-term impacts on the lives of those affected.

Climate change

South Asia is a part of the world that has historically contributed little to climate change but is likely to suffer greatly from the phenomenon. According to the fourth Assessment Report of the Inter-governmental Panel on Climate Change, by the middle of the twenty-first century, crop yields in the region could decrease by as much as 30 per cent due to climate

Higher education levels lead to better health and nutrition outcomes by increasing farm and non-farm productivity and improving food utilization

change,[32] with maize and wheat yields likely to decrease by 6 to 23 per cent and 40 to 45 per cent, respectively.[33] Between 2000 and 2050, it is expected that the number of children suffering from malnutrition will steadily fall from 76 to 52 million. However, the figure is likely to decrease to only 59 million by 2050 in the presence of climate change.[34]

The threats to food security from climate change will come from a variety of sources. Faster than average glacier melt in the Himalayas will threaten the long-term availability of water supplies and lead to more frequent and extreme flooding. Rising temperatures and changing precipitation patterns will increase the probability of droughts, hurt pastures, rangelands, livestock, forests, and crops, and increase the frequency of old and new weed and pest infestations. Rainfed agricultural areas are likely to suffer even more than irrigated areas as there are few coping mechanisms for increased variability in natural precipitation. Finally, sea level rise, storm surges and cyclones can lead to the salinization of freshwaters, hurting fisheries and reducing drinking water supplies. South Asia will require massive investments in its rural areas, particularly in more efficient water usage and storage, and in drought, flood, and pest resistant crop varieties, to cope with the changing climate of the region.

Demographic trends

While population growth rates in South Asia have declined over the past few decades, the region is still home to one of the most rapidly growing populations in the world. Average annual population growth rates between 1990 and 2008 in Pakistan, Nepal, and Bangladesh were 2.4, 2.3 and 1.8 per cent, respectively, far higher than the global average of 1.3 per cent.[35] As shown in table 1.5, the population of South Asia will continue to expand rapidly over the next two decades. This increase in population is of tremendous significance for continued food insecurity. During the past two

Table 1.5   Population projections in South Asia, 2010–30

(thousands)

	2010	2020	2030
India	1,214,464	1,367,225	1,484,598
Pakistan	184,753	226,187	265,690
Bangladesh	164,425	185,552	203,214
Nepal	29,853	35,269	40,646
Sri Lanka	20,410	21,713	22,194
Bhutan	708	820	902
Maldives	314	362	403

Note: These projections are under the 'medium variant'.
Source: UNPD 2011.

decades, technological progress and investments in agriculture have helped alleviate Malthusian concerns that population growth rates will exceed growth in food production. However, not only have agricultural production growth rates slowed down from their earlier rates but more and more farmers, particularly poorer farmers, have been forced to cultivate smaller landholdings and marginal lands.[36] The risks associated with, and inputs required to tend to these marginal landholdings, especially in the face of a changing climate, are quite high. Furthermore, the government is quite likely to find it very challenging to expand food-based welfare programmes and food imports at the current population growth rates. Consequently, it is quite probable that demographic pressures will create serious challenges to ensuring the adequate availability of and access to food supplies in South Asia.

Impact of food insecurity

Food insecurity hurts economic growth, educational achievement, health security, and societal stability. It has a particularly debilitating impact on marginalized groups such as the poor and women, and if left unchecked, can slow down, halt and even reverse years of progress on human development.

Economic insecurity

Poverty and economic well-being are closely linked to food insecurity,

Food insecurity has a particularly debilitating impact on marginalized groups such as the poor and women

particularly when the latter is the consequence of rising food prices (box 1.1). A recent study by the World Bank estimates that poverty increased by an average of 3 percentage points and approximately 73 to 105 million people across the world became poor as the result of rising food prices between 2005 and 2007.[37]

Even though spending on food as a proportion of total expenditure has declined over the years, food purchases still account for a significant proportion of the overall basket of expenditures in South Asia (table 1.4). For low-income families, this number is often higher than 60 per cent of total expenses. Rising food prices diminish the potential for these families to meet their dietary requirements, often leading them to switch from relatively expensive nutrient and protein rich foods, to less nutritious, calorie and energy dense foods and to curtail their expenditures on non-essential social services such as healthcare and education. While higher prices can benefit net sellers of food, net buyers are greater in number in South Asia and comprise of both the urban poor and most of the rural poor, particularly those

who are landless or small landholders. As many farmers sell their produce immediately after the harvest, they may not even reap the benefits of higher prices if prices rise a significant period of time after the post-harvest season.[38] Rising input prices and unresponsive government procurement prices also reduce the benefit of higher prices to many farmers.

Consequently, in the short and medium run, rising food prices have the potential to push millions of South Asians into poverty and worsen the conditions of those already below the poverty line. In the long run, food insecurity through inadequate or interrupted availability, access or utilization, often leads to inter-generational cycles of economic deprivation. For example, malnutritioned children often start school later than healthier ones, have reduced cognitive abilities, and thus, lower lifetime earnings.

Furthermore, at the national level, escalating food insecurity often leads to undesirable macroeconomic consequences, particularly for countries dependent on food imports. Rising food prices lead to high inflation, a deterioration of the current account, worsening terms of trade and a fall in foreign exchange reserves. If monetary policy is tightened to reduce inflation, it can lead to a contraction in demand, slowdown in employment and economic growth rates, and a fall in the tax to gross domestic product (GDP) ratio.[39] Together, these outcomes limit the government's ability to spend on social services such as social protection schemes, health, sanitation, and education, further hurting the economic well-being of the poor.

Social and psychological crises

To adjust to rising food insecurity, households are often forced to adopt a number of actions and behaviours that lead to reduced psycho-social well-being through their impact on mortality and morbidity, cognitive abilities and emotional well-being. For example, a survey of over 10,000 households across

---

Box 1.1 The link between rising food prices and poverty levels

The impact of rising food prices on poverty is not uniform across countries. It depends on a number of factors, including the following:

- The extent to which world market prices are passed on to domestic prices.
- Initial poverty levels and the number of people clustered around the poverty line.
- The number of net buyers and sellers of the commodities in question.
- The share of poor people's budgets devoted to food overall and key staples in particular.
- The ratio of own-consumption to market purchases.
- The effect of food price increases on real wages of poor people.

Source: World Bank 2008.

Table 1.6 Underweight, stunting and wasting in children under-five, 2006–08*

(%)

	India	Pakistan**	Bangladesh	Nepal	Sri Lanka	Bhutan***	Maldives**
Underweight	43.5	31.3	41.3	38.8	21.1	14.1	25.7
Wasting	20.0	14.2	17.5	12.7	14.7	2.5	13.4
stunting	47.9	41.5	43.2	49.3	17.3	47.7	31.9

Notes: *: Data refer to recent year available. **: Data refer to 2001. ***: Data refer to 1999.
Source: World Bank 2011d.

Bangladesh between November 2008 and January 2009, found that families who could not cover food and essential non-food expenditures often adopted negative coping mechanisms, such as reducing expenditure on healthcare.[40] Those who adopted food-based coping strategies also embraced approaches that eventually led to sub-optimal educational and health outcomes, such as reduced portion sizes and relying on cheaper, less preferred food.

Inadequate nutrition is often a consequence of food-based coping strategies and is particularly harmful for child development. Undernutrition is responsible for approximately a third of the 8.8 million child deaths every year globally and leads to high rates of morbidity.[41] Maternal malnutrition and food insecurity during pregnancy hurt the physical and mental growth of the unborn child. Mothers who are underweight tend to give birth to underweight babies, heightening the risk of infant mortality.[42] Good nutrition continues to be most important in the early years of a child's life, particularly in the first three years of life, when even short

term, transitory food insecurity can lead to long-term consequences. During this phase, children are no longer exclusively breastfed and they have high nutritional requirements because they are growing fast and have immature immune systems that cannot adequately protect them.[43]

In South Asia, the health impacts of food insecurity manifest themselves in the poor state of child and maternal nutrition. Table 1.6 shows the prevalence of underweight children, including stunting and wasting among children under-five years of age across various countries in the region. Table 1.7 indicates the high prevalence of iodine, vitamin A and iron deficiencies. Iodine deficiency often leads to stillbirths, miscarriages and preventable mental retardation. Vitamin A deficiency is a leading cause of blindness and weakens the immune system's ability to fight childhood diseases such as malaria, diarrhoea and measles. Anaemia is most prevalent in pregnant mothers and children under-five years of age and can lead to fatigue and cognitive deficiencies.[44] Concentrated efforts to improve nutritional

Inadequate nutrition is often a consequence of food-based coping strategies and is particularly harmful for child development

Table 1.7 Nutrition indicators

	Consumption of iodized salt (% of households)	Vitamin A supplementation (% of children 6–59 months)	Prevalence of Anaemia (2000–06*)	
	2002–08*	2009	(% of children under-five)	(% of pregnant women)
India	51	66	74	50
Pakistan	17	91	51	39
Bangladesh	84	91	47	47
Nepal	63	95	48	42
Sri Lanka	93	64**	30	29
South Asia***	51	72	68	48

Notes: *Data refer to latest year available. **: Data refer to 2005. ***: Data for South Asia is the weighted average of seven countries, India, Pakistan, Bangladesh, Nepal, Sri Lanka, Bhutan and Maldives.
Sources: World Bank 2010 and 2011d and MHHDC staff computations.

outcomes among women (particularly in the adolescent stage before they become pregnant, during pregnancy and lactation), and children (especially during their first few years of life), can help mitigate some of the most serious health impacts of malnutrition.

An often overlooked implication of food insecurity is the emotional distress that it can cause. Studies indicate that food insecurity at the household level leads to high stress levels, anxiety, feelings of powerlessness, exclusion and inadequacy, decreased participation in constructive social activities, and erosion of conviviality among households and broader members of society.[45] Food insecurity is also associated with above average levels of maternal depression.[46] While the direction of causality is not clear, it seems likely that there is dual causality. Maternal depression also acts as an additional channel through which food insecurity hurts child development as it can diminish parental energy levels, weaken mother-child bonds and interaction and lead to child abuse and neglect. Furthermore, empirical evidence shows that hungry children are more likely to exhibit both external and internal social and behavioural problems than the well-fed ones.[47] Commonly exhibited external behaviour includes actions such as cheating, lying, bullying, hyper-activism and aggression, while internal behavioural problems include feelings of worthlessness, fear, and being unloved.

Food insecurity is also an important causal determinate of educational achievement. It has been found to lead to delayed school enrolments, higher absenteeism and lower learning even when children are in school. Moreover, the psychological disturbances brought on by food insecurity lead to further disturbances in learning. There is no doubt that good health and nutrition are essential development goals in and of themselves. However, the benefits of investment in food security far outweigh the immediate outcomes through its instrumental value in terms of its impact on educational achievement.

Conflicts and instability

Food insecurity can aggravate the likelihood of violent conflicts, unrest and instability in society. While such conflicts are rare at the inter-state level, food insecurity has repeatedly been associated with protests, riots, communal and civil conflicts and democratic fragility and failure at the local and intra-state level.[48] These acts of hostility have repeatedly hurt political, community, and individual security.

Illustrations of the violence associated with food insecurity were seen all over the world in 2007–08, when rising global food prices caused protests and violent rioting in 48 countries.[49] South Asia was no exception. In Dhaka, the capital city of Bangladesh, police had to open fire and release tear gas to disperse a crowd of thousands of protestors who had turned violent when they were demanding higher wages to cover rising food prices in April 2008.[50] In Karachi, Pakistan's financial capital and most populated city, 20 women and girls lost their lives in a stampede to collect free bags of food.[51] These incidents are not without precedent. They have periodically occurred all over the world as a result of rising food insecurity. For example, the earlier rise in global food prices during the 1970s and 1980s had led to an escalation in protests and riots across the world. The removal of government subsidies on basic foodstuffs and energy, often mandated as a prerequisite for assistance from international financial institutions, have also caused much popular unrest worldwide.

Empirical evidence suggests that the link between food insecurity and conflicts arises from the impact of the former on economic and social grievances and the perceived costs and benefits of participating in violent action.[52] Changes in the price of foodstuffs, particularly sudden changes through events such as exchange rate fluctuations and export restrictions, can erode real incomes, lead to high stress levels and increase grievances against the state and others perceived to be relatively better off. This is particularly true for low- and middle-income families who spend a significant proportion of their incomes on food and have few coping mechanisms. Under such circumstances, the benefits of resorting to violence can supersede the costs.

Natural disasters can also lead to sudden changes in the availability of food and other resources, leaving people with little to lose and thus more inclined to engage in acts of aggression. An example of violent rioting in the aftermath of a natural disaster was seen in the eastern Indian state of Bihar, when angry villagers attacked officials and local politicians while demanding food and shelter after the devastating floods that struck much of South Asia in 2008.[53] Hostilities in the face of rising food insecurity are not just limited towards state actors but can also arise among communities that have historically lived at peace. This was witnessed in the Pakistani province of Balochistan, where a five-year spell of drought during 1997 and 2001 led to conflicts between sedentary and migratory pastoral communities over grazing rights to lands that had traditionally been shared by both. The reality of climate change is likely to lead to an increase in such catastrophes and their consequences over the next few decades.

Furthermore, food insecurity can also lead to 'extraordinary' behaviours among individuals. One study conducted in Pakistan links actions such as selling body organs, exchanging children (particularly female children) for food, entering bonded labour, committing suicide, and participating in other anti-social activities to food insecurity.[54] It further postulates that the chronically food insecure, many of whom harbour grievances against an establishment perceived to be indifferent to their plight, present easy potential recruits for militants who pose a threat to socio-political stability and domestic and global security.

Given the spectre of violence presented by food insecurity, governments, non-state actors and the international community must put their collective efforts into eradicating the problem of hunger. This is not just a moral and humanitarian imperative but also a mean to ensure individual well-being and promote local, national, and global harmony.

Conclusion

This report comes at a time when South Asia is witnessing soaring food prices, economic and financial crises, stagnant agricultural production, concerns about climate change, liberalization of agricultural trade, protracted conflicts, and a continuously growing population. The report provides a holistic analysis of the state of food security in the region, discusses the impact of food insecurity on people, and provides policy makers with comprehensive policies to ensure the availability of, individual access to, utilization of, and stability of food supplies.

The remainder of the report is structured as follows: chapters 2, 3, and 4 provide country case studies on food security in India, Pakistan, and Bangladesh, respectively; chapter 5 discusses the gender dimension of food security; chapter 6 highlights the threats that climate change presents to food security in South Asia; and chapter 7 concludes the report with an analysis of global commitments to food security.

Governments, non-state actors and international community must put their collective efforts into eradicating the problem of hunger

Chapter 2

Food Security in India: A Critical Analysis*

Mass poverty and malnutrition continue to plague India. Despite specific policies and initiatives to the contrary, India has been unsuccessful in providing access to enough food to the people. The pursuit of economic growth has been accompanied with chronic food deficiency and hunger, amongst the highest globally. For example:

- Eighty per cent of the rural population, 64 per cent of the urban population, and 76 per cent of the total population suffers from inadequate calorie and food consumption.
- According to the *National Family Health Survey*,[1] a little less than half of India's under-three population was underweight or malnourished in terms of the weight-for-age criterion, which has remained virtually unchanged in the last decade.
- More than half of India's women and three-quarters of children are anaemic, with incidence among pregnant women an even higher 59 per cent.
- According to the *Economic Survey of India*,[2] food grain production in India has declined by 11 per cent from 208 kg per annum per capita in 1996–97 to 186 kg in 2009–10. Notwithstanding falling production, India has on average exported seven million tonnes of cereals every year, causing a further fall in availability by 15 per cent from 510 gms per day per capita in 1991 to 436 gms in 2008.
- Unemployment among agricultural labour households grew from 9.5 per cent in 1993–94 to 15.3 per cent in 2004–05.[3] The National Sample Survey Organization (NSSO) data on consumer expenditure on food shows a continuous fall in the annual per capita consumption of cereals for 95 per cent of the population.

The inability of policy to address this crucial issue has very serious long-term implications, since a generation of unhealthy and undernourished girls will grow up to become anaemic mothers producing low birth weight children, thus setting forth a vicious cycle. The inability to provide dependable and adequate access to affordable food is only compounded by the government's inability to control food price inflation, which has hit record highs in the past two years. This is likely to push even more people into hunger and starvation.

India promised to halve hunger by 2015, as stated in the Millennium Development Goal (MDG) 1, but this target will not be met if current trends continue. After India undertook economic reforms two decades ago, it has witnessed the paradox of high economic growth and low food security (in terms of nutrition levels, consumption of food grains as well as per capita availability of food grains).

Food security has several dimensions, in terms of intake as well as outcomes. Energy deficiency, higher anaemia, low body mass index, greater proneness to disease, stunting of children, lower life expectancy, etc., are some of the indicators of the extent and outcome of hunger. Clearly, adequate and balanced food intake, the provision of safe drinking water and the availability of decent sanitation facilities are important elements in food security.

Food security exists 'when all people at all times have access to sufficient, safe, nutritious food to maintain a healthy and

After India undertook economic reforms two decades ago, it has witnessed the paradox of high economic growth and low food security

---

* This is an edited version of a paper written by Smita Gupta of the Institute of Human Development, Delhi. The author is solely responsible for the views expressed in this chapter.

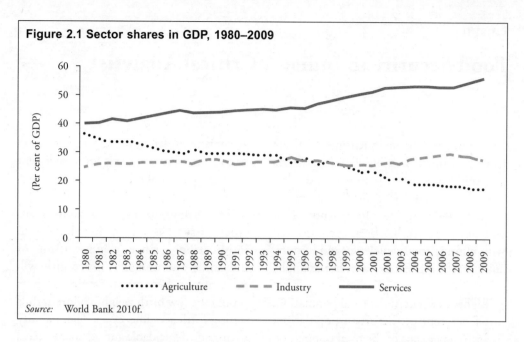

Figure 2.1 Sector shares in GDP, 1980–2009

(Per cent of GDP)

······· Agriculture   – – – Industry   —— Services

Source: World Bank 2010f.

active life.'[4] The concept clearly requires the physical availability of, and economic access to, food that fulfils people's dietary needs in accordance with their customary food preferences. Thus, there are three necessary conditions for food security.

- Self-sufficiency in food production at the regional level on a sustained basis.
- Purchasing power to ensure access to the individual through adequate resources and/or employment to get proper food for a nutritious diet.

- A hygienic and healthy body and environment that allows the body to absorb nutrients from food.

Availability of food grain and self-sufficiency

After 1990, Indian agriculture faced an unprecedented crisis which pushed rural India towards impoverishment, food shortages and hunger. The per capita availability of food grains fell to levels that were seen last during the worst years of colonial rule and famines. The declining growth rate of productivity and production in agriculture is one important reason for this; equally important is the fall in purchasing power due to the deflationary macroeconomic policies and consequent contraction of the public works programmes and employment generation activities of the state. Together these adversely affected food security by reducing availability of food and purchasing power to buy it.

The share of the agricultural sector declined from 35.7 per cent in 1980 to 17.8 per cent in 2009. However, this was not replaced by a commensurate expansion in the manufacturing sector, which rose sluggishly, but by the services sector that often acted as the residual sector with very low incomes and distress wages (figure 2.1).

Figure 2.2 Decade average food grain output growth and population growth rates, 1980–2008

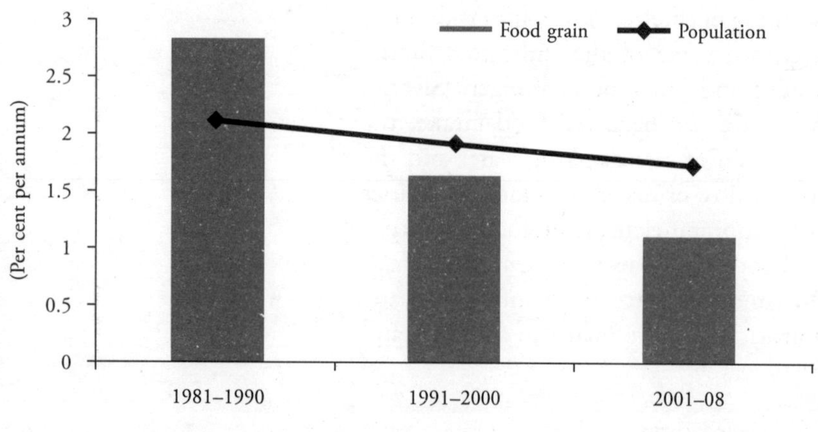

—— Food grain   ◆ Population

(Per cent per annum)

Source: GOI, *Economic Survey of India* (various issues).

Table 2.1 Area, production and yield of food grain, 1991–2007			
	Area (million hectares)	Production (million tonnes)	Yield (kg per hectare)
1991–92	121.87	168.38	1382
1998–99	125.17	203,61	1627
2006–07	124.07	211.78	1707

Source: GOI, *Agricultural Statistics at a Glance* (various issues).

There was a deceleration in both population growth and agricultural growth, but agricultural growth slowed down more than population growth, resulting in falling availability of food grain (figure 2.2).

Looking at the statistics of area, production, and yield of food grain in India from 1991–92 to 2006–07, both area and production increased: area by 2.2 million hectares, and production by 43.4 million tonnes. However, the largest gain took place in productivity improvement— from 1991–92 to 2006–07 productivity increased by 325 kg per hectare (table 2.1).

However, looking at it from a regional perspective, it seems there was a failure to disperse agricultural growth and development to the whole country. The alluvial plains of the snow-fed areas of the north and northwest continue to be the granaries of India, at huge cost to their environment and soil fertility. Far from expanding the areas that have higher production and productivity, the shares of all other regions in food grain production has fallen while that of the north and northwest has increased from 26 to 40 per cent (table 2.2).

The trend in net availability shows a decline in the case of pulses, which are the most important source of protein for the poor. The increase in wheat has been offset by a massive decline for 'other cereals' and a smaller decline in rice. It is well known that many of these other cereals are the millets and coarse cereals grown in the rain dependent drylands with a large presence of poor tribal cultivators in central and eastern India. Rice and pulses, too, are cultivated in uplands, through dry broadcasting for rice and by traverse intercropping in the case of pulses in the hilly and undulating areas in these regions. Thus, the regional neglect has also meant that availability of these groups of food grains has suffered a serious setback (figure 2.3).

Figure 2.4 and table 2.3 show that per capita net food grain availability per day and per year have gone down from 1990 to 2007.

Per capita net food grain availability per day and per year have gone down from 1990 to 2007

Table 2.2 Share of regions in food grain production for selected states (triennial average), 1960–2006					
					(%)
Zone	1960–62	1972–74	1984–86	1990–93	2000–03
North and northwest region (Punjab, Haryana and Uttar Pradesh*)	26.1	30.4	39.8	38.82	41.74
West-central region (Rajasthan. Madhya Pradesh, Maharashtra and Gujarat)	29.1	25	23	25.61	24.22
East region (Bihar**, West Bengal, Assam and Orissa)	23.2	22.7	20.2	18.5	20.42
South region (Andhra Pradesh, Karnataka, Kerala and Tamil Nadu)	21.5	21.9	17	17.07	13.61

Notes: *: Including Uttarakhand. **: Including Jharkhand.
Source: MSSRF and WFP 2008.

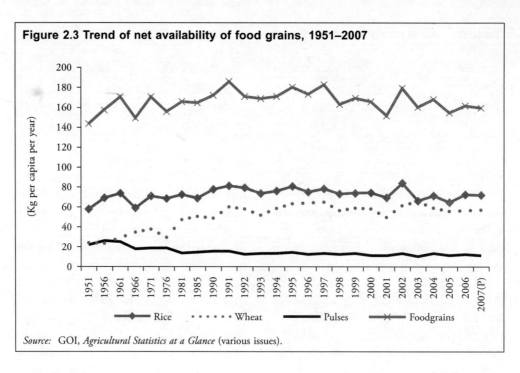

Figure 2.3 Trend of net availability of food grains, 1951–2007

(Kg per capita per year)

Rice ◆ ◆ ◆ Wheat • • • • • Pulses ——— Foodgrains ✕ ✕

Source: GOI, *Agricultural Statistics at a Glance* (various issues).

The high economic growth of the past few years has been accompanied by the failure in rural development, employment generation and poor investment and delivery of public services

Access to food

Employment

Access to adequate and remunerative employment is a very important determinant of food security since it puts purchasing power in the hands of the people in an economy marked by disguised unemployment.

The high economic growth of the past few years has been accompanied by the failure in rural development, employment generation and poor investment and delivery of public services. Poverty is greater in rural areas, though it is also alarming in urban areas. In rural areas, poor farmers and farm labourers are more susceptible to poverty than workers with non-farm income. Unemployment has grown faster than population (table 2.4).

Looking at workforce participation rates (WFPRs), the usual status WFPRs for rural males declined from 55.3 per cent in 1993–94 to 54.6 per cent in 2004–05 in reversal of the prior increase from 54.7 per cent in 1983 to 55.3 per cent in 1993–94. The WFPRs of rural females were relatively unchanging during 1993–94 and 2004–05. WFPRs for urban females increased for two decades except for a fall in 1999–2000 (table 2.5).

The incidence of poverty amongst unorganized sector workers in urban areas is higher across all categories of workers, with the highest difference being for regular workers (table 2.6).

The largest number of workers outside agriculture in rural and urban areas is in the unorganized self-employed sector, which has a very high incidence of poverty. However, the highest incidence of poverty is amongst the unorganized workers in casual labour, whose number is a fourth of the total. The higher incidence in the casual workers category, who are largely manual workers, is due to low availability

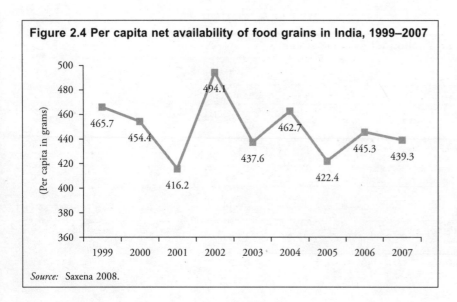

Figure 2.4 Per capita net availability of food grains in India, 1999–2007

(Per capita in grams)

Source: Saxena 2008.

Table 2.3 Net availability of food grains in India*, 1990–2007

(Kg per capita per year)**

Years***	Rice	Wheat	Other cereals	Cereals****	Gram	Pulses****	Food grains****
1990	77.4	48.4	31.7	157.5	3.9	15.0	172.5
1995	80.3	63.0	23.7	167.0	5.4	13.8	180.8
2000	74.3	58.4	21.5	154.3	3.9	11.6	165.9
2005	64.7	56.3	21.7	142.7	3.9	11.5	154.2
2007(P)	71.8	57.0	20.8	149.6	4.3	10.7	160.4

Notes:

*: The net availability of food grains is estimated to be gross production (-) seed, feed and wastage, (-) exports (+) imports, (+/-) change in stocks. **: The net availability of food grains divided by the population estimates for a particular year indicate per capita availability of food grains in terms of kg/year. Net availability thus worked out and further divided by the number of days in a year i.e., 365 days, gives us net availability of food grains in terms of grams/day. Figures in respect of per capita net availability given above are not strictly representative of actual levels of consumption in the country especially as they do not take into account any change in stocks in possession of traders, producers and consumers. ***: For calculation of per capita net availability the figures of net imports from 1981 to 1994 are based on imports and exports on Government of India accounts only. Net imports from 1995 onwards are the total exports and imports (on the government as well as private accounts). ****: Cereals include rice, wheat and other cereals, pulses include all kharif and rabi pulses, and food grains include rice, wheat, other cereals and all pulses.

Sources: GOI, *Agricultural Statistics at a Glance* (various issues) and MSSRF and WFP 2008.

Table 2.4 Growth in population, employment and unemployment, 1983–2005

	Usual Principal Status (millions)				Compounded annual rate of growth (%)	
					Pre-reform period	Post-reform period
	1983	1993–94	1999–2000	2004–05	1983 to 1993–94	1993–94 to 2004–05
Population	720	898	1,001	1,090	2.03	1.78
Labour force	277.34	343.56	377.88	428.35	1.97	2.03
Work force	269.36	334.52	367.37	415.27	1.99	1.99
Unemployment	7.98	9.02	10.51	13.1	1.12	3.45
Unemployment rate	2.88	2.63	2.78	3.06	...	...

Sources: Economic Survey of India (various issues) and GOI, *Employment and Unemployment Situation in India* (various issues)

Table 2.5 Work force participation rates (WFPRs), 1983–2005

(%)

NSS Round No.	Year	Period	\[Usual Status\] PS	All (PS+SS)	CWS	CDS	PS	All (PS+SS)	CWS	CDS
			Rural male				Rural female			
61	2004–05	July–June	53.5	54.6	52.4	48.8	24.2	32.7	27.5	21.6
55	1999–2000	July–June	52.2	53.1	51.0	47.8	23.1	29.9	25.3	20.4
50	1993–94	July–June	53.8	55.3	53.1	50.4	23.4	32.8	26.7	21.9
43	1987–88	July–June	51.7	53.9	50.4	50.1	24.5	32.3	22	20.7
38	1983	January–December	52.8	54.7	51.1	48.2	24.8	34.0	22.7	19.8
			Urban male				Urban female			
61	2004–05	July–June	54.1	54.9	53.7	51.9	13.5	16.6	15.2	...
55	1999–2000	July–June	51.3	51.8	50.9	49.0	11.7	13.9	12.8	13.3
50	1993–94	July–June	51.3	52.1	51.1	49.6	12.1	15.5	13.9	11.1
43	1987–88	July–June	49.6	50.6	49.2	47.7	11.8	15.2	11.9	12 11
38	1983	January–December	50.0	51.2	49.2	47.3	12.0	15.1	11.8	10.6

Notes: PS means Principal Status, SS means Secondary Status, CWS means Current Weekly Status, CDS means Current Daily Status and NSS means National Sample Survey.

Source: GOI, *Employment and Unemployment Situation in India* (various issues).

Table 2.6 Size, distribution and poverty of the organized and unorganized workers in non-agriculture, all India, 2004–05

Category of workers	Number of workers (in million) in non-agriculture			Poverty ratios among non-agricultural workers by category of workers in India, 2004–05 (%)	
	Organized sector	Unorganized sector	Total	Organized sector	Unorganized sector
Self-employed	2.9 (3.15)	89.2 (96.85)	92.1 (100)	11.4	21.4
Regular worker	41.9 (62.82)	24.8 (37.18)	66.7 (100)	6.8	20.2
Casual worker	11.7 (29.4)	28.1 (70.6)	39.8 (100)	35	41.5
Total	56.5 (28.46)	142.1 (71.58)	198.5 (100)	10.4	24.1

Note: Figures in parenthesis are percentages with respect to different category of workers
Source: GOI 2007c.

Table 2.7 Distribution of workforce in India, 1999–2005

(%)

Employment status	1999–2000	2004–05	1999–2000	2004–05
	Rural		Urban	
1. Self-employed	55.76	60.2	42.23	45.4
2. Hired	44.24	39.9	57.77	54.5
(i) Regular	6.83	7.1	40.03	39.5
(ii) Casual	37.41	32.8	17.74	15

Source: Karan and Selvaraj 2008.

Table 2.8 Average daily wages of regular and casual workers (15–59 years), 2004–05

(INR)

	Regular	Casual
Rural	133.81	48.89
Urban	193.73	68.68

Source: Karan and Selvaraj 2008.

Wages

The workforce comprises wage labour and non-wage labour, and the former in turn comprises the more secure regular salary/wage earners and casual workers. The latter or non-wage labour is a mixed bag comprising self-employed persons like own account workers, home-based workers who earn piece rate wages, employers, and unpaid family workers, and can include high degrees of insecurity through uncertainty, irregularity, and inadequacy. For casual workers, both employment and income is precarious. For India, 60 per cent of rural workers and 45 per cent of urban workers are self-employed. This is where employment grew in the early 2000s of work and low wages whereas the self-employed are a mixed bag of very poor people using this as a residual sector, and well-off independent entrepreneurs.

replacing casual employment. Regular employed has remained unchanged at a low 7 per cent for rural and 40 per cent for urban India (table 2.7).

The clear trends in terms of wages are the rural-urban differentials, the casual-regular differentials and the male-female differentials. Regular rural workers earn less than their urban counterpart. Further, casual workers earn only about one-third of what regular workers earn across the board (table 2.8). The fall in this gap in the latest period is on account of a fall in regular wages and not any great increase in casual wages.

Female regular workers receive far lower wages than males, with a difference of 40 per cent in rural areas and 25 per cent in urban areas for regular workers (2004–05). The gender differential in this segment has shot up in rural areas, even as it fluctuates in urban areas. The differential among rural casual workers has remained unchanged while it has declined somewhat in urban areas. For regular wage workers, the inequality is about 25 per cent in urban areas and has remained so, but it has increased from 30 to 40 per cent in rural areas. Workers from the socially disadvantaged groups like Scheduled Castes (SCs) and Scheduled Tribes (STs) also earn lower wages than others due to the operation of multiple social discriminations. These differentials are more marked for regular workers than for casual workers and for male workers than for female workers (table 2.9).

Food inflation

There has been very quick and continual rise in food prices in the last three years and food price inflation has been in double digits for prolonged periods. This has had an adverse impact on the living standards of the vast majority. This has in part been exacerbated by some policies like the deregulation of petrol prices.

Furthermore, the retail prices of food have increased far more than wholesale prices, and the Ministry of Consumer Affairs, Food and Public Distribution data for mid-2010 indicates that the average retail prices increased on average by about 75 per cent for pulses and sugar and by 20 per cent for rice and wheat and 33 per cent each for onions and potatoes (over the previous two years). The situation is no better for vegetables, putting them out of reach for the common people. Thus, the effective rate of inflation for consumers is far higher than the Wholesale Price Index (WPI) calculation indicates, with significant regional variations.

The price monitoring cell of the Department of Consumer Affairs, Ministry of Consumer Affairs, Food and Public Distribution collects the retail and wholesale prices of essential commodities from 37 cities and towns. If seen over a three-year period, this data reveals a consistent and fast rise in the cost of the food basket, comprising cereals, pulses, sugar, tea, milk, onions, etc.

Consider the following:
Price per kg of 'fair average' quality of rice rose by 42 per cent on an average from January 2008 to December 2010. In 12 urban centres the increase is over 50 per cent. Price rise for a kg of *toor dal* (one of the most popular pulses) is 46 per cent, with an over 50 per cent increase in 11 urban centres. Price rise for wheat is over 30 per cent in 10 centres. Average increase for loose tea is 38 per cent (in 11 cities and towns it is between 40 and 100 per cent).

Table 2.9 Average daily wages/earnings across social groups in India, 2004–05

(INR)

	Rural		Urban	
	Casual			
	Male	Female	Male	Female
STs	45.63	33.33	62.69	42.49
SCs	54.92	36.06	72.35	44.31
Others	56.05	34.35	74.98	46.57
	Regular			
STs	130.38	78.04	207.02	123.06
SCs	120.53	59	147.95	93.56
Others	178.67	113.37	240.04	197.36

Source: Karan and Selvaraj 2008.

Sugar price increase is 102 per cent on an average. *Gur* (a crude non-centrifugal sugar in lump) prices over the same three-year period rose by an average of 118 per cent. The per litre price of milk rose by 37 per cent. Prices per kg of onion increased by 197.5 per cent on average. The average increase per kg potatoes was 39.5 per cent.

The rise in prices of essential food items in the last five years implies the higher cost of the per capita consumption of these items as reported by the 61st round of the *National Sample Survey (2004 July to 2005 June)*. This has resulted in low levels of per capita calorie consumption, and a decline or stagnation in these levels over time.

The *Consumer Expenditure Survey 2006–07* reports that 50 per cent of rural households spend less than INR19.33 per day at 2006–07 prices while the average expenditure of all rural households is INR23.17 only at 2006–07 prices.[5] In urban India, the average is INR43.73 per day at 2006–07 prices. These figures reflect both the low level of household food security and rural-urban inequality.

The quantum of trade in agricultural commodities in the commodity futures markets grew by 102.6 per cent in the eight months after April 2009 to January 2010. The increase in volume and value of futures trade was due to extreme speculation that caused inflation and resulted in huge profiteering. The decontrol and hike in petroleum product prices would only strengthen inflationary

There has been very quick and continual rise in food prices in the last three years. This has had an adverse impact on the living standards of the vast majority

Table 2.10 Mean per capita consumption of calories, protein, and fats, 1983–2005								
Year	Round	Calories (kcal)		Protein (gms)		Fats (gms)	
		Rural	Urban	Rural	Urban	Rural	Urban
1983	38	2,240	2,070	63.5	58.1	27.1	37.1
1987–88	43	2,233	2,095	63.2	58.6	28.3	39.3
1993–94	50	2,153	2,073	60.3	57.7	31.1	41.9
1999–2000	55	2,148	2,155	59.1	58.4	36	49.6
2004–05	61	2,047	2,021	55.8	55.4	35.4	47.4

Source: Deaton and Dreze 2008.

Farmers and producers do not benefit from higher prices and consumers bear the burden, with the intermediary corporate and trading interests earning the high margins

tendencies and increase the suffering of the poor and common people.

The central government is opening up the retail trade to domestic and foreign companies. This will lead to further concentration, create monopolies and increase trade and retail margins and further widen the gap between farm gate and wholesale prices; and between wholesale and retail prices. This creates a situation when farmers and producers do not benefit from higher prices and consumers bear the burden, with the intermediary corporate and trading interests earning the high margins.

Food absorption

Food and calorie consumption

The Planning Commission constituted a 'Task Force on Projection of Minimum Needs and Effective Consumption Demand' which in 1979 recommended a national norm of 2,400 kcal/person/day and 2,100 kcal/person/day for rural and urban areas respectively, to be adjusted for age, occupation, and sex respectively. The Food and Agriculture Organization of the United Nations (FAO) uses a far lower

norm of 1,820 kcal/person/day. Despite the centrality of calories in analysing food security, having a judicious mix of micronutrients, fruits, vegetables, and fats, besides cereals, as well as infrastructure/facilities impacting retention of calories like hygiene, clean water, and sanitation too, are important.

Looking at calorie deficiency, the mean per capita consumption of calories, protein, and fats as calculated by a study for various National Sample Survey (NSS) rounds in rural and urban areas is shown in table 2.10.[6] The table shows the continuous fall in average per capita calorie and protein consumption during the 25 year period, the only food group that has increased is fat.

The proportion of rural persons below 2,400 calories energy intake crossed 70 per cent after economic reforms, and by 2004–05 it was about 80 per cent. In urban India, calorie deficiency has widened and deepened, covering more areas with a higher level of deprivation (table 2.11).

There is an increase for India as a whole in the proportion of urban households who cannot get 2,100 calories daily, from 57.0 per cent in 1993–94 to over 64.5 per cent in 2004–05. The sharpest rise is in the more prosperous states, namely Maharashtra, followed by Kerala, and Delhi (table 2.12).

The anthropometric indicators of nutritional status of women and children in India, too, are among the worst in the world and worsening over time. According to the *National Family Health Survey*, the percentage of underweight children stuck at around 46 per cent between 1998–99 and 2005–06 in the

Table 2.11 Population living in households with per capita calorie consumption below 2,100 kcal in urban and 2,400 kcal in rural areas, 1983–2005				
				(%)
Year	Round	Rural	Urban	All India
1983	38	66.1	60.5	64.8
1987–88	43	65.9	57.1	63.9
1993–94	50	71.1	58.1	67.8
1999–2000	55	74.2	58.2	70.1
2004–05	61	79.8	63.9	75.8

Source: Deaton and Dreze 2008.

Table 2.12 Urban poverty by major states and all India, 2004–05		
	Direct calorie estimate (ratio) (<2,100)	
	2004–05	1993–94
Andhra Pradesh	75.5	63.0
Assam	47.0	49.0
Bihar	65.2	47.5
Delhi	57.0	35.0
Gujarat	58.0	57.0
Haryana	66.4	49.0
Himachal Pradesh	43.5	17.5
Jammu and Kashmir	21.0	25.0
Karnataka	75.5	57.0
Kerala	87.0	67.0
Madhya Pradesh	67.5	52.5
Maharashtra	85.0	52.5
Orissa	48.5	32.0
Punjab	68.8	51.5
Rajasthan	69.5	36.0
Tamil Nadu	70.5	69.0
Uttar Pradesh	47.5	57.0
West Bengal	68.5	49.0
All India	64.5	57.0

Source: Patnaik 2008.

0–3 years' age group.[7] Children fare far worse when we look at the number of anaemic children, whose proportion rose from 74 to 79 per cent.[8]

A commonly used measure of nutritional status is the Body Mass Index (BMI), defined as weight in kg divided by height in metre squared. A BMI of below 18.5 per cent for adults indicates chronic energy deficiency (CED), which reflects calorie deprivation over a long period of time. The percentage of rural women with BMI below 18.5 per cent in 2004–05 was twice that of the urban women and was worst for women in the most vulnerable reproductive age group. Overall for women, this was 36 per cent.

The situation is far worse for the socially and economically disadvantaged groups. Over one-third of women from STs suffer from the double burden of CED and anaemia together, which is twice that of the general female population. Women belonging to the poorest quintile also suffer a higher incidence of the double burden. One in four SC women has both

anaemia and CED, higher than the average. Women from the highest quintile are not spared and every second woman suffers from either anaemia or CED (table 2.13).

Anaemia, CED and stunting: Rural

At least one in three rural Indian women in the reproductive age group is anaemic, and with the exception of Kerala, Punjab, and Himachal Pradesh, it is more than half with an all India average of 58.2 per cent. With the exception of six states, it has increased between the two reference periods, with an all India increase of four percentage points. In the same age group of rural women, CED plagues 39 per cent. There is a strong correlation between states with high anaemia and CED. This has declined somewhat everywhere with an all India decline of 1.8 percentage points, with the exception of Haryana, Madhya Pradesh, Bihar, and Assam where it has increased (annex table 2.1).

Rural children with anaemia in the age group 6–35 months is even higher at 81.2 per cent, with only Kerala and Himachal Pradesh reporting less than 60 per cent. Except for six states, the prevalence of childhood anaemia has actually increased everywhere else with a six percentage points

At least one in three rural Indian women in the reproductive age group is anaemic

Table 2.13 Women's nutrition for social and economic groups					
					(%)
	CED	Anaemia	CED and Anaemia		
			Both	Either	Neither
Social groups					
STs	46.6	68.5	33.5	47.8	18.7
SCs	41.1	58.3	25.7	47.7	26.6
OBC*	35.7	54.4	20.8	48.3	30.9
Others	29.2	51.1	16.8	46.6	36.6
STs/others	1.60	1.34	1.99	1.03	0.51
Wealth groups					
Lowest	51.5	64.3	34.0	47.5	18.5
Second	46.3	60.3	29.0	48.3	22.7
Middle	38.3	56.0	22.9	48.2	28.9
Fourth	28.9	52.2	16.4	48.2	35.4
Highest	18.2	46.1	9.4	45.5	45.1
Lowest/highest	2.83	1.39	3.62	1.04	0.41

Note: *: Other backward castes.

Source: Saxena 2008.

increase for India as a whole. It should therefore come as no surprise that the percentage of children with stunted growth is a high 40 per cent, with a decline in each state except Karnataka. Once again, there is a strong correlation between stunting and anaemia (annex table 2.1).

Anaemia, CED and stunting: Urban

Though it is less than their rural counterparts, urban women too have a very high incidence of anaemia (51 per cent) and CED (25 per cent) in the reproductive age group. Both indicators have worsened over time for India as a whole. In nine states more than half of urban women suffer from anaemia, and in seven states more than a fourth suffer from CED. With the solitary exception of Assam, the incidence of anaemia has increased everywhere, with the highest increase in Gujarat and the three southern states of Andhra Pradesh, Karnataka, and Kerala. Interestingly, the poorer states of Orissa, West Bengal, Bihar, and Uttar Pradesh managed a fall in the incidence of CED amongst urban women (annex table 2.2).

The percentage of urban children (6–35 months) who are anaemic and stunted is lower than their rural counterparts, but the incidence has increased over time, and is a high 72 per cent for anaemia and 37 per cent for stunting. At least half the children in this age group are anaemic in all states, with Karnataka having the highest incidence of 82 per cent. More than a fourth of all children in the reference age group are stunted, with a high of 42 per cent in Gujarat (annex table 2.2). Thus three important conclusions can be drawn:

1) Besides the unacceptably high incidence of CED, anaemia, and stunting, the incidence of all three has increased over time in most states.
2) There is a strong positive correlation between the various indicators of health and nutrition, thereby indicating that the same factors determine all of them.

3) The performance of the high growth states which also have high levels of income is extremely disappointing both in terms of the extent of incidence of anaemia, stunting, and CED, and the efforts made for their reduction.

Drinking water and toilets: Rural

One in every four rural households does not have access to safe drinking water and/or access to a toilet within the residence according to the decadal census. Between 1991 and 2001, the decline in households without safe drinking water was by 17 percentage points and 12 percentage points for toilets (annex table 2.3).

Drinking water and toilets: Urban

It is well known that in urban areas the availability of open fields for defecation or a small private area for a bath, especially for women, is very difficult and has safety implications. Additionally, sanitation, waste disposal, hygiene and health are inextricably linked to each other, and in the urban context, inadequate infrastructure and facilities can have dire consequences for good health. All data sources point to the fact that 7 to 10 per cent of the urban population does not have access to safe drinking water, which has been almost halved between the mid-1990s and mid-2000s. Madhya Pradesh, Tamil Nadu, Orissa, and Assam face maximum deprivation despite their greater efforts to increase drinking water facilities (annex table 2.3). About 17 per cent of urban households do not have access to toilet facilities.

The very rich and the very poor states in terms of income and growth are both plagued by precarious and low food security. The most important conclusion that emerges from the preceding discussion is that high levels of state income and high economic growth are neither necessary nor sufficient conditions for food security, either in terms of its level or the ability to attain food security. A special effort has to be made to attain food security and the

High levels of state income and high economic growth are neither necessary nor sufficient conditions for food security

Box 2.1 State of hunger in India

The Global Hunger Index (GHI) underlines the fact that endemic hunger continues to badly affect a large section of the Indian people. It places India in the category of nations where hunger is 'alarming', ranking 67 out of the 88 developing countries. The International Food Policy Research Institute (IFPRI) estimate of the hunger index for the 17 major states in 2008 (more than 95 per cent of the population of India), put 12 into the 'alarming' category, and one into the 'extremely alarming' category. High levels of hunger are seen even in high growth states. Expectedly, the backward eastern and central region has the worst performance (tables 2.14 and 2.15).

Table 2.14 Data underlying the calculation of the 1990 and 2010 Global Hunger Indices: India and her neighbours

| Country | Proportion of undernourished in the population (%) | | Prevalence of underweight in children under-five years (%) | | Under-five mortality rate (%) | | GHI | | | |
| | | | | | | | Value | | Rank | |
	1990–92	2004–06	1988–92	2003–08	1990	2008	1990 (with data from 1988–92)	2010 (with data from 2003–08)	1990	2010
China	15.0	10.0	15.3	6.0	4.6	2.1	11.6	6.0	14	9
Sri Lanka	27.0	21.0	33.4	21.1	2.9	1.5	21.1	14.5	37	39
Myanmar	44.0	17.0	32.5	29.6	12.0	9.8	29.5	18.8	61	50
Pakistan	22.0	23.0	39.0	25.3	13.0	8.9	24.7	19.1	51	52
Nepal	21.0	16.0	47.2	38.8	14.2	5.1	27.5	20.0	56	56
India	24.0	22.0	59.5	43.5	11.6	6.9	31.7	24.1	67	67
Bangladesh	36.0	26.0	56.5	41.3	14.9	5.4	35.8	24.2	71	68

Source: IFPRI 2010.

Table 2.15 The Indian State Hunger Index and its underlying components

| State | Prevalence of calorie undernourishment (%) | Proportion of underweight among children under-five years (%) | Under-five mortality rate (%) | India State Hunger Index | |
				Value	Rank
Punjab	11.1	24.6	5.2	13.6	1
Kerala	28.6	22.7	1.6	17.6	2
Andhra Pradesh	19.6	32.7	6.3	19.5	3
Assam	14.6	36.4	8.5	19.8	4
Haryana	15.1	39.7	5.2	20.0	5
Tamil Nadu	29.1	30.0	3.5	20.9	6
Rajasthan	14.0	40.4	8.5	21.0	7
West Bengal	18.5	38.5	5.9	21.0	8
Uttar Pradesh	14.5	42.3	9.6	22.1	9
Maharashtra	27.0	36.7	4.7	22.8	10
Karnataka	28.1	37.6	5.5	23.7	11
Orissa	21.4	40.9	9.1	23.8	12
Gujarat	23.3	44.7	6.1	24.7	13
Chhattisgarh	23.3	47.6	9.0	26.6	14
Bihar	17.3	56.1	8.5	27.3	15
Jharkhand	19.6	57.1	9.3	28.7	16
Madhya Pradesh	23.4	59.8	9.4	30.9	17
India	20.0	42.5	7.4	23.3	...

Source: Menon *et al.* 2009.

strategy of economic growth becomes a crucial factor.

Agricultural policy

Evolution of development policy for agriculture in a historical perspective can provide some insights into the present crisis in food security. In the nationalist phase of development immediately after Independence, state-sponsored agricultural development was the cornerstone of national policy of independent India. Food security—in the sense of national self-sufficiency in domestic production as well as protection of deficit areas and people through food distribution—was seen as the foundation of self-reliant and sovereign growth. The importance of agriculture (for raw materials, exportable surpluses and wage goods) was recognized in fighting inflation and the early national five-year plans reflected this. By the fourth plan, it also became clear that agriculture was strategic to self-reliance and non-alignment. The country made significant advances in agricultural (including food) production, due to active state support through public investment in infrastructure; land legislation and laws that attempted to break some constraints to capitalist production;[9] the Green Revolution technological strategy and the introduction of high-yielding seeds, chemical fertilizers and pesticides along with improved implements;[10] price policy based on minimum support price and procurement operations for some crops; expansion in agricultural credit and extension services etc. Land reforms were seen as an intervention to promote equity and break the shackles on investment; expand the availability of the principal wage goods, and raw material; increase the size of the home market; and generate effective demand for goods of mass consumption. Thus, the agrarian sector was seen as an important part of the growth project. The home market and peasantry were protected through tariff and non-tariff restrictions on the import and export of agricultural commodities. These helped achieve agri-cultural growth, self-sufficiency and establish a public procurement and distribution system for some crops.

Despite these achievements, there were fundamental unresolved contradictions and structural constraints that were allowed to persist such as the inability to discipline the rural elite and carry out effective land reforms; the unwillingness to address the locational technological specificities of the drylands, especially in peninsular, central, and eastern India resulting in their gross neglect; the high degree of regional and class concentration of the gains from the Green Revolution technology; the high degree of centralization and bureaucratization of government institutions resulting in a lack of accountability and transparency at the local level; the exclusive technological focus on groundwater extraction and high dams-based storages and canal irrigation resulting in waterlogging and salinization in the canal irrigated tracts and irreversible depletion of groundwater in the tubewell areas; the inability to implement minimum wage legislation and protect the agricultural labourers, etc. Along with the relatively unaltered production relations, these prevented unleashing of agricultural growth with regional and class equity and environmental sustainability.

The present crisis in food security is not entirely a product of the weaknesses of the path of development based on high dams or the Green Revolution strategy, or even the failure of the land reforms programme which resulted in the shift in focus away from egalitarian measures to technocratic solutions in the Fourth Plan. Nor is it an outcome of drought or other natural phenomena. It is clearly an outcome of trade liberalization, deflationary policies and specific structural adjustment measures undertaken in the agrarian sector since 1990. Structural Adjustment Programmes and trade liberalization measures in agriculture demand that the sector be opened up to compete with agricultural production globally. Thus, the state is doing away with all forms of protection to the Indian farmers. The measures include

After Independence, state-sponsored agricultural development was the cornerstone of national policy of independent India

reduction in public investment; privatization; removal of subsidies for fertilizers, energy, water and power; restructuring of credit norms for agriculture; dismantling of the public food distribution system; dismantling land reform legislation; promotion of cash cropping and contract farming; reduction in (and often removal of) tariffs on food imports; fall in employment generation; etc.

Food and nutrition schemes of the government

As a response to the low level and fragility of food security in India, various regimes have formulated policies to (1) increase availability, and (2) improve access. Each of these has in turn changed over time, with a shift in availability over time from import-based availability combined to large irrigation led 'grow more food' strategy; land reforms in the nature of tenancy reforms and distribution of surplus land, towards self-reliance in food production through the high-yielding varieties (HYV)-led Green Revolution; to an emphasis on crop diversification to high value crops based on regional comparative advantage in spices, horticulture, floriculture, etc. Access has been addressed in three ways: by generating wage employment in public works with cash or food payment, by distributing subsidized food and food grain through public procurement to initially the entire population, and later a target group, to the most recent attempt to shift from public provisioning to cash transfers. In this section, the existing food and nutrition schemes are discussed.

The public distribution of food in India

Till 1997, access to the Public Distribution System (PDS), was universal and open to all rural and urban households. Entitled households were given a ration card using which they could buy set amounts of rations of specified commodities. There were a total of 222.2 million families with ration cards, which became a symbol of citizenship. There were inter-state varia-

tions in the entitlements in terms of quantity, commodities, and prices. A network of half a million fair price shops was designated to provide the commodities. These were mostly run by private agents, a few co-operatives and in some cases they were state-owned.

Historically, the PDS has gone through four phases after Independence.[11]

- The first that lasted till about 1960 can be called the phase of import-dependent food security, when more cities and regions were brought within its ambit and the grain was largely imported.
- The second phase, till 1978, can be called the period of national self-sufficiency in production and procurement, when the government set up the Agricultural Prices Commission and the Food Corporation of India to build up domestic procurement and storage, and launched the Green Revolution to boost production.
- The third phase, till 1991, can be called the period of expansion and stock-building with a massive expansion of the PDS through more outlets, procurement and stock maintenance.
- The fourth phase, till the present, may be called the phase of targeting and narrowing, where the policies have resulted in the dismantling of the universal PDS and ushering in of a scheme targeted at the poor (in terms of income).

The Targeted Public Distribution System (TPDS)

The TPDS was adopted as a measure to restrict the food subsidy and was a direct outcome of a 1996 World Bank report. The income poverty line was used to separate households into the 'poor' and 'non-poor', thus dividing the entire population into below poverty line (BPL) and above poverty line (APL) categories. The income poverty line was defined by the Planning Commission. The two groups of households had differentiated entitlements in the PDS both in terms of

Present policies have resulted in the dismantling of the universal PDS and ushering in of schemes targeted at the poor

quantities and prices. Thus the system has dual pricing, and a third price was introduced in 2001 through the Anna Antyodaya Yojana (AAY) that is meant for the most vulnerable groups or the 'poorest of the poor' who receive a higher subsidy than BPL households. In March 2000, the entire APL population faced a massive increase in PDS prices through a denial of the subsidy whatsoever.

Unlike the universal system, the size of the BPL population and entitlements, and therefore quotas, for state governments at the sub-national level are decided by the central government on the basis of the Planning Commission estimates of poverty. Allocations to states are linked to previous utilization. So even as the state governments are responsible for much of the social and economic development in their respective states, vital decisions regarding price, quantity and beneficiary numbers cannot be taken by them. In fact, the ineffectiveness of the TPDS has been admitted by a *2005 Performance Evaluation by the Planning Commission* itself, where it is stated that 'the transition from universal PDS to TPDS has neither benefited the poor, nor helped reduce budgetary food subsidies.[12]

According to M. Swaminathan: 'It is clear that the TPDS has not been effective in ensuring food security to the needy. . . . There are many problems with the TPDS, the most relevant among them are the following: first, targeting has led to large-scale exclusion of genuinely needy persons from the PDS. Secondly, targeting has affected the functioning and economic viability of the PDS network adversely and led to a collapse of the delivery system. Thirdly, TPDS has failed to achieve the objective of price stabilization through transfer of cereals from surplus to deficit regions of the country. Lastly, there are reports of large-scale leakages from the PDS, that is, of grain being diverted and not reaching the final consumer.'[13]

Contrary to its supporters, the TPDS has failed miserably in including and reaching the poor. There are two types of errors that are inevitable in a targeted programme due to flawed estimation and identification. There are huge errors of wrong exclusion, when the deserving get left out, and there are errors of wrong inclusion when the non-poor get included. From the point of view of welfare, clearly, exclusion has far more serious consequences and is completely undesirable since it leads to malnutrition. In its obsession to cut subsidies, the central government is far more concerned about higher numbers and wrong inclusion rather than effective selection. Obviously, a universal programme does not suffer from exclusion problems. However, the government chooses to lower financial costs rather than human costs.

Rural PDS

Several remote and food-insecure areas in the northeastern hilly tracts and in the eastern and central plateau areas of Orissa, Madhya Pradesh, Chhattisgarh, Jharkhand and Bihar have a far higher exclusion than the all India average (annex table 2.4).

The mere holding of a card does not imply the same protection of food security, which varies according to the type of card held. The difference between APL and BPL/AAY prices has increased significantly over the years after 2000, and since the APL prices were hiked at a time when market prices stagnated, APL households stopped lifting grain from the PDS. However, the moment APL offtake fell, future availability was affected since the central government decided to link quotas to offtake. So, paradoxically, when prices in the market rose, APL entitlements were cut. This virtually means the exclusion of APL households from the PDS. The percentage of such households was a staggering 65 per cent in Uttar Pradesh, 78 per cent in Rajasthan, and 60 per cent in Bihar, which together are home to vast numbers of India's poor.

Households without ration cards and households with 'other' ration cards (or the non-BPL/AAY households) can be considered to be the population that is excluded from the PDS as it is currently structured. With a whopping 70 per cent as the all India average, in no state is this exclusion under 43 per cent. With the exception of four states, it is above 60 per cent everywhere else. This is the aggregate picture. If the social composition of those excluded is considered, the more vulnerable socio-economic groups are not adequately protected. The government concedes this point. According to the *XI Plan of the Planning Commission*, there are huge exclusion and inclusion errors in identifying the poor.[14] When the entire sample surveyed by NSS is analysed, the errors of targeting in the inclusion and exclusion across the official poor and non-poor are stark.

Firstly, except for some of the central and eastern states of Orissa, Chhattisgarh, Madhya Pradesh, Tripura, Bihar, and Jharkhand, in all the other states of India the inclusion of the officially poor is far less than the inclusion of the officially non-poor. Secondly, in what can at first appear to be a paradox, except for Tripura, all these states that have more poor than non-poor in their BPL or AAY lists are also amongst the group with the highest absence of the poor.

When the possession of cards by occupation, social group, land ownership and expenditure is analysed, the features of the excluded households become clear. The NSS has five categories of rural households based on sources of income: self-employed in agriculture, self-employed in non-agriculture, agricultural labour, other labour, and other households. Agricultural labourers are amongst the most food-insecure sections of rural society, and more than half of them do not have access to the BPL card. The only states where two-thirds or more rural manual labourers in agriculture were included are Andhra Pradesh, Karnataka, Jammu and Kashmir, and Tripura. Uttar Pradesh, and Bihar, which are amongst the more backward regions with low agricultural wages and employment, excluded over 70 per cent agricultural labour households.

It is also a well known feature of Indian society that SCs status, landlessness and poverty are closely linked to each other with a high degree of overlap. Sixty per cent SCs households in rural India are not covered under the BPL category, and the north and northwest which is home to a large SCs population (Haryana, Uttar Pradesh, Himachal, Punjab and Rajasthan) and the two populous eastern states of Bihar and Assam exclude between 68 and 84 per cent SCs from the BPL category.

However, does the TPDS at least include those households that are considered officially poor according to the Planning Commission's poverty line? In 14 states, more than half of those households who are designated as poor by the official yardstick do not have BPL or AAY cards.

Despite the problems in coverage, the rations from the PDS constitute a high share of rice and wheat consumption of rural households, at over one-fourth for the country as a whole (annex table 2.5). The BPL and AAY households rely heavily on the PDS and the exclusion of needy households is a very important reason that there is low food security in India.

Urban PDS

A larger share of India's population now lives in cities and urban areas, many of them leading precarious lives without proper housing, employment, and social welfare measures. Migrants dependent on manual labour are particularly vulnerable, but the failure of policy and schemes to cover them by food security and other welfare measures is visible on the streets and pavements, in the slums and under the flyovers of every city of India.

The urban situation is far worse when it comes to coverage and incidence of exclusion. At the all India level the incidence of exclusion is a whopping 88.7 per cent, with eight states having the dubious distinction of being above the national average. The same states, with the addition of Tamil Nadu, report the highest exclusion of SCs with an all India average

In 14 states, more than half of those households who are designated as poor by the official yardstick do not have BPL or AAY cards

of 81.1 per cent (who are without doubt the most vulnerable in urban areas too). The exclusion of STs is an even higher 85 per cent. Equally startling is the fact that three-fourths of the lowest expenditure class is excluded from the PDS. Here again, there is a massive overlap with states excluding other vulnerable urban groups (annex table 2.6).

When it comes to households classified by occupation type, the most vulnerable people are likely to be concentrated within the casual labour households, and therefore it comes as no surprise that the exclusion here is relatively less than other categories, but it is still a high 70 per cent. Again, the same set of states that have the highest overall exclusion also excludes the poorest the most.

This exclusion is all the more disturbing when seen in light of the importance of PDS rice and wheat in the total consumption of the poorer expenditure classes, with an all-India average of 23 per cent for rice and 11 per cent for wheat. The four southern states of Karnataka, Kerala, Andhra Pradesh, and Tamil Nadu report the highest reporting households in the bottom 30 per cent, and these are also the states where PDS rice accounts for 40 per cent or thereabouts of total rice consumption. Interestingly, Kerala and Karnataka appear to have the highest outreach of wheat too, along with Gujarat and Maharashtra (annex table 2.6).

The exclusion of APL households from the PDS has severely compromised the financial viability of fair price shops due to the huge decline in offtake (by about 45 per cent). The lower volumes and fixed margins have meant that the profitability of fair price shops are too low for the owners and dealers as their fixed costs of transportation, rent, etc., have remained.

The price stabilization role of the PDS would be most effective under a universal PDS, since the demand for grain from fair price shops will go up when the market price rises relative to the fair price shops price. However, with a large section of the population dependent on the market under the TPDS, the ability of the PDS to stabilize prices has got considerably undermined.

Supplementary nutrition programmes in schools and Anganwadis

Mid-day Meal Scheme (MDMS) and Integrated Child Development Scheme (ICDS)

The National Programme of Nutritional Support to Primary Education, which later became the MDMS, was launched nationally in 1995. Originally, the Scheme would link the provision of a cooked meal at school or three kg of food grain to each child for 80 per cent attendance at school. Only after 2001 in light of a public interest litigation, the Supreme Court of India ordered the government to 'implement the MDMS by providing every child in every government and government-assisted primary school with a prepared mid-day meal with a minimum content of 300 calories and 8–12 gms of protein each day of school for a minimum of 200 days.' While the quality and extent of implementation varied across states, Tamil Nadu and Gujarat are pointed out as success stories.[15]

As in the case of universalization of the PDS, Tamil Nadu was the pioneer in 1982 in covering pre-schoolers, all primary school children, children up to 15 years of age in rural areas, old age pensioners, the destitute, widows and from 1995, all pregnant women under a noon-meal scheme. Of course, children from poorer and socially deprived sections participated more enthusiastically and consistently.[16] It is obviously not very easy to assess the impact of this on nutrition, but surely decline in severe malnutrition (grades III and IV) among children aged 0–36 months from 12.3 per cent in 1983 to 0.3 per cent in 2000 may in part be an outcome of the state's feeding programme.[17]

The ICDS, which began on an experimental basis in 1975, is now an all India programme and provides the under-six children with a number of integrated services. The institutional structure is based

The ICDS, which began on an experimental basis in 1975, is now an all India programme and provides the under-six children with a number of integrated services

on an ICDS centre or *Anganwadi* (government sponsored child-care and mother-care centre), and the services include nutrition, health and pre-school education. In response to a public interest litigation, the Supreme Court has directed the government to make the programme universal, with a functioning *Anganwadi* centre in every settlement, and coverage of all children below six, and eligible (pregnant and lactating) women by the programme. The inter-state variations in quality and coverage are large, and while some states provide cooked hot food, elsewhere ready-to-eat snacks are served. Evaluations report irregular food supply and poor quality of food. The government has institutionalized a system based on thinly spread and very poor infrastructure with an army of unskilled and underpaid workers who do not receive even minimum wages.

Rural ICDS and MDMS: The data for 2004–05 shows that the percentage of rural households with at least one member benefiting from MDMS during the last 365 days was 22.8 per cent for the country as a whole. This is far higher than the ICDS at 5.7 per cent. The worst performers in terms of this indicator for MDMS are, Jammu and Kashmir, Punjab, Bihar, Jharkhand, Haryana, Uttar Pradesh, and Assam. The laggard states for ICDS add Rajasthan to this list (table 2.16).

Urban ICDS and MDMS: In no state of India did even half the children of the relevant age group receive any service at all. When all expenditure classes are taken together, the percentage of urban households benefiting from MDMS is only eight per cent, which, though higher than for ICDS, is still very low. Almost 20 per cent of the lowest 30 per cent receive some benefit, and both these figures are well below the corresponding rural figure (table 2.17).

Allocation, offtake, procurement and stocks

The huge amount of exclusion discussed above manifests itself in falling allocation and offtake on the one hand, and

Table 2.16 Rural households with at least one member benefiting from ICDS/MDMS during the last 365 days, 2004–05

(%)

States	ICDS	MDMS
Andhra Pradesh	4.4	21.6
Assam	6.6	18
Bihar	0.7	10.7
Chhattisgarh	14.7	40.6
Gujarat	9.8	27.2
Haryana	9.4	15.8
Himachal Pradesh	5.7	27.7
Jammu and Kashmir	2.2	1.3
Jharkhand	0.9	11.2
Karnataka	4.5	33.4
Kerala	7.4	21.7
Madhya Pradesh	3.1	32.3
Maharashtra	13.2	26.6
Orissa	15.5	26.5
Punjab	1.3	3.1
Rajasthan	1.5	21.6
Tamil Nadu	5.7	31.8
Uttar Pradesh	0.9	16.1
West Bengal	9.5	29.8
All India	5.7	22.8

Source: GOP 2007b.

The percentage of rural households with at least one member benefiting from MDMS was 22.8 per cent

commensurate excess stockholding on the other, without any increase in procurement activities. The allocation of food grains began to decline very sharply from 2004–05 onwards with a fall by 50 per cent. The decline in wheat accounted for a significant share in total decline (figure 2.5).

Total offtake continued to rise in absolute terms throughout this period. Offtake under BPL rose till 2004–05, to fall in subsequent years. Offtake of food grains declined after 2004–05 and increased slightly in 2007–08, but was still lower than 2003–04. While BPL offtake decreased, AAY offtake increased, keeping the offtake of BPL and AAY more or less stagnant during the reference period (figure 2.6).

Allocations and offtake under the MDMS declined throughout the period despite there being a larger number of children in schools, though there was a slight turnaround in 2007–08 (figure 2.7).

Table 2.17 Aspects of access to supplementary nutrition and services under ICDS and MDMS in urban areas

(%)

	Mothers who received any services from an AWC during pregnancy	Mothers who received Supplementary food	Children age 0–71 months who received some service from an AWC	Children age 0–71 months who received Supplementary Food	Urban households with at least one member benefiting from	
					ICDS	MDMS
Andhra Pradesh	18.2	17.7	22.4	20.5	1.0	8.6
Assam	16.9	16.9	21.2	17.8	0.5	2.0
Bihar	6.3	6.1	14.2	8.2	0.0	2.2
Gujarat	16.6	14.8	29.0	21.6	4.4	8.7
Haryana	2.9	2.9	4.3	2.9	3.0	2.8
Karnataka	13.2	12.5	16.0	11.2	1.1	11.3
Kerala	18.1	16.3	32.8	24.4	5.3	12.5
Madhya Pradesh	35.2	32.2	45.3	39.3	1.3	11.4
Maharashtra	11.8	9.9	23.9	21.5	3.2	9.3
Orissa	20.2	8.7	41.3	26.9	4.9	9.0
Punjab	0.0	0.0	0.0	0.0	0.1	0.3
Rajasthan	5.9	4.6	4.6	2.0	0.2	3.8
Tamil Nadu	38.6	37.1	36.1	25.2	3.0	15.6
Uttar Pradesh	4.6	4.5	10.6	8.3	0.1	3.1
West Bengal	13.3	12.9	18.4	16.2	1.2	9.3
All India	16.8	15.6	...	...	...	...

Note: AWC means *Anganwadi* centre. AWC services for children include distribution of supplementary food, growth monitoring, immunization, health check-up and pre-school education.

Source: GOP 2007a.

The food security legislation

Universal access to affordable food grain was brought on the national political agenda ever since the problems in the TPDS became clear. The present Congress-led United Progressive Alliance government at the centre promised to enact legislation to guarantee access to food security to all Indians by providing 25 kg of grain at INR3 per kg. This task was given to the National Advisory Council (NAC).

The decision taken by NAC on 23 October 2010 and the subsequent Draft Bill rechristens BPL as 'priority', and APL as 'general'. It increases the percentage of priority households for rural areas by four percentage points, and for urban areas by two percentage points when compared to government estimates. The share of each state is to be in accordance with the Planning Commission ratios. To these households, the proposed bill gives 35 kg rice, wheat or millets at INR3, INR2 and INR1, respectively. The general category

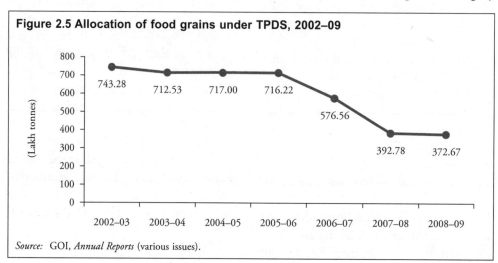

Figure 2.5 Allocation of food grains under TPDS, 2002–09

(Lakh tonnes)

743.28 712.53 717.00 716.22 576.56 392.78 372.67

2002–03 2003–04 2004–05 2005–06 2006–07 2007–08 2008–09

Source: GOI, *Annual Reports* (various issues).

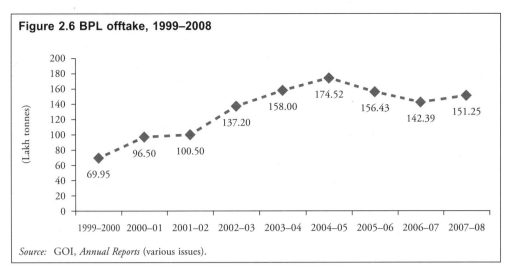

Figure 2.6 BPL offtake, 1999–2008

Source: GOI, *Annual Reports* (various issues).

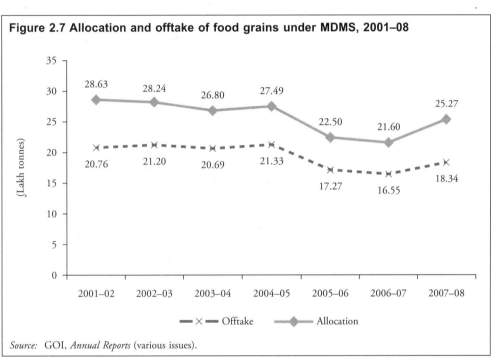

Figure 2.7 Allocation and offtake of food grains under MDMS, 2001–08

Source: GOI, *Annual Reports* (various issues).

The NAC recommendations reduce the number of 'priority' households by 2.11 crores

households will comprise 44 per cent of the rural households and 22 per cent of the urban households, and will be entitled to 20 kg per month at half the minimum support price. Thus 90 per cent rural households and 50 per cent urban households are to be covered with unequal and differentiated entitlements. The mechanism and criteria for their identification/selection is to the central government.

The NAC recommendations in fact reduce the number of 'priority' households by 2.11 crores (11 crore persons) as compared to the present number of actual

cardholders. In fact, the current situation is that 56 per cent of the 2001 population has already got BPL cards. This will come down by 14 percentage points in the NAC formulation, a removal of 3.4 crore households (18.8 crore persons).

Availability of food grain is an essential prerequisite for food security. Roughly a hundred million tonnes of cereals are required for a universal PDS (with 80 per cent offtake and 35 kg per household), which is 57 per cent of total production, net of seeds and wastage. Currently, procurement is about 30 per cent of production. Given the geographically

Sustained food security requires self-reliance in food grains production to feed the 1.15 billion-plus population which in turn requires adequate public investment

unequal concentration of production and procurement in India, most of this is from four or five states. Expanding guaranteed procurement to all states and crops, announcing cost-covering minimum support price in advance, strengthening the decentralized procurement scheme, building storages and godowns in many more places, giving incentives to local doorstep procurement, and making timely payments to farmers are measures needed to increase procurement.

These are of course steps to be taken immediately. In the medium term, it is essential to improve production and productivity of food production through public investment, provision of extension services, inputs at controlled prices, appropriate land use policies with guaranteed fair prices for farmers through a stronger network of geographically dispersed procurement centres. A special package for *adivasi* (tribal people) farmers and dryland farming will encourage the production of pulses, millets, and coarse grains suited to dry and non-irrigated land.

In any case, the ground reality in India today is not of a supply-constrained system but excessive stock-holding. The fact is that the government is holding 60 million tonnes, well over the buffer norms. The holding in excess of storage capacity (roughly 15 million tonnes) is lying in the open, and often rotting even as vast sections of the Indian population go hungry.

It is the fiscal concern to reduce subsidies that have led to the pricing policy that links the minimum support price or cost of acquisition to the issue price, to sell the food at some proportion of the economic cost. However, food security has two aspects; production and consumption. Farmers or producers need to cover their cost of production and if farming is to once again become a viable activity, profitability has to be maintained through assured procurement. Consumers, on the other hand, are constrained by their ability to pay, and prices for them have to meet the yardstick of affordability. If both consumer affordability and producer

profitability have to be ensured for food security, the two prices cannot be the same.

Financing food security

The Indian economy witnessed a negative growth rate in agriculture (–0.2 per cent in 2009–10) accompanied by massive inflation of prices of many essential commodities since 2008–09.[18] This was accompanied by the recession induced job loss in the manufacturing and textile industries and the urban construction sector. According to a Government of India Commission on the Unorganized Sector, 77 per cent of the rural population spends less than or equal to INR20 per day as consumption expenditure which underlines the low purchasing power in the hands of the rural population.

Agriculture

Even as the overall gross domestic product (GDP) grew at an average 8.62 per cent per annum from 2004–05 to 2010–11, agricultural GDP grew by only 3.46 per cent per annum in the same period. Thus the share of agriculture in the country's GDP has continuously fallen over the years to 14.2 per cent as per 2010–11 estimates at constant 2004–05 prices, compared to 19 per cent in 2004–05. Sustained food security requires self-reliance in food grains production to feed the 1.15 billion-plus population which in turn requires adequate public investment. The decline in performance is due to many reasons, in particular the shrinking share of public investment in this sector.

The share of agriculture in the total expenditure from the Union Budget has fallen sharply from 15.7 per cent in 2007–08 to 10.3 per cent in 2011–12 (budget estimate). The Union Government's expenditure on the rural sector as a whole (agriculture and allied activities; rural development; special area programmes; irrigation and flood control; and village and small industries) fell from 3.34 per cent of GDP in 2008–09 to 2.3 per cent

Table 2.18 Spending on rural economy as a proportion of total Union Budget expenditure and GDP, 2004–12

Year	Expenditure on rural economy*		Expenditure on agriculture and allied activities	
	As a % of total Union Budget expenditure	As a % of GDP at current market prices	As a % of total Union Budget expenditure	As a % of GDP at current market prices
2004–05	9.9	1.5	7.3	1.1
2005–06	11.3	1.6	7.4	1.0
2006–07	14.6	2.0	8.3	1.1
2007–08	13.1	1.9	9.6	1.4
2008–09	21.1	3.3	15.7	2.5
2009–10	15.7	2.5	11.4	1.8
2010–11 RE**	17.9	2.8	11.9	1.8
2011–12 BE**	16.4	2.3	10.3	1.4

Notes: *: Expenditure on rural economy includes: agriculture and allied activities; rural development; special area programmes; irrigation and flood control; and village and small industries. **: RE means revised estimate and BE means budget estimate.

Source: CBGA 2010.

of GDP in 2011–12. Even in Central Plan allocation, the share of agriculture and allied activities has fallen since 2005–06 (table 2.18)

Food subsidy

Food subsidy has hovered at values less than one per cent of GDP, therefore demonstrating the failure to transfer any benefits of the high growth to food security. Total subsidies have declined after 2008, both as a share in GDP and in total budgetary expenditure. The budgetary allocation for food subsidy in 2011–12 has fallen in relation to both the total Union Budget and to the GDP; it

also fell in absolute terms relative to the preceding year's revised estimates. This has been done in a year when it intends to start implementation of the proposed National Food Security Act. At a time when food inflation was in the neighbourhood of 18 per cent, the share of food subsidy as a proportion to the GDP has remained below one per cent in the seven years preceding 2011–12 (figure 2.8). Various estimates have been made regarding the cost of a universal system of food security, and even if all households were to be given 35 kg per month at INR2 per kg, and assuming that they all bought this grain, the food subsidy bill would be two per cent of the GDP.

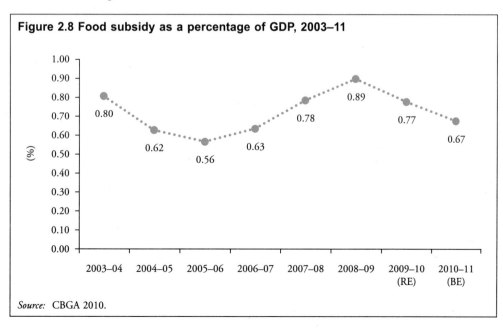

Figure 2.8 Food subsidy as a percentage of GDP, 2003–11

Source: CBGA 2010.

Conclusion

The recurrent story in the international news media as well as the Indian corporate media has been to project the Indian story as a reflection of its arrival as a world economic power. This is despite the overwhelming indictment of India as a poor performer on human and social development and its growing ranks of citizens suffering chronic hunger and malnutrition. There can be no getting away from the undeniable conclusion that India has failed abysmally in designing and implementing interventions that pull its people out of chronic and widespread undernutrition.

What makes this failure worse is that India knew what to do after the wake up call in the 1960s after successive droughts. In the mid-1960s, it put in place a sound matrix of policies for food security, through production, procurement, storage, and distribution. Problems notwithstanding, the outcome was positive from the point of view of national availability and price stabilization of cereals. However, this was dismantled and thrown out with liberalization since the primary aim was to cut the food subsidy rather than provide full fledged food security. This has compromised food security with inflation compounding the problem.

The most startling instance of the destruction of food security was the introduction of the TPDS which paradoxically led a high incidence of exclusion of the more vulnerable groups and a sizable section of even those whom the government defines as income poor. The *National Sample Survey in 2004–05*[19] demonstrates that a large proportion of agricultural labour and other manual labour households, households belonging to the SCs and STs, households with little or no land, and households in the lowest expenditure classes, are excluded from the PDS today.

The path of economic reforms that has resulted in high economic growth in some regions and sectors has been accompanied by utter failure on the food security front,

in terms of food security in all aspects— production, availability, distribution, affordability, absorption and nutrition— which makes India one of the most undernourished countries in the world. The government's own *Economic Survey* reports that food grain production has declined by 11 per cent from 208 kg per annum per capita in 1996–97 to 186 kg in 2009–10. Despite this negative growth rate in per capita production, perversely, the Government of India has continually exported an average seven million tonnes of cereals per annum, resulting in a further fall in availability by 15 per cent from 510 gms per day per capita in 1991 to 436 gms in 2008. It is no surprise that there is a commensurate fall in the annual per capita consumption of cereals across all expenditure classes. As India became more affluent in the last two decades in terms of national income, the cereal consumption of the rural population continued to be low and falling. The inequality across expenditure groups remains high with the lower most deciles consuming roughly 60 to 73 per cent the quantity consumed by the highest. This is clearly a reflection of their distress in terms of dwindling incomes and employment; increasing burden of other expenses (such as healthcare, schools, fuel, light and transport) and the inability of the TPDS to intervene effectively. The food expenditure of the poor has been constricted due to the privatization of other services pushing up the cost of non-food requirements. Inflation and rising prices of food has meant that there is inadequate access of the poorer sections of the population to expensive foods, such as pulses, vegetables, oil, fruits, and meat products which provide essential proteins, fats, and micronutrients. Lack of access to safe drinking water and toilets within easy distance too results in poor absorption of whatever is consumed. The patriarchal norms and low social status of women and the girl child leads to their poor health outcomes, early age at marriage, low weight at pregnancy, poor nutrition and low weight of new born babies. The

The path of economic reforms that has resulted in high economic growth in some regions and sectors has been accompanied by utter failure on the food security front

government schemes and programmes were meant to overcome these constraints. The poor and worsening spread and reach of government infrastructure and services has only compounded the problem to such an extent that the situation seems to be spiralling out of hand and the MDG to halve hunger by 2015 recedes more and more. This is happening at a time when there is excess stockholding in the government system (at about three times the norm).

Policy recommendations

The problem is multi-faceted requiring a multi-pronged approach. The following emerge as the factors that must be addressed by public policy:

Increase food production

Stagnation in agricultural growth, income and rural employment after the mid-1990s caused a massive crisis in rural areas. In the medium and long term, there is a very high likelihood of slowdown in cereal production in the existing five surplus producing states, and if India is to retain self-sufficiency in food, growth must be more dispersed and spread to the eastern and central states. The most significant intervention that is needed is larger investment in infrastructure like irrigation, power, and roads; agricultural extension services; more and cheap credit for investment; assured procurement at cost-covering prices for all crops and regions; and availability of subsidized and improved inputs. The producers have to be protected against the volatility of international prices to avert the repetition of huge losses a decade ago. Furthermore, it is essential to increase productivity and reduce variability in production in the drylands and in central and eastern India, where the concentration of poverty is increasing.

Disperse growth to the drylands

The importance of the drylands can be gauged from the fact that half the Indian workforce is engaged here and a similar proportion of the agricultural sector is in the rain-fed areas. Except for the 1970s, productivity in the dry districts has grown far more slowly than the non-dry, and the gap has widened over time. Despite the significance of drylands in Indian agriculture, from the point of view of national income, food production, employment and growth, it has suffered serious neglect.

The central and eastern plateau and hill regions are predominantly drylands, with large poverty-affected and agriculture dependent tribal populations and a very harsh ecological setting. The uninterrupted neglect of these regions has led to regionally imbalanced agricultural growth, ultimately resulting in a slow overall agricultural growth rate. This has been in part due to concentration of public irrigation in the alluvial plains; and unchanged class relations due to ineffective land reforms, resulting in high ground rent in many low growth areas. Growth has occurred where state intervention altered unfavourable initial conditions, either through investment in infrastructure and irrigation, or through land reforms.

To ensure production stability and growth, public investment in soil and water conservation as well as micro irrigation in a location specific manner is a must here. Despite a modest average size of operational holding, these areas are plagued by severe malnutrition and hunger. Thus, farming by these small and marginal farmers has to be revamped with a far greater attention to technology and profitability. Furthermore, increased soil moisture and soil retention will boost production on small and marginal farms. Higher bio-mass as private and common property improve access of the poor to more fodder, fuelwood, water, etc. Millets are robust and sturdy crops grown in the drylands and can grow on the worst soils under dry conditions. They have an unexplored potential to contain hunger and poverty. They should be procured and used for food and nutrition programmes.

It is essential to increase productivity and reduce variability in production in the drylands and in central and eastern India, where the concentration of poverty is increasing

Mahatma Gandhi National Rural Employment Guarantee Scheme needs to be strengthened and extended to urban areas in order to increase mass purchasing power

The Mahatma Gandhi National Rural Employment Guarantee Act (MGNREGA) offers the perfect opportunity to take up labour-intensive works that increase rural assets for irrigation, drought proofing, and land and soil conservation on public lands, and on the lands of some categories of socially disadvantaged farmers (SCs, STs, BPL households and beneficiaries of land reforms and Indira Awaas Yojana) and all small and marginal farmers. This should be strengthened by promoting decentraliz-ed local area development.

Improve land use policies

Land use policies have far-reaching implications for livelihood security, food security, common property access, housing patterns, industrial zoning, etc. In an economy with widespread nutritional poverty and hunger, national and regional self-sufficiency in food production has to be the first priority when determining land use for agricultural land. Even the so-called barren and wasteland can be reclaimed for dryland farming and many poor communities depend on such marginal land through agro-silvi-pastoral systems. Forest areas are home to the traditional forest dwellers (as farmers, gatherers and nomads) as well as to huge mineral and hydro-electric wealth. The genuine livelihood and food security needs of people must get a high priority and should be protected against the corporate search for lands for forest wealth, minerals, etc. It is crucial to make the so-called barren and wastelands available to the poor for agro-silvi-pastoral systems instead of diverting them for biofuels and to the corporate sector. Fruit trees can be planted on degraded forests and homestead lands and given to local communities for cons-umption and management.

Furthermore, despite the passage of the Scheduled Tribes and Other Traditional Forest Dwellers (Recognition of Forest Rights) Act 2007, the implementation is very tardy. This Act must be more vigorously implemented.

Ensure remunerative and assured employment

It is extremely vital to create more jobs opportunities at decent minimum wages by undertaking massive public works in both rural and urban areas. Furthermore, the Mahatma Gandhi National Rural Employment Guarantee Scheme is restricted only to rural areas and even there the average days of work generated is less than half the promised number of 100 days, and the real wage is continually falling due to inflation. The legal guarantee of 100 days at statutory minimum wages promised under MGNREGA has been met in only three per cent of the cases. Additionally, the linkage of wages to productivity and very unrealistic pro-ductivity norms have resulted in the non-payment of minimum wages. The average days of work remains below 40 per house-hold per year. Therefore, the programme needs to be strengthened and extended to urban areas in order to increase mass purchasing power.

The entitlement should be increased in both cases to 100 days per person and wages should be paid fully and indexed to inflation. A larger menu of works should be permitted, so that it is not difficult to generate employment. The assets and the income multiplier will both contribute to increase in growth and productivity.

Universalize and expand public distribution and other nutrition schemes

A well-functioning universal PDS can be the means to ensure adequate physical access to food at the local and household levels. The suggestions for a universal public distribution system, for universalization of good quality ICDS, and for a mid-day meal to all primary and secondary school children have huge inter-generational welfare implications.

ICDS reaches only 12.5 per cent children in the age group 6 months to 6 years with allocations by-passing vulnerable children of poorer households, lower castes and remote hamlets. The MDMS, too, has limited reach. Both programmes have to be strengthened through universalization and by creating legal entitlements. Workers in the ICDS and the MDMS, too, must be regularized and paid minimum wages. Their skills and capacities must be enhanced.

The PDS must cover all households in an undifferentiated manner and provide at least 35 to 50 kg of food grain per household per month at affordable prices. Pulses, oil, millets, and sugar must be brought under a guarantee in the food security legislation. Universal PDS must be accompanied by universal procurement, regional self-sufficiency must be ensured through a match between procurement and distribution, and to the extent possible, local self-sufficiency should be pursued. This requires a massive revamp of the decentralized procurement scheme.

There is a great need to reform the PDS by bringing the outlets into the government sector and making it more transparent and accountable in order to plug leakages. *Panchayats* (a legislative body of five wise and respected elders chosen and accepted by the village community) and *Gram Sabhas* (a meeting of all adults who live in the area covered by a *Panchayat*) must have the powers to monitor fair price shops. Their viability must be increased both by universalization and sale of other items.

Control inflation

There is for the last year or thereabouts galloping food price inflation (WPI), which crossed 19 per cent in the week ending 28 November 2010, and in early 2011 stood at 18 per cent. There is spiralling inflation in several food articles with the prices of vegetables (particularly potatoes and onions), pulses and cereals witnessing the highest increase. One of the main reasons for this is the black-marketeering and hoarding whenever there are any shortages due to weak laws and inadequate monitoring.

The government, central and state, must initiate a nationwide onslaught against hoarding and black-marketing. Private traders of food must be required to disclose their stocks and release surpluses.

Improve healthcare, water and sanitation

A higher public investment in primary health centres and clinics, disease prevention and control, water and sanitation, rural electrification and rural roads is the need of the hour. The systems of service delivery have to be improved. Recent trends of privatization by the withdrawal of the state or by providing cash rather than service has proved detrimental, especially in areas with inadequate infrastructure.

Cash transfers not a solution

There have been several suggestions for large scale substitution of PDS by direct cash transfers. The whole idea behind cash transfers involves a shift from public provisioning to cash, which in turn places consumers at the mercy of the market. It tends to exacerbate inequalities since deficit areas with poor availability of grain and infrastructure would not be able to convert the cash into the grain that it is meant for. It will give a boost to private traders who will once again monopolize food sales. In a situation which has supply constraints, the higher liquidity is likely to push up prices and speculation if the government does not supply the grain. The ability of cash transfers to meet the ends of nutrition are severely undermined by inflation, and the growing cost of other services like health, transport, and lighting that erode expenditure on foods. Policy alternatives by way of conditional or unconditional cash transfers instead of food grains are wrong because they do not ensure food availability in an inflationary situation.

Since procurement serves the dual purpose of garnering food surpluses to provide food security to food deficit areas

The government, central and state, must initiate a nationwide onslaught against hoarding and black-marketing

and people, along with providing remunerative prices to farmers, dismantling of the PDS after the introduction of cash transfers will be to the detriment of both consumers and producers. Finally, there is every likelihood of leakages through cash transfers, too, since low banking will involve middlemen and commission agents, especially in the unbanked areas. Therefore, shifting to cash transfers will not be effective in terms of food security.

Expenditure on agriculture, employment generation and the PDS must be expanded significantly

Increase public expenditure

Expenditure on agriculture, employment generation and the PDS must be expanded significantly. Food production, procurement and distribution are extremely important aspects of food security as are remunerative employment, health, water and sanitation. All these require a massive increase in expenditure, by at least three to four per cent of GDP, which is entirely a question of political will.

Annex table 2.1 Status of rural women (15–49 years) and children, 1998–2006

(%)

States	Rural women with anaemia (15–49 years)		Rural women with CED (15–49 years)		Rural children with anaemia (age 6–35 months)		Rural children stunted (age 6–35 months)	
	1998–99	2005–06	1998–99	2005–06	1998–99	2005–06	1998–99	2005–06
Andhra Pradesh	50.6	63.7	43.2	37.5	73.3	82.7	41.6	37.3
Assam	69.9	69.5	27.9	39.5	63.8	77.4	50.9	35.5
Bihar	63.9	68.2	40.3	45.9	81.3	89.0	55.0	43.7
Chhattisgarh	59.4	...	...	45.7	...	82.1	...	47.9
Gujarat	51.3	59.2	47.7	41.9	78.5	83.6	46.7	45.6
Haryana	47.5	56.9	30.8	32.5	83.0	83.3	53.0	38.9
Himachal Pradesh	40.7	41.2	31.0	25.8	70.3	59.8	42.2	26.7
Jammu and Kashmir	59.9	53.6	30.4	26.1	71.7	67.3	41.0	28.3
Jharkhand	73.7	...	...	47.8	...	80.5	...	44.2
Karnataka	46.0	52.5	47.0	38.2	72.7	84.3	39.3	43.3
Kerala	23.4	32.4	19.9	14.3	43.2	57.9	22.7	21.1
Madhya Pradesh	57.0	61.0	41.8	44.98	75.4	84.9	54.3	41.6
Maharashtra	51.2	51.1	49.3	44.2	78.0	76.8	44.2	40.3
Orissa	64.1	64.0	49.9	43.7	72.7	75.8	44.8	39.1
Punjab	42.5	37.4	20.5	14.5	80.9	80.0	42.7	28.7
Rajasthan	49.1	54.9	38.7	36.5	82.6	80.1	54.1	36.4
Tamil Nadu	59.1	53.9	35.2	30.0	70.5	71.0	30.6	24.4
Uttar Pradesh	49.4	49.8	39.1	37.2	73.9	85.7	57.3	42.0
West Bengal	64.2	65.6	49.8	44.9	81.5	71.9	45.1	35.4
All India	53.9	58.2	40.6	38.8	75.3	81.2	48.5	40.7

Sources: GOI 2000 and 2007a.

Annex table 2.2 Status of urban women (15–49 years) and children, 1998–2006

(%)

States	Urban women (15–49 years) with anaemia		Urban women with CED		Urban children (6–35 months) with anaemia, 1998–99 and 2005–06		Urban children (6–35 months) who are stunted, 1998–99 and 2005–06	
	1998–99	2005–06	1998–99	2005–06	1998–99	2005–06	1998–99	2005–06
Andhra Pradesh	47.4	59.7	19.7	22.1	69.5	73.5	29.7	33.2
Assam	67.2	65.9	18.8	26.4	52.3	70.4	37.1	35.3
Bihar	59.6	61.2	31.1	30.5	80.7	69.1	42.2	38.2
Gujarat	39.5	50.9	22.8	24.6	67.9	73.8	38.5	42.4
Haryana	45.8	55.2	13.7	20.6	86.6	79.8	40.3	36.1
Karnataka	35.7	48.3	23.8	26.3	66.3	81.6	30.9	33.9
Kerala	20.4	34.1	14.7	15.2	46.8	53.2	18.5	27.3
Madhya Pradesh	46.2	48.0	28.2	30.7	3.7	75.4	39.8	41.1
Maharashtra	44.8	46.0	26.2	26.6	72.8	65.7	33.3	40.0
Orissa	54.8	55.9	32.9	28.6	68.3	63.2	37.0	36.0
Punjab	39.0	39.1	9.2	17.2	77.2	80.5	29.4	32.9
Rajasthan	46.7	48.0	28.5	30.9	81.3	78.5	44.0	29.4
Tamil Nadu	51.6	52.0	17.5	22.8	66.2	74.2	27.1	30.1
Uttar Pradesh	46.0	49.6	23.3	22.9	74.1	73.5	46.7	33.1
West Bengal	57.8	59.4	24.5	23.3	64.1	58.2	25.5	29.6
All India	45.7	50.9	22.6	25.0	70.8	72.2	35.6	37.4

Sources: GOI 2000 and 2007a.

Annex table 2.3 Population without access to safe water and toilet facility, 1991–2006

(%)

States	Rural households without access to safe drinking water		Rural households not having access to a toilet within the premises		Urban households without access to SDW*			Households with no toilet facility	
	1991	2001	1991	2001	1991	2001	2005–06	1998–99	2005–06
Andhra Pradesh	51.0	23.1	93.4	81.9	26.2	9.8	3.6	28.1	24.3
Assam	56.7	43.2	69.5	40.4	35.9	29.6	21.8	5.1	2.5
Bihar	43.5	13.9	95.0	86.1	26.6	8.8	12.3	33.5	26.5
Gujarat	40.0	23.1	88.8	78.4	12.8	4.6	4.1	23.1	11.7
Haryana	32.9	18.9	93.5	71.3	6.8	2.7	1.4	17.9	10.8
Karnataka	32.7	19.5	93.2	82.6	18.6	7.9	14.4	19.0	17.0
Kerala	87.8	83.1	55.9	18. 7	61.3	57.2	52.0	6.8	1.6
Madhya Pradesh	54.4	38.5	96.4	91.1	20.6	11.4	8.5	35.2	31.2
Maharashtra	46.0	31.6	93.4	81.8	9.5	4.6	1.5	13.6	12.1
Orissa	64.7	37.1	96.4	92.3	37.2	27.7	21.2	45.0	40.9
Punjab	7.9	3.1	84.2	59.1	5.8	1.1	0.4	7.1	6.3
Rajasthan	49.4	39.6	93.4	85.4	13.5	6.5	2.4	22.9	14.7
Tamil Nadu	35.7	14.7	92.8	85.6	25.8	14.1	11.8	25.3	26.5
Uttar Pradesh	43.4	14.5	93.6	80.8	14.2	2.8	2.0	16.5	10.6
West Bengal	19.7	13.0	87.7	73.1	13.8	7.7	3.6	8.6	9.5
All India	44.5	26.8	90.5	78.1	18.6	10.0	7.0	19.3	16.8

Notes: *: According to Census, SDW means safe drinking water, it refers to water from taps, hand pumps and tubewells. According to *National Family Health Survey (NFHS-3) 2005–06, India* SDW refers to water from piped sources or public taps or tubewells.

Sources: GOI 1991, 2000, 2001 and 2007a.

Annex table 2.4 Distribution of rural households by type of ration card possessed and exclusion in rural areas, 2004–05

(%)

State	Antodaya	BPL	No ration card	Included (with BPL or Antodaya card)	Excluded (with APL or no card)	Exclusion among households with monthly per capita expenditure below the official poverty line	Exclusion among agricultural labour households	Exclusion among SCs households
Andhra Pradesh	2.8	53.7	27.5	56.5	43.5	38.5	29.6	31.4
Arunachal Pradesh	0.7	16.1	23.4	16.8	83.2	68.8	88.7	…
Assam	0.6	11.8	24.6	12.4	87.7	72.6	68.6	80.8
Bihar	2.3	15.1	22.5	17.4	82.6	77.0	70.9	70.4
Chhattisgarh	4.4	34.9	28.6	39.3	60.7	54.3	45.8	53.9
Goa	5.1	13.4	8.7	18,5	81.6	15.0	60.9	…
Gujarat	0.8	36.1	12.7	36.9	63.1	44.9	37.6	42.5
Haryana	2.6	16.0	13.1	18.6	81.4	65.6	50.6	68.3
Himachal Pradesh	6.2	10.6	7.2	16.8	83.2	48.2	53.3	74.9
Jammu and Kashmir	0.5	22.7	3.4	23.2	76.8	28.5	32.4	83.7
Jharkhand	3.0	22.8	23.1	25.8	74.2	67.1	67.2	63.9
Karnataka	9.6	42.1	22.6	51.7	48.3	28.5	30.2	26.9
Kerala	1.8	27.7	13.4	29.5	70.5	50.8	47.4	37.9
Madhya Pradesh	3.3	30.8	27.9	34.1	65.9	54.2	49.2	57.2
Maharashtra	4.4	30.5	18.9	34.9	65.2	48.6	50.3	51.0
Manipur	0.0	22.3	62.2	22.3	77.7	75.8	96.0	…
Meghalaya	2.6	23.6	22.7	26.2	73.7	68.7	38.7	…
Mizoram	1.7	36.4	1.4	38.1	61.9	21.0	85.3	…
Nagaland	0.4	6.3	90.4	6.7	93.3	…	…	…
Orissa	2.0	42.4	33.1	44.4	55.6	44	40.2	45.1
Punjab	0.1	11.9	12.2	12.1	87.9	76.5	76.7	77.0
Rajasthan	2.8	15.7	3.6	18.5	81.5	67.4	67.7	79.3
Sikkim	1.0	39.5	27.2	40.5	59.5	17.5	42.1	…
Tamil Nadu	1.5	18.9	10.8	…	…	…	…	…
Tripura	1.6	38.9	2.4	40.5	59.6	20.2	33.4	54.6
Uttar Pradesh	2.8	13.5	18.5	16.3	83.7	74.3	73.1	72.6
Uttaranchal	2.5	23.2	7.9	25.7	74.3	47.2	56.8	53.4
West Bengal	3.2	27.3	8.4	30.5	69.5	57.0	52.7	58.4
All India	2.9	26.5	18.7	29.5	70.5	…	52.1	60.7

Note: The sample size and data quality for the northeast is questionable, and Tamil Nadu has a universal programme.
Source: GOI 2007b.

Annex table 2.5 Average monthly consumption of rice and wheat (kg) from PDS and other sources, BPL and Antyodaya card households in rural areas, 2004–05

State	PDS	Other sources	Total consumption	PDS as a % of total consumption
Nagaland	0.0	74.9	74.9	0.0
Manipur	0.1	81.2	81.3	0.1
Punjab	0.7	46.9	47.6	1.5
Bihar	2.2	60.8	63.0	3.5
Jharkhand	4.8	56.9	61.7	7.8
West Bengal	5.2	56.8	62.0	8.4
Haryana	6.3	45.3	51.6	12.2
Orissa	8.7	55.6	64.3	13.5
Uttar Pradesh	10.3	59.9	70.2	14.7
Chhattisgarh	15.6	50.7	66.3	23.5
Assam	15.8	46.8	62.6	25.2
All India	13.5	35.4	48.9	27.6
Madhya Pradesh	16.5	35.6	52.1	31.7
Andhra Pradesh	15.7	31.2	46.9	33.5
Arunachal Pradesh	20.7	39.4	60.1	34.4
Goa	13.7	24.5	38.2	35.9
Gujarat	9.3	15.5	24.8	37.5
Meghalaya	19.9	31.5	51.4	38.7
Mizoram	26.7	42.1	68.8	38.8
Uttaranchal	22.6	31.5	54.1	41.8
Kerala	16.7	22.8	39.5	42.3
Rajasthan	17.5	22.3	39.8	44.0
Tamil Nadu	20.1	18.6	38.7	51.9
Tripura	27.8	23.6	51.4	54.1
Jammu and Kashmir	35.8	29.8	65.6	54.6
Maharashtra	16.3	13.5	29.8	54.7
Himachal Pradesh	29.7	20.3	50.0	59.4
Sikkim	31.6	21.3	52.9	59.7
Karnataka	21.4	7.1	28.5	75.1

Source: GOI 2007b.

Annex table 2.6 Exclusion across social, occupational and expenditure groups in urban areas, 2004–05

(%)

	STs	SCs	Other backward class	Others	All	Bottom 30 % MPCE	Self-employed	Casual labour	Regular workers
Andhra Pradesh	74.1	62.6	65.7	83.0	71.9	49.7	65.9	49.4	79.7
Assam	98.9	92.6	94.0	98.0	96.6	88.0	96.7	86.7	96.4
Bihar	78.1	88.9	89.3	98.4	92.6	85.4	89.4	79.0	96.0
Gujarat	94.3	85.5	82.3	96.6	91.5	75.9	90.5	72.7	94.7
Haryana	75.7	78.9	86.4	92.4	88.6	67.8	85.0	63.5	95.2
Karnataka	58.0	68.6	78.6	92.4	83.6	59.9	85.1	54.9	90.6
Kerala	90.1	52.5	77.5	89.0	79.4	53.7	82.5	60.5	86.4
Madhya Pradesh	79.6	73.4	81.3	91.9	84.2	69.2	81.4	67.9	91.2
Maharashtra	87.0	82.8	90.5	95.0	91.7	73.9	91.3	74.1	95.1
Orissa	79.9	79.6	85.0	92.5	86.9	75.2	81.7	74.6	95.9
Punjab	97.9	90.7	96.7	98.5	96.1	87.2	97.2	83.0	96.3
Rajasthan	96.3	94.4	96.7	98.7	96.9	95.3	97.3	91.9	98.5
Tamil Nadu	88.2	87.9	85.5	94.3	86.6	73.9	86.4	75.8	88.6
Uttar Pradesh	60.5	80.1	92.2	97.5	93.0	84.2	93.0	87.7	93.6
West Bengal	79.5	80.3	90.3	93.2	90.4	77.3	89.1	73.7	95.9
India	85.1	81.1	84.7	94.4	88.7	74.6	88.0	70.8	93.6

Sources: GOI 2007b and Swaminathan 2008.

Chapter 3

Food Security in Pakistan: Issues and Choices

Food security, as explained in chapter 1, implies that availability, access, and absorption must simultaneously coexist to ensure food security. Food availability is a necessary but not a sufficient condition to ensure access to food. However, even adequate access to food does not guarantee effective food absorption by the poor. Thus, all three conditions of food security must be simultaneously satisfied.

A comprehensive food security strategy to cover all these elements of food security has not been developed in Pakistan. So the current government set up a Task Force on Food Security to develop such a strategy in 2009. The main elements of such a strategy, as presented in the Task Force on Food Security report, are:

a) 'Ensuring adequate supply of food by achieving an average agricultural growth rate of at least four per cent per annum in the next decade—2010–20.

b) Evolving an efficient and equitable system of food procurement, storage and distribution to ensure that food is available at affordable prices throughout the year in all parts of the country.

c) Improving the access of poor households to food by adopting a pro-poor growth strategy and providing non-farm employment on a substantial scale.

d) Building a transparent and well-managed system of safety nets to provide income support to very poor households.'[1]

Status of food security

In recent years Pakistan's food security has deteriorated as measured by average per capita daily intake of calories. The average consumption remained stagnant around 2,375 kcal/person/day between 1990–92 and 1995–97, but decreased to 2,270 kcal/person/day during 2000–02. Food consumption went down further in 2005–07, falling to 2,250 kcal/person/day. This is low when compared to consumption average of 2,630 kcal/person/day in developing countries.[2]

Availability of food

Availability of food is achieved when sufficient quantity of food is consistently available to all individuals. Domestic production alone does not account for total food availability. Domestic production, combined with imports, determine the total quantity of food available for domestic consumption and exports. Pakistan has shown some improvement in food production; per capita food production index has increased from 99 in 1991 to 106 in 2008. However, there is concern about significant declines in 1991, 1994 and 2002 (figure 3.1).

One factor for poor food availability situation in Pakistan is the declining share of the agriculture sector in gross domestic product (GDP). While the sector once contributed 46.2 per cent to the national

In recent years Pakistan's food security has deteriorated as measured by average per capita daily intake of calories

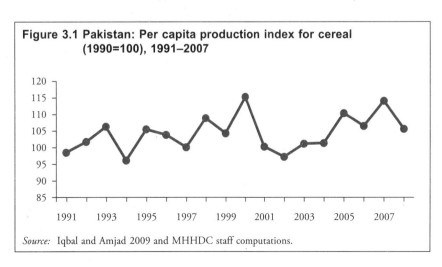

Figure 3.1 Pakistan: Per capita production index for cereal (1990=100), 1991–2007

Source: Iqbal and Amjad 2009 and MHHDC staff computations.

| Table 3.1 | Pakistan: Agriculture sector growth performance, 1960–2010 |
| | (%) |

	Growth rate
1960s	5.1
1970s	2.4
1980s	5.4
1990s	4.4
2000s	3.2

Source: GOP 2010c.

GDP in the 1960s,[3] its share has decreased to 21 per cent in 2009–10.[4] Its role, however, is still very important to the overall economy as 45 per cent of total employment is generated by agriculture.[5] More than 67 per cent of Pakistan's population is dependent on agriculture as the main source of livelihood.[6] Thus agriculture not only provides food to the fast growing population of the country, it also provides employment to the vast majority of the population. With a population growth rate of around two per cent, implying an increase of three million people per year, agriculture sector growth has to be stable to provide food to this growing population.[7]

Historically, Pakistan had been experiencing high growth rate of agriculture especially during the 1960s and 1970s because of the application of the Green

Revolution technology. However the rate of growth of agriculture in recent times has fallen, and has been fairly unstable (table 3.1). Though the sector has grown at an average rate of 3.2 per cent during the present decade, it has shown high volatility, with the rate of growth varying between –0.1 and 6.5 per cent (table 3.2). In 2008–09, the agriculture sector grew at four per cent against the expected rate of 3.5 per cent. However, the growth rate slowed down in 2009–10, registering a growth rate of only two per cent. The recent performance of the agriculture sector has been weaker compared to last year as all the components (major crops, minor crops and fisheries), except livestock, grew slower than the preceding year (table 3.2). The cropping sector has largely followed a cyclical pattern in growth where production of both major and minor crops remains high one year followed by a collapse in the following year (figure 3.2). These kinds of fluctuations in overall agriculture are among the major factors responsible for food insecurity.

Food security in Pakistan depends heavily on the crop sector, especially the three major crops: wheat, sugarcane, and rice. Though their performance as reflected by area of cultivation, production and yield has improved since the Green Revolution of the 1960s (table 3.3), in the last decade the growth rate of the crop sector has been volatile. Wheat production increased from 21,079 thousand tonnes in

Table 3.2 Pakistan: Agriculture sector growth rate by components, 2001–10

(%)

	Agriculture	Major crops	Minor crops	Livestock	Fishery
2001–02	–0.1	–2.5	–3.7	3.7	–12.3
2002–03	4.1	6.9	0.4	2.8	3.4
2003–04	2.4	1.7	3.9	2.9	2.0
2004–05	6.5	17.1	1.5	2.3	0.6
2005–06	6.3	–3.9	0.4	15.8	20.8
2006–07	4.1	7.7	–1.0	2.8	15.4
2007–08	1.0	–6.4	10.9	4.2	9.2
2008–09	4.0	7.3	–1.7	3.5	2.3
2009–10	2.0	–0.2	–1.2	4.1	1.4

Sources: GOP 2003, 2004 and 2010c.

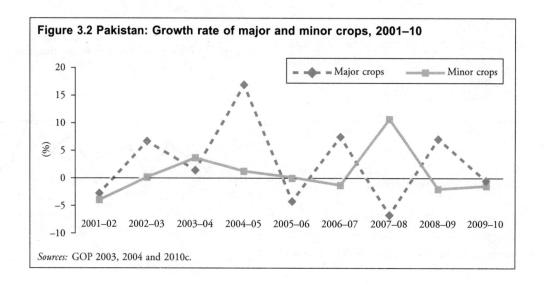

Figure 3.2 Pakistan: Growth rate of major and minor crops, 2001–10

Sources: GOP 2003, 2004 and 2010c.

1999–00 to 23,295 thousand tonnes in 2006–07, and then it declined to 20,959 in 2007–08. In 2008–09, the production rose by 3,074 thousand tonnes before falling to 23,864 thousand tonnes in 2009–10. This, in the context of steadily rising wheat utilization, implies a worsening food security situation (figure 3.3). A similar pattern is observed in sugarcane production where 2007–08 was a bumper year with production fluctuating in other years. The flood of 2010 is likely to further increase instability in the production of major crops, especially sugarcane. Market imperfections and weak governance also contribute to poor agricultural performance.

The performance of the livestock sector —the largest contributor to agriculture value added—has been positive. The sector, important for its additional income generation, especially for rural households, has grown by 4.1 per cent in 2009–10 compared to 3.5 per cent the year before (table 3.2). In contrast, the fisheries sector, despite its immense potential and importance for food security, has not maintained the growth achieved during the boom years of 2005–07, and has fallen drastically since. The sector grew merely by 1.4 per cent in 2009–10 in contrast to an extremely high growth rate of 20.8 per cent in 2005–06.

Table 3.3   Pakistan: Cultivation, production and yield of important crops, 1959–2009

	Wheat	Sugarcane	Rice	Maize
	Production (000 tonnes)			
1959–60	3,909	...	995	439
1969–70	7,294	...	2,401	668
1979–80	10,857	...	3,216	875
1989–90	14,316	...	3,220	1,179
1999–2000	21,079	46,333	5,156	1,652
2004–05	21,612	47,244	5,025	2,797
2005–06	21,277	44,666	5,547	3,110
2006–07	23,295	54,742	5,438	3,088
2007–08	20,959	63,920	5,563	3,605
2008–09	24,033	50,045	6,952	3,593
	Area (000 hectares)			
1959–60	4,878	...	1,204	482
1969–70	6,229	...	1,622	648
1979–80	6,924	...	2,035	701
1989–90	7,845	...	2,107	863
1999–2000	8,463	1,010	2,515	962
2004–05	8,358	966	2,520	982
2005–06	8,448	907	2,621	1,042
2006–07	8,578	1,029	2,581	1,017
2007–08	8,550	1,241	2,515	1,052
2008–09	9,046	1,029	2,963	1,052
	Yield (kg/hectare)			
1959–60	801	...	826	911
1969–70	1,171	...	1,480	1,031
1979–80	1,568	...	1,581	1,248
1989–90	1,825	...	1,528	1,366
1999–2000	2,491	45,874	2,050	1,717
2004–05	2,568	48,906	1,995	2,848
2005–06	2,519	49,246	2,116	2,985
2006–07	2,716	53,199	2,105	3,036
2007–08	2,451	51,507	2,212	3,427
2008–09	2,657	48,635	2,346	3,415

Source: GOP, *Pakistan Economic Survey* (various issues).

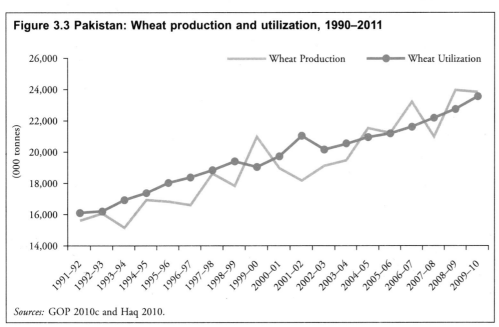

Figure 3.3 Pakistan: Wheat production and utilization, 1990–2011

Sources: GOP 2010c and Haq 2010.

Table 3.4	Pakistan: Import of food commodities, 2001–09			
				(000 tonnes)
	Wheat	Sugar	Pulses	Edible oil
2000–01	1,588	758	37	1,144
2001–02	…	319	68	1,197
2002–03	…	86	67	1,294
2003–04	…	51	87	1,361
2004–05	1,368	…	36	1,605
2005–06	185	267	51	1,696
2006–07	…	1,527	81	1,787
2007–08	1,708	587	89	2,701
2008–09	2,685	…	70	2,489

Sources: FAO 2011a and GOP 2009a.

Food availability is also dependent on food trade. Though food production has gradually improved, the increase in population has necessitated increased imports to satisfy domestic needs. Pakistan has been importing significant quantities of wheat, sugar, edible oil, pulses, and other grains to meet the domestic shortfall (table 3.4).

An issue of concern regarding food availability in Pakistan is legal and illegal exports of food commodities across borders to neighbouring countries, especially Afghanistan. Exports of sugar and wheat have been significantly high due to the price differential between Pakistani and global markets, resulting in domestic shortfall. Based on an analysis in 2008, around 1,800 million metric tonnes of wheat flour was smuggled across the Afghan border every month.[8] Similarly, around 300,000 tonnes of sugar was smuggled to Afghanistan between November and January, 2009, resulting in a shortage of sugar in the country.[9] This not only resulted in food shortage

within the country but also contributed to significant price increases.

Thus, the performance of food production has been mixed. The gap between dietary energy supply (DES) and need has been diminishing since 1995–97 when it was 220 kcal/person/day to merely 70 kcal/person/day in 2005–07 (table 3.5).

Access to food

Access to food is the second important component to ensure food security. Access means adequate economic resources to buy food, with physical infrastructure for distribution of food throughout the country. Enhancing per capita production would do little to ensure food security if the available food is not within people's access. The worsening food security situation has more to do with socio-economic access rather than production. Access to food is not guaranteed until the household has economic resources sufficient to acquire food that meets their nutritional requirements and dietary needs.

Access to food is a function of various factors related to economic, social, political and cultural factors. Economic factors relate to low income, high rate of unemployment, decreasing real wages, and inflation. Social factors include widespread inequality across various income groups and inequitable distribution of resources. Cultural factors involve distribution of resources and allocation of food entitlement based on gender, class, ethnicity, etc.

Economic access to food is largely determined by the purchasing power of people which is reflected by income. Though the per capita income has increased in Pakistan since 1980s, from purchasing power parity (PPP) US$915 in the 1980s to PPP US$2,680 in 2009, its growth has varied significantly over the years. Annual per capita income growth averaged 7.7 per cent in the 1980s, but declined drastically to 2.9 per cent in the 1990s. It increased again during 2003–07, before falling in 2008 and 2009 (table 3.6). In most years the rise in income has been

Table 3.5	Pakistan: Food supply and need, 1990–2007			
				(kcal/person/day)
	1990–92	1995–97	2000–02	2005–07
Average dietary energy requirement (ADER)	2,100	2,120	2,150	2,180
DES	2,210	2,340	2,270	2,250
Surplus DES	110	220	120	70

Source: FAO 2010a.

Table 3.6	Pakistan: Profile of income per capita, 1980–2010		
	Average Income per capita (PPP US$)	Rate of income growth (%)	Inflation (%)
1980–89	915	7.7	7.3
1990–99	1,472	2.9	9.7
2000	1,690	3.7	4.4
2001	1,720	1.8	3.1
2002	1,790	4.1	3.3
2003	1,920	7.3	2.9
2004	2,060	7.3	7.4
2005	2,230	8.3	9.1
2006	2,390	7.2	7.9
2007	2,550	6.7	7.6
2008	2,600	2.0	20.3
2009	2,680	3.1	13.6

Source: World Bank 2010.

Table 3.7	Pakistan: Average monthly household income and consumption, 2007–08					
						(PKR)
Quintiles	Average monthly household income			Average monthly household consumption		
	Urban	Rural	Total	Urban	Rural	Total
1st	8,744	7,639	7,812	8,251	7,343	7,485
2nd	11,019	9,577	9,910	10,038	8,960	9,209
3rd	11,872	10,901	11,172	11,289	10,118	10,445
4th	13,239	13,219	13,227	12,938	11,833	12,235
5th	26,164	22,808	24,659	21,341	18,051	19,866
Total	17,970	12,626	14,456	15,601	11,128	12,660

Source: GOP 2009b.

outpaced by inflation, implying a decrease in real purchasing power. Another issue of concern is the income inequality that persists both between urban and rural and across income groups. An analysis of average income by income quintiles indicates that the richest 20 per cent, both in urban and rural areas, have more than three times the average income levels of the lowest 20 per cent. What makes this a food security concern is that this pattern is translated into a disparity in consumption patterns (table 3.7).

The unemployment rate in Pakistan has gradually increased over the years. From being 3.5 per cent of the total labour force in the 1980s, it increased to 4.9 per cent during the 1990s,[10] and is around 5.5 per cent in 2008–09.[11] There has been a substantial increase in unpaid family helpers who account for around one-third of the total employed labour force, and more females than males are engaged as unpaid family workers. Also, three-quarters of the employed are engaged in the informal sector of the economy which is characterized by low wages and long working hours.[12]

Inflation in Pakistan has become a major concern after the 1990s, with serious repercussions for food security. Historically, inflation rates have been below double digits up to the end of the

1980s.[13] Even in the 1990s, and between 2000 and 2005, average inflation remained below the double digit. Between 2004–05 and 2006–07, inflation rates declined. However, after 2007 inflation increased significantly, and in 2008 inflation reached the peak of 20.3 per cent (table 3.6).

Disaggregating inflation into food and non-food categories reflects that food inflation has largely outpaced non-food inflation since 2005, highlighting the concern for food access in recent years. Food inflation rose by around 20.1 percentage points (from only 3.6 per cent in 2000–01 to 23.7 per cent in 2008–09) compared to the 13.3 percentage points rise in non-food inflation (from 5.1 per cent in 2000–01 to 18.4 per cent in 2008–09). Though food inflation declined to 12.0 per cent in 2009–10 it however is showing an upward trend lately (table 3.8).

Table 3.8	Pakistan: Inflation trends in Pakistan, 2000–10		
			(%)
	General	Food	Non-food
2000–01	4.4	3.6	5.1
2001–02	3.5	2.5	4.3
2002–03	3.1	2.8	3.3
2003–04	4.6	6.0	3.6
2004–05	9.3	12.5	7.1
2005–06	7.9	6.9	8.6
2006–07	7.8	10.3	6.0
2007–08	12.0	17.6	7.9
2008–09	20.8	23.7	18.4
2009–10 *	11.5	12.0	11.0

Note: *: Values are for July to April.
Sources: GOP 2010c and MHHDC staff computations.

Table 3.9 Pakistan: Inflation for selective commodities, 2006–10

(PKR)

Commodity	Unit	2006–07	2009–10*	% increase
Wheat flour	per kg	13.6	29.1	113.0
Rice	per kg	23.1	43.8	89.3
Pulses	per kg	53.2	92.2	73.2
Vegetable ghee	per kg	70.8	111.3	57.1
Sugar	per kg	31.9	56.3	76.6
Tea	per 250 grams	68.4	118.9	73.8
Fresh milk	per litre	26.7	41.7	56.1

Note: *: Values are for July to April.
Source: GOP 2010c.

Within food, prices of essential commodities have risen significantly. The prices of wheat flour, rice, pulses, vegetable ghee, sugar, tea, and milk have risen by over 50 per cent since 2006–07 (table 3.9). Price of wheat flour that accounts for around 15 per cent of a family's monthly expenditure has risen by 113 per cent since 2006–07 (13.6 per kg in 2006–07 to 29.1 per kg in 2009–10).[14] As a result despite increase in monthly consumption expenditures on food which have increased by 20 per cent in 2007–08 compared to 2005–06, monthly consumption of major food items (wheat, rice, and pulses) has decreased significantly, indicating a drop in nutritional intake of people (table 3.10).[15]

High food inflation affects the welfare of the poor in a society. The poorest have suffered proportionately more than the richest as the prices of food commodities that constitute a significant proportion of the poor's consumption basket have risen significantly (table 3.11). High food inflation in the last three years has driven around 11 million people below the poverty line.

Inflation has disproportionately affected certain segments of the society. Fixed income groups, landless daily wage workers in the agriculture sector and domestic workers whose income has not increased proportionately with the price hike are the worst affected.

A new demographic dimension is witnessed here. Food insecurity (due to insufficient access) is more pervasive in urban areas. Population groups that are vulnerable to food insecurity are present more in urban areas (slums or middle-income localities), compared to rural areas.

Both international and domestic factors are responsible for high inflation in the country. Poor governance has increased smuggling, hoarding and profiteering, resulting in artificial shortages and increase in prices. Lack of marketing and shortage of storage facilities have also contributed to demand push inflation. More recently, floods have contributed to supply-side constraints. Standing crops of rice, maize, cotton, sugar, vegetables, fruit orchards and livestock have been destroyed by the flood. Internationally high commodity prices, specifically related to food and energy, have put an upward pressure on domestic prices.

With inflation outpacing growth in income, access to food has become more difficult for people. This, along with inequitable distribution of economic resources, limits access to food in Pakistan.

Table 3.10 Pakistan: Per capita monthly consumption of major food items, 2005–08

(kg)

	2005–06	2007–08
Wheat	8.16	7.75
Rice	1.02	0.89
Pulses	0.27	0.24
Milk	6.37	6.83
Meat	0.53	0.57
Fruit and Vegetables	3.54	4.50

Source: GOP 2009b.

Table 3.11 Pakistan: Percentage of monthly expenditure on major food items by quintiles, 2007–08

	1st	2nd	3rd	4th	5th	Total
Wheat	22.77	19.48	17.23	14.35	9.35	14.93
Pulses	2.67	2.62	2.51	2.44	1.98	4.25
Rice	4.3	4.6	4.16	4.36	4.06	4.25
Vegetable ghee	12.84	11.2	10.33	8.8	5.26	8.71
Sugar	6.42	5.75	5.3	4.66	3.52	4.76
Meat	6.22	7.28	8.26	8.59	8.61	9.35
Fruit and vegetables	11.07	11	11.47	11.71	12.31	11.69

Source: GOP 2009b.

Food absorption

The basic aim of food security is to ensure that everyone has access to adequate food, not only in terms of quantity but also in quality, to enable them to lead a healthy and productive life. This aim requires that a proper hygienic environment is maintained to ensure appropriate utilization of food.

Several conditions need to be met to ensure proper absorption of food. The availability of clean water for drinking and cooking purposes, proper sanitation facilities to prevent water contamination, good healthcare facilities, mother's knowledge about hygienic cooking and maintaining a balance of nutrition in food content, and equitable and need-based intra-household distribution of food are some of the prerequisites that ensure proper food utilization and absorption.

A large number of households in Pakistan, especially those residing in rural areas and urban slums, do not have access to safe drinking water and adequate sanitation facilities. Though Pakistan possessed abundant surface and groundwater, rapid population growth and unplanned urbanization has reduced water availability and deteriorated water quality, resulting in a significant increase in water-related health problems. Per capita water availability in Pakistan is likely to decrease, from 5,300 cubic meters in 1951 to an estimated 659 cubic meters by 2025.[16]

With 37 per cent of the population still lacking access to proper sanitation and a significant increase in untreated industrial and agriculture effluents, water contamination remains a significant concern causing substantial health risks. It is estimated that more than 1.6 million disability-adjusted life years (DALYs) are lost annually as a result of death and disease due to diarrhoea.[17] Children with weak immune systems are the most vulnerable. An estimated 60 per cent of the under-five mortality cases are attributed to water and sanitation related issues.[18] In 2009 alone, 200,000 children died because of diarrhoeal diseases.

Worsening the food utilization situation further are the deteriorating health practices related to nutrition, child, and maternal care. Proper healthcare is essential to meet the physical, mental, and social needs of the whole family, especially children and women. Good healthcare incorporates both the provision for health facilities as well as existence and maintenance of a hygienic environment inside and outside the household. Vaccination and immunization against diseases, specifically infectious diseases, and particularly those of infants and children, are of primary importance to ensure proper food absorption. In recent years, the government has paid specific attention to vaccination of children against diseases. However despite the commitment, the proportion of children under-two years who have been fully immunized against infectious diseases have increased only by one per cent between 2004–05 and 2008–09. The current level of 79 per cent immunization is well below the Medium Term Development Framework target of 90 per cent set for 2009–10. Better results have been achieved in reducing the proportion of children under-five suffering from diarrhoea. The proportion has gone down by 16 per cent from 26 in 1990–91 to 10 per cent in 2009–10.

As a result of weak economic situation of a household, as reflected by low income growth and high inflation, knowledge about hygienic cooking and maintaining a balance of nutrition in food content becomes extremely important to ensure food security. The role of women is important in this regard in view of their involvement in food selection, preparation and distribution. Analysis reveals that women's education is an important factor contributing towards improving food utilization. However, illiteracy remains high among women in Pakistan, with only 45 per cent of female population being classified as literate. Limited access to education deprives them of necessary training and knowledge to maintain food hygiene and dietary standards.

A large number of households in Pakistan, especially those residing in rural areas and urban slums, do not have access to safe drinking water and adequate sanitation facilities

Figure 3.4 Pakistan: Yield of cereals in selected developing countries, 1981–2009

(Kg/hectare)	1981	1990	2000	2004	2009
Bangladesh	1,938	2,491	3,384	3,439	3,890
China	3,092	4,323	4,756	5,190	5,460
India	1,399	1,891	2,294	2,350	2,471
Pakistan	1,670	1,766	2,408	2,431	2,803

Source: World Bank 2010.

Factors affecting food security

Food security is a complex and multi-faceted phenomenon, influenced by a number of factors such as agricultural production and productivity, economic and social factors, institutional setup and natural calamities.

Agriculture production and productivity

Sustained agricultural growth is the most important factor for ensuring food security. Though the population growth rate has decreased to around two per cent per annum, it is still quite high requiring a productive agricultural sector to feed all the people. Historically, Pakistan has

achieved a sustained agricultural growth rate of over four per cent per annum in the past four decades (1960–2000). However, the trend could not be sustained and agricultural growth rates declined to around three per cent per annum in the current decade (2000–10). The sector is undergoing structural transformation as its share in the country's GDP is declining while the sector still absorbs 45 per cent of the country's total labour force.[19] Further agricultural growth is only possible by increasing the area under cultivation, enhancing productivity of existing land, ensuring provision of water, and reducing post-harvest losses. All these factors are facing significant constraints.

Area under cultivation: The total area under cultivation has increased by 40 per cent over the past 60 years. However, land area expansion cannot be sustained over a longer period as in the past two decades the area under cultivation has only increased by 0.25 million hectares.[20] A large part of the remaining land is unsuitable for cultivation and requires significant investment. The cost of increasing the productivity of such land is highly uneconomical and unsustainable. Furthermore, the area under cultivation would in fact be further reduced due to land degradation (waterlogging and salinity) and unplanned expansion of cities.

Productivity and yield: The agriculture sector in Pakistan is undermined by low productivity and yield. Both the labour and land productivity are low compared to neighbouring countries (figure 3.4). Though there has been some improvement in agricultural yield over the years, the yield gap between the progressive farmers and national average of various crops is still significantly high (figure 3.5). The reason for such large productivity and yield gap include limited diversification of crops, unequal distribution of land, poor agricultural technology due to limited research and development, and limited credit availability to the farming sector.

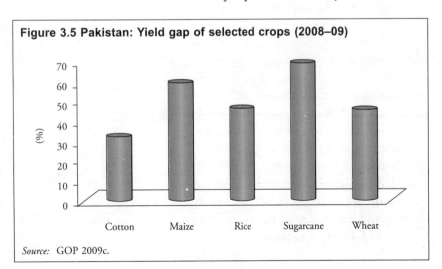

Figure 3.5 Pakistan: Yield gap of selected crops (2008–09)

Source: GOP 2009c.

Diversification and value addition: The cropping pattern in Pakistan is relatively static, dominated largely by food and some cash crops. Major crops like wheat, rice, maize, gram, sugarcane and cotton account for around 70 per cent of the total cultivated area, and this pattern has persisted for the last three decades (table 3.12). This domination by a few crops reduces land productivity and scope of value addition. Diversity in food production, coupled with on-farm livestock, poultry or fish production, is ideal to maintain soil fertility and prevent pest attack. Diversification would also shift the pattern of production to higher value-added activities. There is a significant scope for value addition in livestock and the dairy sector as it contributes around 52 per cent of agriculture value added. So far the sector has largely been a subsistence sector constrained by insufficient and poor quality of feed; limited health coverage and vaccination facilities; inadequate marketing services; poor market infrastructure; and lack of investment in research and development. Horticulture is another sector that can also contribute towards significant value addition, provided proper guidance and resources are extended to farmers.

Unequal land distribution: Land distribution in Pakistan is highly skewed. Even though Pakistan has tried land reforms three times since independence, a weak implementation mechanism has limited its effect on redistribution of land. To put the issue from the perspective of equity, although recent estimates of farm sizes are not available, in 2000 about 58 per cent of total farms were smaller than 5 acres in size, producing 16 per cent of output, while only 6 per cent of farms of over 25 acres in size produced 32 per cent of output. Smaller farm size reduces productivity as small farmers have limited access to factors of production like water, seeds, fertilizers and most importantly credit. Thus, small farmers are deprived from the start.

Table 3.12 Pakistan: Cropping pattern, 1990–2009

(as a % of total land under cultivation)

	Food crops	Cash crops	Pulses	Fruit and vegetables
1990–95	55	18	7	3
1995–2000	55	19	7	4
2000–05	55	19	6	4
2005–06	56	18	6	5
2006–07	55	18	6	5
2007–08	55	19	6	5
2008–09	58	17	6	5

Source: GOP 2009a.

Agriculture credit: Lack of access to credit is an important factor hindering the growth of the agriculture sector. Despite immense contribution of agriculture to the country's GDP, the sector merely receives 5.1 per cent of the total institutional credit. Though there has been a nominal increase in cash disbursement to the sector, the share of agriculture credit as a percentage of total credit has declined from 12.8 per cent in 1999 to the current levels (table 3.13). Out of 6.6 million farming households only two million receive credit.[21]

The government has established several initiatives like the Zarai Taraqiati Bank and the Punjab Provincial Cooperative

Table 3.13 Pakistan: Agriculture credit disbursements, 1999–2009

(PKR million)

Year**	Agriculture credit*	Total credit	Share of agriculture in total credit (%)
1999	92,503	720,924	12.83
2000	98,640	797,474	12.37
2001	97,255	864,261	11.25
2002	102,958	885,008	11.63
2003	111,392	969,872	11.49
2004	113,458	1,242,384	9.13
2005	127,111	1,694,153	7.50
2006	131,542	2,071,191	6.35
2007	144,394	2,376,182	6.08
2008	154,438	2,815,638	5.49
2009	157,163	3,080,346	5.10

Notes: *: Agriculture credit includes agriculture, hunting, forestry and fishing **: Years refer to fiscal year June to May.

Source: SBP 2009.

Table 3.14 Pakistan: Agriculture loan disbursement by landholding, 1999–2009

	Subsistence holding			Economic holding			Above economic holding		
	Borrowers	Amount (million PKR)	per person	Borrowers	Amount (million PKR)	per person	Borrowers	Amount (million PKR)	per person
1999	754,588	23,924	0.03	129,633	10,689	0.08	22,856	1,913	0.08
2000	827,164	28,440	0.03	129,406	11,340	0.09	30,944	2,022	0.07
2001	871,460	34,510	0.04	117,034	10,674	0.09	27,854	3,042	0.11
2002	903,320	35,969	0.04	108,105	11,690	0.11	19,350	3,017	0.16
2003	938,176	44,615	0.05	122,518	14,708	0.12	17,156	4,040	0.24
2004	930,732	64,177	0.07	124,976	21,617	0.17	19,510	7,615	0.39
2005	431,072	34,670	0.08	57,851	11,906	0.21	11,180	7,091	0.63
2006	455,627	40,803	0.09	52,949	14,645	0.28	10,755	6,563	0.61
2007	809,608	90,853	0.11	111,722	32,345	0.29	20,785	20,688	1.00
2008	1,282,617	99,086	0.08	133,156	38,830	0.29	26,259	24,698	0.94
2009	1,087,412	108,951	0.10	124,818	43,279	0.35	24,490	22,165	0.91

Note: Classification of landholding size varies by provinces and is defined in the source document.
Source: SBP 2009.

Bank to provide institutional credit to farmers. In addition, five commercial banks and several domestic private banks are also providing agriculture credit to cope with the increasing demand. Despite these efforts the share of agriculture to the total credit dispersed has been decreasing over the years. The limited credit availability to the sector is severely hampering technological progress and hence productivity.

The distribution of credit is highly skewed in favour of landed elites. Farmers with subsistence level or economic levels of landholdings receive far less credit per person compared to above economic level landholders (table 3.14). There is also inequality in credit disbursement by provinces where Punjab receives 90.6 per cent of the total agricultural credit compared to Sindh (4.6 per cent), Khyber Pakhtunkhwa (KPK) (3.1 per cent) and Balochistan (0.7 per cent) (table 3.15). Agricultural credit is also vital to farmers in the livestock, dairy, and fisheries sectors, and for farm development purposes, including farm mechanization, water conservation and infrastructure development, if any sustained agriculture growth is to be achieved.

Agriculture research and technology: One of the major factors in Pakistan's recent poor record in agricultural growth is the lack of a vigorous agricultural research system at the national and provincial levels. With the advent of the Green Revolution, Pakistan witnessed technological and economic transformation in the late 1960s. The government supported advanced technology, resulting in high-yielding varieties (HYVs) of rice and wheat; improved policy environment; incentive structure in the form of input subsidies; and investment in agricultural infrastructure, including irrigation, research and extension. This resulted in significant high agriculture growth rates and an improved food security situation. However, in recent years the necessary investment in agricultural research and technology at both public and private sectors has declined. Public sector investment has declined from US$223 million in 1991 to

Table 3.15 Pakistan: Distribution of agricultural credit by provinces, 2008–09

	PKR millions	%
AJK and NA	101.33	0.86
Balochistan	85.68	0.73
KPK	369.81	3.14
Punjab	10,690.83	90.65
Sindh	546.5	4.63
Pakistan	11,794.1	100

Notes: *: AJK means Azad Jamu and Kashmir, and NA means Northern Areas. **: KPK means Khyber Pakhtunkhwa.

Source: GOP 2009a.

US$185 million, highlighting significant state withdrawal from the agriculture sector. The government extension system is also limited as there are deficiencies in delivering research results to farmers. Poor farmers do not have financial resources to pay for the needed technical services.

Along with the reduction in public investment, the government has also gradually reduced subsidies on agricultural inputs including fertilizers, insecticides, seeds, irrigation water, tubewell installations and tractors thereby reducing incentives to undertake farm mechanization. Technological innovation is necessary for agricultural development as it results in improving productivity, adaptability to changing weather patterns, and enhancing high-nutrition crops. Unless public investment in agriculture is scaled up, long-term agricultural productivity will decline, seriously hampering Pakistan's efforts to improve food security.

Water: Availability of water is one of the most serious constraints of the agriculture sector in Pakistan. Issues of water availability to the agriculture sector include those of water shortage, inefficient use of water, and escape of water to the sea.

Being one of the world's most arid countries, the per capita availability of water has decreased to 1,066 cubic meters, placing Pakistan in the high water stressed countries category.[22] The irrigated area in Pakistan has increased by 17 per cent since 1990–91. This increase in cultivated area over the last two decades has not been accompanied by any effort to use water efficiently, nor have any steps been taken to increase water storage and reduce its escapage to sea. The efficiency of irrigation in Pakistan is very low; around 60 per cent of the water is lost at watercourses and canals before reaching the farms.[23] The water that does reach farms is often used inefficiently. Pakistan produces only 0.13 kg of cereal per cubic meter of irrigated water which is significantly lower than India and China.[24] The country's further reliance on producing water-intensive crops like sugarcane and rice for consumption and export purposes further strains water availability. Despite acute water shortages, Pakistan has not undertaken any major steps since 1976 to increase water storage capacity which at present is only nine per cent. Annually, Pakistan loses 31.5 million acre feet of water to the Arabian Sea. Understanding the need for water conservation and efficiency, the government allocated PKR5.1 billion for improving watercourses. However, the government failed to implement its policies and utilized only PKR672 million. If the current trend continues, by 2020 water scarcity in Pakistan would reach a level where it could disrupt economic activity and hamper health and well-being of people.

Post-harvest losses: Post-harvest losses contribute significantly to reduction in food available for consumption. Post-harvest losses of various food commodities in Pakistan is about 10–15 per cent of their total production, and for fruits and vegetables the figure is around 40 per cent of total production.[25] Therefore, one way to improve food security is to reduce these post-harvest losses.

Post-harvest losses occur at every stage of the production system, starting from the producer and ending with the consumer. The primary factors responsible for both pre- and post-harvest produce losses are: poor pre-harvest measures—adoption of poor production techniques (varieties with low shelf life, imbalanced use of nutrients and insecticides); improper harvesting procedures (harvesting at improper stage and improper care at harvest); and post-harvest problems (dumping and packaging procedure, improper transportation and storage, and distant and time consuming market distribution).

Food distribution system: A timely and smooth transfer of food (produced or imported) to consumers is important to ensure physical access to the food. In the case of Pakistan, where only around 20 per cent of the districts produce surplus food,

Unless public investment in agriculture is scaled up, long-term agricultural productivity will decline, seriously hampering Pakistan's efforts to improve food security

Though external factors may have triggered the current food crisis, it is the political action, or inaction, that has determined its severity

an efficient and equitable food distribution system becomes a necessity to ensure food security.

Distribution of food in Pakistan involves the role of both private and public sectors. The private sector intermediaries include the shopkeepers, *arthies* (commission agents), wholesalers and *beparies* (traders), with *arthies* the main market functionary. They are engaged with supplying inputs (seeds, fertilizers, machinery and pesticides) and purchasing output from farmers. They also determine prices of most commodities like fruits, vegetables, poultry, etc.

In Pakistan, the role of government in food distribution is weak, unlike in India where the public food distribution network is extensive since Partition. Pakistan used to have a food rationing system in place that ensured supply of pre-determined quantities of food to consumers. However, the system was gradually phased out in 1980s, increasing the role of private traders in the food trade. Currently, the state is involved mostly in the wheat market where Pakistan Storage and Supply Corporation (PASSCO) procures wheat from farmers and supplies it to flour mills. It also determines the procurement price of wheat and sugarcane and hence influences their market price. The government also plays a role in food distribution when there is a local shortage of certain food commodities. This is done through the Trading Corporation of Pakistan (TCP) that issues licenses and monitors import of particular food commodities. Additionally, the government, through the Utility Store Corporation (USC), provides essential food items to the public at subsidized rates. The USC is also instrumental in reducing artificial shortages, hoarding, and black marketing, as it ensures a regular supply of basic commodities at its outlets.

The existing food supply and marketing system has various shortcomings that undermine access to food. The existing infrastructure is insufficient to cater to market needs. The retail and wholesale markets in urban areas have not increased with the rate of urbanization and population growth. The absence of adequate rural infrastructure like roads, warehouses, storage facilities and agriculture markets impedes farm to market linkages. The government pricing policy is also flawed as it fails to transfer benefits to poor consumers. For example, the subsidy on wheat benefits the flour millers but not the poor consumers, as they do not have access to wheat distribution outlets. Similarly, the subsidies on fertilizers also benefit large farmers rather than small and marginal ones. The provision of subsidized food through the USC is a blanket subsidy, not targeting the extremely poor and vulnerable.

Governance and food security

The role of government is vital in guaranteeing food security. Poor governance in Pakistan, as reflected in the absence of rule of law, violent conflicts, lack of transparency and accountability, endemic corruption, and weak public administration, is the single most important reason for human insecurity, including food insecurity, in the country. Though external factors, such as financial and oil crises, may have triggered the current food crisis, it is the political action, or inaction, that has determined its severity. The severity of food insecurity, as demonstrated by shortages of wheat and sugar resulting in high prices in an apparently food self-sufficient country, explains the nexus between food insecurity and poor governance.

At the policy level, food security has never been reflected in the national policy discourse. There is hardly any policy document (except the current *Task Force on Food Security* report)[26] that specifically targets food security in its complete definition: production, access and absorption. The thrust of policy makers and government so far has been on ensuring adequate production without realizing that the concept of food security goes beyond the production of food. It is the access and absorption of food that is the missing link between sufficient production and people's well-being. In

Pakistan, there were several years when agricultural production, specifically of wheat and sugar, recorded a surplus, yet consumers suffered deprivation.

There is inadequate awareness and capacity to understand the global factors underlying the recent food insecurity prevailing in the world, and its impact on the local food security situation. Even where understanding exists, the response is too slow to prevent the crisis from becoming severe. The wheat crisis that originated in 2007 is a classic example of the failure of governance (box 3.1).

The wheat crisis described in box 3.1 highlights another dimension of poor governance: lack of transparency and accountability, and pervasive corruption. The government machinery, from the food department to the border security forces to local administration in tribal areas, failed to curb smuggling across borders. The local authorities also failed to stop excessive hoarding and panic buying that prevailed in the wake of the brewing wheat crisis. This reduced wheat supplies, further aggravating the crisis. It is estimated that around 1.5 million tonnes of wheat was hoarded locally, apart from 1.0 million tonnes that was smuggled across Pakistan's western borders.[27]

Mixing political interests with public policy and functioning of markets is another dimension through which poor governance increases food insecurity. This is evident in almost all food markets but has been most pronounced in the case of the sugar industry where political patronage is predominant (box 3.2), the cost of which is faced by consumers and

The wheat crisis that originated in 2007 is a classic example of the failure of governance

---

Box 3.1 Case of governance failure

In 2007, Pakistan had surplus wheat production of 23.3 million tonnes and an additional 0.5 million tonnes as carried forward stock from the previous year. This was sufficient to meet the consumption needs of roughly 21 million tonnes. The crisis however erupted because of a government policy in the wake of global trends in food prices. While the world price of wheat was hovering around US$450 per ton, the government maintained the local support price of PKR425 per 40 kg set in 2006–07. The price differentials with Afghanistan and Iran were over 30 per cent. Thus, huge amounts of wheat were smuggled through the porous borders in the northwest. Not realizing the repercussions of the price differential, the government, in anticipation of a surplus of around 2.0 million tonnes of wheat, allowed export of 1.5 million tonnes in April and May 2007 at US$225–232 per tonne. This resulted in wheat shortages in the local market around October, forcing the government to import one million tonnes of wheat from the international market in December when the prices were at US$380–400 per tonne. This mismanagement not only lost the country an opportunity to make financial profit from surplus wheat, it, in fact, also resulted in exporting wheat when international prices were low and importing when prices were high.

Each year the government takes on the task of procuring wheat from farmers. Delays in wheat procurement either due to shortage of funds or non-availability of gunny bags have become an annual feature. The after effects are worse for both government and farmers. Farmers in their haste to plant for the next season sell to private traders at less than the support price, thereby not getting their due remunerative return. During the current fiscal year, growers in Sindh were forced to sell wheat in the open market at a price which was PKR100 below the support price, because the Sindh Food Department failed to provide sufficient gunny bags. The growers were getting PKR840 to PKR890 per 40 kg against the official rate of PKR950. The government failed to achieve the procurement targets and much of the wheat was hoarded with private millers and traders. The government also had insufficient and inefficient storage capacity. The total wheat storage capacity in Pakistan is for about 6.5 million tonnes, which is extremely low compared to over 20 million tonnes of estimated annual produce. As a result, the procured wheat lies in open fields damaging the grain.

Sources: GOP 2009a and 2010c and Shah 2011.

Box 3.2 Another case of government mismanagement

The sugar crisis has been a recurrent feature of Pakistan's food industry. The triggering point of the crisis can be international factors like shortage in global markets due to sugarcane being used as a source of energy, or rise in its global prices, its impact is always magnified when it hits Pakistan. The underlying reason is the link between sugar mafia and the political powers of the country. Of the nearly 78 sugar mills in the country more than 50 per cent are owned by the politicians or their family members. This brings into conflict personal against public interest that can easily be tampered through control over public policy that these politicians enjoy. The politicization of sugar industry started in 1980s when loans were sanctioned to newly privatized sugar mills through state-owned commercial banks. The political tycoons were the main beneficiary through their influence over bureaucracy, political parties and parliament. Most of these loans were written off during the politically

manoeuvred debt write-off in the 1990s. These industries were economically inefficient with their survival based on exploiting farmers and altering public policy in their favour.

Along with inefficient industry, the markets are distorted against consumers and farmers and in favour of mill owners. This is done through hoarding and by manoeuvring public policy to serve their interests. The sugar cartel working under Pakistan Sugar Mills Association (PSMA) has strong lobby in the Economic Coordination Committee (ECC) that control policy-making. They use their influence to prevent timely import and also distort production incentives for sugarcane growers. This was apparent during the sugar crisis in 2009–10 when the lobby delayed import of sugar for five months despite 'apparent' shortage resulting in immense price hike, benefiting the millers and traders to the tune of PKR25 billion.

Source: Malik 2009.

producers whereas the middlemen, in many cases the politicians or their cronies, reap the benefits. The sugar industry has largely been established through subsidized loans and subsequent debt write-offs. The setting up of an inefficient industry is the main reason behind the sugar crisis in the country. It created market imperfections

that resulted in shortages requiring imports at higher prices. This was then subsidized, using populist tools financed from public revenue. The beneficiaries of these political interferences are the middlemen, traders and millers who gained at the cost of both the initial producers who failed to get the remunerative reward of their crop, and the final consumers who paid a higher price.

Natural calamities: Flood and food insecurity in Pakistan

The heavy monsoon that struck Pakistan in 2010 resulted in flooding, causing large scale destruction all across the country. The devastation spread across 160 thousand square km directly affecting 18.1 million people, causing physical loss, loss to livelihoods and infrastructure.[28] More than 2,000 people lost their lives and around 11 million heads of livestock and poultry were lost. Loss of infrastructure included destruction of more than 1.7 million houses and 13,042 water courses (table 3.16).[29] The floods also damaged health and education infrastructure: 7,600 schools, and 436 health facilities.

The flood affected around three-fifths of the country (82 of the total 122 districts).[30] Unfortunately, many of the districts affected by the floods were already vulnerable to food insecurity as was presented in a recent study (table 3.17).[31] The worst affected amongst the victims of the floods were predominantly small and marginal farmers, and unskilled workers. The loss of homes, livelihoods and assets further deteriorated their food security.

Table 3.16 Pakistan: Flood damage, 2010

	Human casualties	People displaced (000 people)	Crop area (000 hectares)	Animal (000 head)	Poultry (000 head)	Water course (Nos.)	Total damage (US$ millions)
AJK	71	…	33	1	12	657	24
Balochistan	48	218	132	1,176	626	47	427
Gilgit Baltistan	183	…	8	12	13	960	22
KPK	1,677	652	121	140	621	1,790	396
Punjab	103	2,666	747	5	2,012	2,598	1,838
Sindh	186	4,596	1,044	176	6,895	6,990	2,302
Total	2,268	8,132	2,093	1,524	10,279	13,042	5,045

Sources: FAO 2010d, UNDP 2010a and WFP-P 2010.

Provinces	Severely effected	Moderately effected
AJK	*Neelum, Muzaffarabad, Sudhanutti*	Hattianbala,*Bagh*,Mirpur, *Bhimber*
Balochistan	Jaffarabad, Nasirabad, *Jhal magsi, Barkhan, Kohlu, Sibbi, Kech*	Harnai, Lasbela, *Loralai, Zhob*
Gilgit Baltistan	*Diamer,Hunza Nagar, Gilgit, Ghizar*	*Skardu, Ghanche*
KPK	*Swat, Charsadda*, Nowshera, Upper Dir, Kohistan, Shangla, *Tank, DI Khan*	Rest of KPK
Punjab	*Rajanpur, Muzaffargarh, DG khan*, Layyah, Bhakar, Rehim Yar Khan, Mianwali	Khushab, Multan
Sindh	*Khairpur*, Shikarpur, Dadu, Larkana, Thatta, Jacobabad, Kashmore, *Sukkur, Ghotki* and Noshero Feroz	Qambar Shahdadkot, Jamshoro, *Tando Allahyar*, Hyderabad

Note: Districts in italics are food-insecure districts.

Sources: Haq 2010, SDPI, SDC and WFP-P 2010 and UNDP 2010a.

The flood caused unprecedented disaster to agriculture. Overall, the flood destroyed over two million hectares of standing crop, mainly rice, sugarcane, maize, cotton, some pulses, and vegetables. The extent of the damage was more severe in Punjab and Sindh where very destructive riverine and riverine delta floods caused significant damage to standing crops. According to the Ministry of Agriculture and Livestock, the flood destroyed 37 per cent of rice crop, 17 per cent of cotton crop and 15 per cent of sugarcane crop.[32] In monetary terms, the accumulated loss was over PKR250 million (table 3.18). Though the wheat crop survived as it was harvested prior to the flood, over one million tonnes of stored wheat and wheat seeds for next year's plantation were destroyed.

The flood created food security concerns both at the national and household level. At the household level, the destruction of property, crops and livestock deprived people of the immediate food supply. The flood impact assessment by the World Food Programme (WFP) reveals that 58 per cent of the total households surveyed had completely lost their stored wheat. Similarly, 32 and 38 per cent of the households have reported loss of pulses and cooking oil.[33] In addition to the loss of stored food stock, the affected areas also witnessed loss of livelihoods. The destruction of cash crops, especially cotton,

created problems for agriculture-based industries like cotton ginning, jute textile and ready-made garments. Rice, sugar and flour mills were also affected severely. This hampered non-farm livelihoods of those living in flood affected areas. As a result, the food consumption went down and around one-third of the households had recorded poor food consumption.[34] Destruction of property and loss of livelihood also forced around 8.1 million people to migrate out of the flood affected areas, 40 per cent of these were internally displaced people.

At the national level, the vast scale of destruction of crops and livestock resulted in scarcity of food supplies. Deteriorating the food availability scenario further, the destruction of infrastructure like roads, bridges and markets severely damaged the food distribution network. The worst affected in terms of loss to community-based infrastructure (CBI) were the mountainous regions of KPK and Balochistan that received flash floods. In

The flood caused unprecedented disaster to agriculture, destroying over two million hectares of standing crop

Table 3.18 Pakistan: Crop damage due to flood, 2010

(PKR million)

	Sugarcane	Paddy	Cotton	Other crops	Total
Punjab	12.5	3.7	50.0	37.5	103.7
Sindh	7.8	31.3	25.0	15.6	79.6
KPK	2.9	1.4	...	21.1	25.3
Balochistan	...	15.1	1.9	24.4	41.4
Pakistan	23.2	51.4	76.9	98.5	250.0

Source: Ahmed and Farooq 2010.

KPK alone, around 6.6 million people were reportedly inaccessible due to damaged road infrastructure. In Swat, all the connecting bridges between the two sides of the river were destroyed over a distance of 140 km.[35]

The shortage of food supply and its inability to reach the markets due to damaged infrastructure translated into significant food inflation. Inflation based on Sensitive Price Index (SPI) surged to 20.5 per cent in the weeks immediately after the floods. This was primarily due to higher prices of perishable items such as fruits, vegetables, and poultry goods. The significant increase in the prices of basic food items made the access to food for flood affected households extremely difficult, making them vulnerable to increased food insecurity.

Social implications of food insecurity

Food security is fundamental for achieving poverty reduction and human development. Poverty and food insecurity are closely linked in the sense that poor people are generally food insecure. Food insecurity leads many vulnerable people deeper into the poverty trap, making it difficult for them to recover. As households adopt various coping mechanisms to mitigate the impact of food insecurity, they reduce expenditures on education, health, and nutrition, negatively affecting human development.

Poverty: Pakistan made significant progress over the last decade to reduce poverty as indicated by the decline in the proportion of population below the calorie-based food plus non-food poverty line (figure 3.6). The percentage of population below the poverty line decreased from 34.5 per cent in 2001–02 to 23.9 per cent in 2004–05; significant progress over a span of three years. Poverty was reduced further by 1.6 percentage points (from 23.9 to 22.3 per cent) during the fiscal year 2005–06. However, since 2006 the economy has come under severe pressure. First, the global financial crisis had its repercussions on the domestic economy. This was followed by the global hike in food and fuel prices which strained government finances even further. Though the local economy was largely insulated from the international financial crisis itself, the impact of the crisis was transmitted to the domestic economy through the increase in the price of oil which, in turn, affected food security, and hence, the welfare of the population. The government passed the burden of higher prices to local consumers, thereby undermining any poverty reduction gains made earlier. The rising food prices not only increased food

Food security is fundamental for achieving poverty reduction and human development

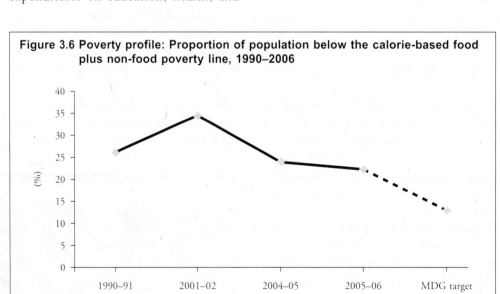

Figure 3.6 Poverty profile: Proportion of population below the calorie-based food plus non-food poverty line, 1990–2006

Source: GOP 2010b.

insecurity but also resulted in increasing poverty. Higher fuel prices increased the prices of goods and services. This resulted in an increase in poverty. The dietary requirement of 2,350 calories was translated into the poverty line of PKR673 per capita per month in 1998–99. The inflation adjusted poverty line figure increased to 944.5 in 2005–06. It is estimated that food inflation during 2006–09 impoverished around 11 million more people making poverty figures go up to 33 per cent.[36]

Inflation: Increased prices and the resultant food insecurity affects everyone adversely. However, the impact varies across households based on income groups and geographical location (provinces and rural/urban). Inequality has increased across different income groups as inflation has disproportionately affected the poorest. The prices for the basket of essential goods have usually been higher for the poor as indicated by table 3.19. It is not only the price of essential food that has been higher for the poor, in recent years the poor have witnessed higher inflation compared to the rich (table 3.19).

The impact of the price hike on food security has also varied according to geographical location. Food consumption of the households that produce their own food has not been affected much compared to those who buy food. Since food production is a rural phenomenon, agriculturally dependent rural households either gained from rising food prices through farm product sales, or through subsistence farming by improving their own consumption. On the other hand, the rising prices have adversely affected food consumption of urban households as food inflation outpaced growth in income. However, not everyone in rural areas benefited from the price hike as around 60 per cent of the rural population buys food from markets. Similarly, in urban areas the profit margin of traders has gone up as they have transferred the burden of higher prices to the consumers. Overall, the producers of food or food traders have benefited from the price hike while consumers have suffered. Another reason for the differential impact of the price hike on urban and rural households is the difference in the nature of diet. While urban households eat a more varied and diversified diet of meat, fruits, vegetables, and dairy products, rural households are more dependent on wheat. Hence, food expenditures are higher in urban areas compared to rural areas but the calorie intake is lower. According to the *Household Income and Expenditure Survey 2005–06*, one-third of urban households consume less than 1,700 kcal/person/day compared to around one fourth in rural areas.[37]

There is also a provincial dimension to food security in Pakistan. While the provinces of Sindh and Punjab are largely self-sufficient in cereal production, the provinces of Balochistan and KPK are deficient. Since wheat markets are controlled by provinces (there exists a ban on inter-provincial transfer of wheat), there is a disparity in wheat prices between provinces with wheat prices higher in Quetta and Peshawar compared to Karachi and Lahore. Balochistan and KPK are also vulnerable in the sense that during the crisis the prices in these markets increased substantially compared to other provinces. In 2008, wheat prices in Quetta and Peshawar increased by over 100 per cent and 80 per cent respectively compared to around 30 and 40 per cent increase in Karachi and Lahore.[38]

Coping with inflation: Households adopt different coping strategies to deal with

The producers of food or food traders have benefited from the price hike while consumers have suffered

Table 3.19 Pakistan: Price indices by income groups, 1990–2010

	All income	Lowest	Highest
2006–07	141.9 (7.8)	143.5 (8.3)	141.2 (7.4)
2007–08	158.9 (12.0)	164 (14.3)	156.3 (10.7)
2008–09	191.9 (20.8)	200.2 (22.1)	186.9 (19.5)

Note: The figures in parentheses are computed inflations.

Sources: GOP 2010b and 2011.

Despite the government's commitment to the United Nations (UN) Millennium Development Goals (MDGs) to reduce the number of undernourished people by half, not much success has been achieved thus far

food insecurity. A recent assessment of coping strategies adopted by households in Pakistan in the wake of the floods shows that some households reduced the quantity of food intake by cutting down daily meals, while others preferred to reduce quality rather than quantity and shifted to less nutritious and cheaper food sources. Some resorted to activities that have long-term implications, such as curtailing spending on health or education, while some households opted for additional incomes by increasing the number of income earners, with children being the primary casualty resulting in high school dropout rates. Sometimes households also resorted to selling productive assets like animal, livestock, and land for current consumption at the expense of future income. The recent flood witnessed 12 per cent of the households selling their domestic and productive assets including animals to compensate for their dwindling incomes.[39]

Higher food prices also forced households to increase their expenditure on food at the expense of non-food expenditures. An earlier assessment undertaken in 2008 had revealed increase in food expenditure all over the country between 2005 and 2008 (table 3.20). The share of food in total expenditure is higher for Balochistan and KPK (47 and 40 per cent, respectively), the two most vulnerable provinces in terms of food security compared to Sindh and Punjab (34 and 32 per cent, respectively).

Malnutrition: Deteriorated food quality and reduced food quantity resulted in undernourishment. Despite the government's commitment to the United Nations (UN) Millennium Development Goals (MDGs) to reduce the number of undernourished people by half between 1990 and 2015, not much success has been achieved thus far. The proportion of the undernourished in total population is still very high, as around one in every four of the population is still malnourished and the situation has deteriorated since 2006.[40] Child nutrition has not shown much improvement either. The proportion of

underweight children under-five is around 38 per cent, way above the MDG 2015 target of less than 20 per cent.[41] Chronic malnutrition (stunting) in children under-five has been reported to be around 37 per cent and acute malnutrition (wasting) around 13 per cent in 2003 (table 3.21).[42] Both stunting and wasting are associated with food poverty, poor socio-economic conditions and inappropriate feeding practices. As a result the health profile of children in Pakistan is extremely poor, characterized by high mortality rates.[43]

Among those with specific nutrition needs, the nutritional status of women, especially pregnant and lactating mothers, is not much different than that of children. Around 17 per cent of pregnant and lactating women are malnourished in Pakistan. These nutritional deprivations result in women suffering from anaemia which is currently affecting around 1.9 million pregnant women. Similarly, four out of 10 women in the child-bearing age are anaemic.[44] Though recent estimates are not available, data collected by the *National Nutrition Survey 2001–02* reflect that women in Pakistan are also suffering from other micronutrient deficiencies like iron, zinc, iodine and vitamin A.[45] Inadequacy to meet the specific needs of women, a consequence of malnutrition, has translated into high maternal mortality rates (260/100,000 live births).[46]

As mentioned earlier, food insecurity has forced households to alter expenditure pattern with a greater share being allocated to food expenditure at the cost of non-

Table 3.20 Pakistan: Food share in total expenditure, 2005–08

(%)

	2005–06	2008
Punjab	30	32
Sindh	32	34
KPK	37	40
Balochistan	44	47

Source: UN 2008.

Table 3.21 Pakistan: Prevalence of malnutrition in Pakistan, 1965–2003

(%)

	underweight	Stunted	Wasted
1965	...	49	11
1977	...	43	9
1985	51.5	45	11
1992	40.4	42	17
1998	38.8	43	9
2000	38.0	40	12
2003	...	37	13

Sources: Khalil 2007 and UN 2008.

food expenditure. Within non-food expenditures, the share of education which was already as low as 6–7 per cent of the total non-food expenditures has dwindled further. The households, in order to meet food expenditure, are forced to take children out of school and send them to work. In rural areas around 5–8 per cent of children are employed as farm labour.[47] The prevailing food insecurity will encourage more families to use children in farm and other activities to generate additional income. Thus, increased food insecurity would result in increased child labour, higher dropout rates, and lower enrolment rates, undermining any improvement that was made in education indicators of the country.

Food policies and the way forward

Pakistan lacks a comprehensive food security policy that covers all the aspects of food security. Over the years, the government has undertaken several initiatives to ensure adequate production of food and its access to people. In this regard, a number of agricultural policies were adopted to ensure sustainable growth of the agriculture sector to increase food availability. Realizing that a large proportion of the population was extremely poor and lacked purchasing power to buy food, various social security programmes were introduced to increase food entitlements of the needy.

Policies to increase food supply

On the supply side, the main objectives of governments' agricultural policies have been to increase agriculture productivity to achieve food self-sufficiency and ensure availability, especially of staple crops like wheat. To achieve these objectives, governments have intervened in the food market by providing direct and indirect subsidies for agricultural inputs and announcing minimum support price for agricultural outputs. The support price mechanism is the most effective instrument to influence prices of agricultural commodities. The instrument has largely been used for wheat and sugarcane where the government guarantees a minimum support price to producers. This monitoring of commodity prices ensures that producer receives a fair price for their products but not at the cost of the consumer who is also ensured of a reasonable and stable price. Farmers also benefit as it removes price uncertainty.

In addition to guaranteeing these support prices, the federal government also ensures access through procuring, storage, and distribution of food commodities (largely wheat). This is implemented through PASSCO and provincial food departments that run wheat procurement drives annually during the harvesting season to procure and store the required quantity. The policy is designed to assist farmers and consumers, but it has some flaws that undermine their interests. To maximize consumers and farmers benefits, PASSCO procures wheat from the farmers at a high price and sells to flour mills at a subsidized price. Resultantly the middle men, mainly the flour and sugar mill owners, draw the major chunk of the benefits while the state exchequer incurs heavy losses. The government suffers due to inefficiencies within the system. It lacks the storage capacity to store the procured wheat, and private storage facilities add an additional burden to the government's financial resources.

In the past, the government has also provided direct subsidies for agricultural inputs such as fertilizers, electricity, irrigation and seeds. Apart from these direct input subsidies, the government also provides indirect subsidies in the form of concessionary loans. This has been largely targeted towards improving farm mechanization, especially tractors; land development; installation and maintenance of tubewells; and farm transportation. The provision of input subsidies benefits small and marginal farmers who otherwise lack financial capacity to utilize these productivity enhancing measures.

The government has also contributed in extending agricultural research and

Pakistan lacks a comprehensive food security policy that covers all the aspects of food security

development, and laying down infrastructure that includes development of the irrigation system, roads, and markets. In Pakistan, the government undertakes most of the agricultural research and development activities, accounting for 92 per cent of such activities. The Pakistan Agriculture Research Council is the main federal agency with the mandate to conduct, support, coordinate and promote agricultural research and development. The government also supports a number of agricultural universities and agencies in this regard.

Policies for social protection

Considering the number of people with serious financial needs, the government has traditionally provided relief to vulnerable groups through its various social protection and safety net programmes. These social protection programmes comprise social security and welfare, food support programmes, food subsidies, and some targeted programmes for people with disabilities, child labourers and others. The overall share of social protection and safety net spending as a share of total poverty reduction spending have fluctuated over the years but largely remained below 10 per cent (table 3.22). However, after 2006–07, there has been a significant increase in social protection spending largely attributed to the increased spending on food subsidies and social

security. Pakistan's social security system offers pension benefits to workers in the private and the public sector through the Employees Old Age Benefit Scheme, Workers Welfare Fund, and Employees Social Security Institutions. However, these are restricted only to formal sector employees. The share of food subsidies has also increased significantly over the years from PKR4.3 billion in 2001–02 to PKR178.3 billion in 2009–10 peaking to around PKR400 billion in 2007–08.

For the purpose of targeting the welfare of the chronically poor and vulnerable, Pakistan has safety net programmes, providing cash transfers to meet their basic food requirements. This safety net system includes three main federal cash transfer programmes: *Zakat*, Pakistan *Bait-ul Maal* (PBM), and the recently established Benazir Income Support Programme (BISP). The *Zakat* and *Usher* scheme is a cash transfer programme that provides a monthly subsistence allowance of PKR500 and rehabilitation grant of up to PKR5,000 to the needy and the poor. The programme especially targets widows, orphans, and the disabled. Within the PBM programme a major component is the food specific Food Support Programme (FSP). The FSP targets households with an income of PKR2,000 per month or less and provides annual cash transfer of PKR3000 per household to buy food. Pakistan's FSP also provides food stamps/coupons for the purchase of basic food items. In 2009–10

Table 3.22 Pakistan: Social protection and safety nets spending, 2001–10

(PKR billion)

	2001–02	2002–03	2003–04	2004–05	2005–06	2006–07	2007–08	2008–09	2009–10
Social security and welfare	3.7	1.3	41.0	2.0	7.6	4.5	22.5	29.1	73.5
Food support	2.0	2.0	2.8	2.7	3.1	3.5	4.3	12.4	11.8
Subsidies	4.3	10.9	8.5	5.4	6.0	5.5	398.5	220.6	178.3
Peoples work programme	0.8	0.8	0.6	0.1	0.0	0.0	1.9	3.3	2.9
Natural calamities and disasters	0.2	0.4	0.5	0.9	19.1	5.0	7.4	10.0	3.5
Total social protection and safety nets	11.0	15.4	17.0	11.4	36.1	18.8	435.2	276.1	271.6
Total social sector and poverty reduction expenditure	166.1	209.0	261.3	316.2	376.1	426.7	1042.0	977.2	860.0
As a % of poverty reduction spending	6.6	7.4	6.5	3.6	9.6	4.4	41.8	28.3	31.6

Source: GOP 2010c.

the programme provided PKR1.65 billion to 1.11 million beneficiaries. The project is planned to disburse PKR2 billion during the current fiscal year.

Recently, in order to cushion the negative effects of the food crisis and inflation on the poor, the government launched the BISP that provides cash grants to the poor and vulnerable segments of the population. This cash transfer programme offers a monthly payment of PKR1,000 per household. The government spent PKR34 billion during 2008–09 on BISP, doubling the federal government's social safety nets spending from 0.3 per cent in 2003–04 to 0.6 per cent of GDP. It covered five million families in FY2009–10, and intends to provide relief to seven million in 2010–11, increasing the spending on social safety net programmes to one per cent of the GDP.

These unconditional cash transfers directly improve consumption and income levels of the beneficiaries, and help in reducing poverty, improving health and nutrition, and increasing income generation.

These cash and food support programmes work towards ensuring food and nutrition for the extremely vulnerable. However, there are certain flaws that need to be addressed to achieve the desired results. These programmes have different implementing agencies: *Zakat* and *Usher* by the Ministry of Religious Affairs, Zakat and Usher; PBM by the PBM Board; and the BISP by the Ministry of Finance. Thus, the delivery mechanism of the safety net programmes is fragmented. The multitude of administrative authorities required to manage the cash transfer programmes, without any coordination mechanism between them, also results in duplication of beneficiaries.

A higher level of spending on safety net programmes does not necessarily translate into more coverage for the poor if the programmes are poorly targeted. The implementation of BISP lacks transparency, increasing chances of corruption and nepotism in identifying poor households, and hence, exclusion

of the needy. It is extremely important that the BISP establishes a proper targeting mechanism. The initial practice whereby parliamentarians nominated the beneficiaries was flawed as it led to political patronage. The new method of the poverty scorecard based on household surveys is still in the early stage of implementation.

Expanding the safety net programme comes at a huge financial cost, especially at a time when the country is undergoing severe financial crisis. The importance of the cash transfer programmes to ensure smooth income and consumption at a time when many households' economic situation is at its lowest point can also not be denied. These initiatives are currently needed as peoples' income sources are severely stretched in the wake of natural calamities such as earthquakes and floods, and the ongoing 'war on terror'. The government needs to create a balance between its social protection needs and financial cost. It has to implement stringent conditions for targeting beneficiaries to ensure that only the most deserving receive these benefits. It also needs to enhance coordination between its various administrative departments to avoid duplication of beneficiaries. Stringent accountability mechanisms need to be implemented to minimize loss due to corruption. There is also a vital need to curtail the administrative expenses incurred in running these programmes to ensure that the maximum number of beneficiaries is included within the allocated financial resources. The safety net programmes have to be complemented with the development of a pro-poor growth strategy so that employment opportunities are created to provide graduation/exit strategies to the beneficiaries of the safety net programmes.

The way forward

The preceding sections have discussed the status of food security in Pakistan, the factors that affect food security, and the social implications of deteriorating food security situation. The analysis suggests

A higher level of spending on safety net programmes does not necessarily translate into more coverage for the poor if the programmes are poorly targeted

that policy makers need to evolve a comprehensive food policy, addressing both the supply and demand side constraints in order to ensure food security of all people. The country has to increase agricultural growth and improve its productivity to ensure sufficient food to the rapidly growing population. It has to ensure adequate production to meet domestic needs. To ensure that production translates into food availability, the government needs to implement a coherent plan for ensuring proper procurement, storage, and distribution of food. The government also needs to ensure that available food is within access to people and thus adopt a pro-poor growth strategy that leads to adequate employment and livelihood opportunities for all. Further, social safety net programmes specifically targeted towards those households who fail to meet their food requirements must be implemented efficiently.

Adequate production to meet domestic needs: Sustained agricultural growth can only be achieved by actively supporting agricultural research and extension including developing improved crop varieties and crop management technologies, and promoting these to the farmers. Currently, the focus has been on a few major and minor crops. In addition to enhancing productivity of the existing crops that Pakistan produces, agricultural research should focus on crop diversification to exploit the diverse ecological zones in the country. It should also promote the notion of multiple cropping—growing more than one crop on the same land during the season. This technology increases the efficiency of inputs such as water, fertilizer, etc.; maintains soil fertility; and increases output per unit of land.

Accompanying crop diversification, farmers should also be encouraged to diversify their income sources and livelihoods. For this on-farm livestock, poultry and fish ponds should be encouraged through provision of better breeding facilities and improved animal feed. Horticulture is another sector that

adds significant value addition and has the potential to generate secondary livelihood opportunities for farmers.

Water scarcity poses a grave threat for the future of the agriculture sector in Pakistan. Therefore, the focus of agricultural research, while enhancing productivity, should be towards efficient use of this resource. In this regard, cultivation of less water-intensive crops should be promoted. Agricultural research should also develop water-saving technologies like drip irrigation and sprinkler irrigation. Wastage of water in water channels and canals should also be curtailed by proper lining of water courses.

Available land for cultivation should be expanded by giving state lands to small farmers and to implement meaningful land reforms. There is an urgent need to streamline land records and simplify land sale procedures. Methodologies like cooperative farming need to be designed where small farmers can retain ownership of their individual land while working collaboratively to produce crops.

In addition to availability of land and water, agricultural productivity can be enhanced by ensuring timely provision of farm inputs, such as quality seeds, fertilizers, machinery, pesticides and other farm-related services. For this the existing markets need to be expanded or village sale centres should be established. These sale centres could serve an additional purpose of disseminating new technology by providing training and guidance to farmers for improved technology.

Credit is a significant factor of production that determines farmers' ability to cultivate new crops. There is an urgent need to develop credit guarantee schemes for small and marginalized farmers and simplify the lending procedures. Strategic lending to farmers associated with livestock, dairy, and the fisheries sectors and those for development purposes like water conservation and infrastructure development should be encouraged.

Improve food procurement, storage and distribution: Post-harvest losses due to weak food procurement, storage and distribution systems significantly undermine agricultural produce. Therefore, any improvement in production and productivity has to be balanced by improving post-harvest handling of products. This would involve:

- Setting up a pricing policy for food procurement to ensure reasonable returns to farmers.
- Ensuring a centralized administrative control (provincial/federal) regarding food procurement and distribution.
- Improving storage capacity of government godowns.
- Developing a trade strategy to ensure timely exports and imports during surplus and deficit. In this regard the government should build the capacity to understand the food supply and demand factors of basic commodities. It should be able to adopt a forecasting mechanism to understand food supply and foresee its demand. This would enable government and policy makers to be proactive in preventing a crisis rather than having to act when the crisis has already hit.
- Minimizing the role of cartels/hoardings/smuggling networks through strengthening the Competition Commission of Pakistan and other legal and administrative bodies.

Developing a pro-poor growth strategy and ensuring social safety nets for poor: Any effort to improve the food security situation in Pakistan depends on policies to reduce poverty. For this, it is extremely important that the poor are part of the growth process, and policies should specifically target their increased participation.

Such a strategy would involve:

- Promoting non-farm employment by increasing public and private investment in physical and social infrastructure like building roads, and education and health facilities. Diversification of livelihoods in the rural economy through farm and non-farm employment opportunities is extremely vital to ensure their food security.
- Enhancing human development through improving education and health facilities.
- Equitable distribution of land and provision of state land to poor landless farmers.
- Extending agriculture credit and finances to small farmers,
- Promoting farm research results to poor farmers for efficient land use.

The current food insecurity situation in the country demands that a reasonably well-targeted social safety net programme is in place to supplement efforts for pro-poor growth. There are many such programmes that government is running through its various departments. It is important that a strong verification and monitoring system of beneficiaries is in place to ensure that there is no duplication of beneficiaries.

It is extremely important that the poor are part of the growth process, and policies should specifically target their increased participation

Chapter 4

Food Security in Bangladesh: Challenges and Response*

To talk about food security for all people and at all times in Bangladesh—a country prone to floods, droughts, and cyclones, and with the 40 per cent of the population in poverty—is a difficult task. And yet the country has been able to mobilize the political will and technical capacity to put in place policies and initiatives that seek to avert food insecurity for its vulnerable people. Bangladesh is addressing the issues of both availability and access to food seriously and showing some good results.

Availability of food

Availability of food depends on both domestic production and imports. Major items of food production in Bangladesh include rice, wheat, pulses, potato, vegetables, spices, and fish. These food items account for almost 80 per cent of total calories and protein intake. Of these, rice and wheat alone contribute to 74 per cent and 57 per cent of total per capita calorie and protein intake respectively. The production trend of major food items are provided in table 4.1.

Rice production has shown respectable growth due to adoption of high-yielding varieties supported by expansion of minor irrigation. In fact, the growth in rice production kept pace with population growth in the 1980s and has surpassed it by a significant margin since. The growth in rice production, however, decelerated during the first half of the current decade. The easy sources of increasing rice production have already been exhausted. Sustaining the growth will be difficult without development and diffusion of technologies in the unfavourable ecological areas. Bangladesh does not have a favourable agricultural climate for growing wheat. Wheat is mostly grown in the northwestern region of the country which has a relatively longer winter period. Yet wheat showed some healthy growth during the last three decades, registering growth of over 10 per cent over the 1971–2000 period. The growth, however, has significantly decelerated in the current decade, accounting for less than four per cent of total cereal production now. In recent years, maize has been replacing wheat because of its higher yield and profitability and suitability to the agro-ecological conditions in Bangladesh.

The production of cereal has become more resilient to natural disasters over time because of dramatic change in the seasonal composition of production.[1] This has important implications for food security. *Boro* rice, together with wheat, now constitute about 60 per cent of the cereal production during the March to June period; their share of the total cereal harvest was less than 10 per cent in the early 1970s. The change in the seasonal composition of production had a smoothening effect on the seasonal variation in prices as well.[2]

Bangladesh has been able to mobilize the political will and technical capacity to put in place policies and initiatives that seek to avert food insecurity for its vulnerable people

Table 4.1 Long term trend in the production of major food crops, 1970–2009

(000 tonnes)

	1970–72	1990–92	1999–2001	2008–09
Cereals	10,584	19,223	26,002	32,167
Rice	10,393	18,157	24,126	31,318
Wheat	111	986	1,807	849
Potato	1,637	1,715	3,342	5,268
Sugar	1,367	991	995	80
Pulses	376	518	379	196
Oil crops	250	466	486	337
Vegetables	1,120	1,354	1,794	1,862*
Fish	1,384	13,384	1,369	2,701

Note: *: Vegetable production in 2006–07.
Source: Hossain and Deb 2009a.

* This is an edited version of a paper prepared by Quazi Shahabuddin and Uttam Kumar Deb from Bangladesh. The views expressed are those of the authors.

The rapid expansion in the production of cereals was partly achieved through reductions in area for production of pulses, oilseeds and sugarcane. Pulses and oilseeds are important sources of protein and micronutrients, especially for the poor. The reduction in the production of these crops has had an adverse impact on nutritional balance among the people. There has been a perceptible decline in the production of pulses and sugarcane. The production of potato, on the other hand, has shown robust growth in recent years (table 4.1).

Bangladesh has a substantial biological and physical resource base for production of fisheries. From the nutritional point of view, fish occupies a significant position in dietary habits of the people. The growth in fish production, which was rather sluggish in the 1970s, picked up in the 1980s, and has been very rapid in recent years due to rapid expansion of pond aquaculture. The growth in the production of meat and milk, however, has remained rather unsatisfactory, despite the expansion of the poultry industry, while their demand has been growing fast. The growth in livestock and poultry farming has been constrained by lack of feed, risk imposed by avian flu and other animal diseases, and poor marketing infrastructure.

Availability of food at the national level depends not only on domestic production but also on imports (and exports).[3] The country is heavily dependent on import of almost all food items to meet the demand of the growing population. The import of rice remained stagnant at around 0.5 million tonnes per year, with a substantial increase in imports in years following poor harvests due to floods and droughts. Thus, Bangladesh imported over two million tonnes of rice during 1973–75, 1988–89 and 1998–99, periods following disastrous floods or droughts. After the disastrous floods of 1998, for example, Bangladesh imported over 3.5 million tonnes of rice and wheat. In some years (1991, 2000), following bumper harvests, the government declared self-sufficiency in rice production, only to find the country slipping back to import dependence due to increasing demand from growing income and population.[4]

Commercial import of wheat has increased steadily over time despite growth in domestic production due to reduction in food aid in recent years. The volume of imports increased from one million tonnes in the early 1970s, to 1.4 million tonnes in the early 1990s, and further to two million tonnes during 2000–02, and continues to grow since then. The food items for which imports have been increasing fast are oils, pulses, sugar, milk and fruits. The rapidly rising imports of these food items are becoming a major drain on the limited foreign exchange earnings of the country. Attempts have been made to promote crop diversification to reduce dependence on imports, but without much success.

To sum up, food availability at the national level barely kept up with population growth till the end of the mid-1990s. The situation has improved since the late 1990s, particularly for food grain and potato, due to both acceleration in the growth of production and the success achieved in reducing the growth of population.[5] The per capita availability of most other food items, however, declined over the last four decades, despite upward trend in imports.

Access to food

The major determinant of food entitlement of a household and hence its access to food is obviously the level of income. In Bangladesh, per capita income remained almost stagnant until the end of the 1980s due to slow growth in gross national product (GNP) and high growth in population. Income growth has accelerated since 1990, reaching 6.0 to 6.5 per cent in recent years. As a result, per capita income has been growing at a faster rate of about 4.5 per cent recently. However, available evidence from *Household Income Expenditure Survey* indicates growing urban-rural disparity in incomes. The concentration of income as measured by

Gini coefficient was estimated to be 0.30 for rural areas and 0.38 for urban areas in 2005. The increase in income inequality was moderate in the 1980s but became worse in the 1990s in both rural and urban areas. As a result, the impact of recent acceleration in income growth on poverty reduction has remained modest.

Wages

The trend in real wage rate, especially of the agricultural labour, is often used as an alternative indicator to assess changes in the living conditions of the poor. It should, however, be mentioned that the wage rate may reflect changes in income of the extreme poor and not necessarily of the moderate poor. The latter group may earn their livelihood more as marginal and small farmers, while the former may derive the major portion of their income from participation in the labour market.[6] The estimates of real wage (as deflated by the price of rice) show a steady increase in real wages since 1983–84, except in years of recent global inflation (2007 and 2008) when rice prices significantly increased (table 4.2).

The increase in real wage can be attributed to growing scarcity of labour in agriculture which has been caused by (a) movement of labour to rural non-farm activities due to expansion of trade and transport operations, and rapid growth of microcredit used for generation of self-employment in the informal sector; and (b) rapid migration from rural to urban areas. The scarcity of agricultural labour is reflected in the rising trend towards mechanization of farm operations. The recent food inflation, however, had a negative impact on real wages in agriculture. Although agricultural wages responded positively to the increase in rice prices, the adjustment was only partial. It is estimated that in 2007 and 2008, food prices increased by 65 per cent while agricultural wages increased by 35 per cent, which led to a substantial downward movement in real wages for agricultural labourers over the two years.[7]

Access to real income and hence food can be examined in terms of the movement of real wage over time. The time series data on real wages are presented in table 4.3. It shows that the indices of real wages—both general as well as sectoral indices—displayed an upward trend over the last three decades. However, this is lower in agriculture, which employs most of the labour force, as compared to those in the manufacturing and construction sectors.

Movement in real wage determines affordability to those who are already employed. In order to have an idea about overall economic accessibility, one needs to look at the trend of underemployment in the country (see table 4.4). The rate of underemployment has declined from 43.4

The recent food inflation had a negative impact on real wages in agriculture

Table 4.2 Trend in real agricultural wages in Bangladesh, 1983–2008

	Nominal wage rate (BTK per day)	Poverty line deflator (2003=100)	Rice price deflator (2003=100)	Real wage (BTK per day)	
				With poverty line deflator	With rice price deflator
1983–84	19.58	38.70	54.50	50.59	35.92
1988–89	32.71	55.70	72.60	58.73	45.05
1991–92	41.77	67.80	82.80	61.60	50.45
1995–96	45.58	78.20	103.00	58.29	44.25
2000	63.60	91.50	96.80	69.51	65.70
2003	72.23	100.00	100.00	72.73	72.73
2004	75.83	106.75	103.09	71.04	73.56
2005	84.42	...	117.36	...	71.93
2006	94.83	...	120.99	...	78.38
2007	109.50	...	147.82	...	74.08
2008	135.67	186.88	218.10	72.60	62.21

Sources: Authors' calculations based on Hossain and Bayes 2010 and Hossain and Deb 2009a.

Table 4.3   Index of real wage (1969–70=100), 1980–2009

	General	Manufacturing	Construction	Agriculture
1980–81	87	79	94	86
1981–82	86	80	96	85
1982–83	88	82	99	82
1983–84	90	95	99	75
1984–85	86	91	91	75
Average	87	85	96	81
1985–86	95	102	100	82
1986–87	102	109	106	89
1987–88	106	108	117	93
1988–89	107	110	120	92
1989–1990	110	115	113	96
Average	104	109	111	90
1990–91	107	114	107	95
1991–92	107	113	104	98
1992–93	113	119	109	105
1993–94	114	121	106	106
1994–95	111	121	100	103
Average	110	118	105	101
1995–96	114	123	106	104
1996–97	120	130	111	109
1997–98	122	137	114	107
1998–99	118	131	113	102
1999–2000	121	137	116	103
Average	119	132	112	105
2000–01	125	142	118	107
2001–02	130	150	121	112
2002–03	141	169	127	118
2003–04	146	177	125	121
2004–05	149	181	124	123
Average	138	164	123	116
2005–06	149	183	123	124
2006–07	150	184	124	125
2007–08	154	206	141	140
2008–09	174	243	171	169
Average	157	204	140	139

Source: GOB, *Bangladesh Economic Review* (various years).

Therefore, despite the gains achieved by Bangladesh in augmenting food availability, public food distribution in general, and social safety net programmes in particular, are needed to assist the poor to be food secure by increasing their access to food through such transfer programmes. There are a number of food distribution programmes in operation, each with its own specific objective and target population. Some are relief programmes that aim primarily at relieving immediate distress, generally due to natural disasters. Other programmes have explicit development objectives.[8] Although relief provision remains an important objective, most targeted programmes have gradually shifted in emphasis from relief to development.

In an attempt to reorient food transfers to the poor, the government abolished the poorly targeted urban and rural rationing channels. A number of safety net programmes have evolved from being purely relief measures to having a development dimension. These include 'Food-for-Work', 'Food-for-Education' and 'Vulnerable Group Development'. The size and composition of the Public Food Distribution System (PFDS) has changed significantly over the last two decades (table 4.5). The share of food grain distributed to targeted food assistance programmes has increased over time; about two-thirds of the total food grain channelled through the PFDS is now

per cent in 1989 to 31.9 per cent in 1999–2000, and further to 28.7 per cent in 2009, thereby indicating an improvement in economic accessibility over the last two decades. However, it is somewhat worrying to note that the rate of decline has slowed down considerably over the last decade compared to the preceding one.

Public Food Distribution System

Bangladesh, by virtue of its geographical location, is often at the mercy of natural calamities such as floods and cyclones.

Table 4.4   Underemployment rate in Bangladesh, 1989–2009

	Rate of underemployment (%) (among 10+ years aged labour force)
1989	43.4
1990–91	42.8
1995–96	34.6
1999–2000*	31.9
2002–03*	34.0
2005–06*	24.5
2009*	28.7

Note: *: These years' data are for 15+ years aged labour.

Sources: GOB, *Labour Force Survey* (various years) and 2009b.

directed towards these programmes. The remaining one-third passes through other so-called monetized, sales channels of the PFDS.

Poverty trends in Bangladesh: Economic accessibility

Poor people are generally food insecure. Hence rapid and sustained reduction in poverty is essential to ensure food security at the household level. The poverty trend in Bangladesh shows the economic accessibility of food in the country.

Although inter-temporal estimates of poverty reveal substantial variation due to differences in underlying assumptions and methodologies, some trends can nevertheless be established with available information. The typical sources of data which are nationally representative for measurement of poverty at the household level are several rounds of the *Household Income Expenditure Survey* of the Bangladesh Bureau of Statistics (BBS). The poverty estimates based on these data are presented in table 4.6 for the 1983–84 through 2005 period.

As can be seen from table 4.6, the incidence of poverty, as measured by the headcount ratio, declined from about 58.5 per cent in 1983–84 to 40.0 per cent in 2005. Both rural and urban poverty declined. The incidence of rural poverty, however, remained higher than that of urban poverty.

The estimates reveal two contrasting trends. Urban poverty declined at a faster rate than rural poverty between 1983–84 and 1995–96—from about 50.2 per cent in 1983–84 to about 29.4 per cent in 1995–96. During this period, rural poverty declined only marginally—from about 59.6 per cent in 1983–84 to about 55.2 per cent in 1995–96. In contrast, the later period (1995–2005) witnessed considerable decline in rural poverty (from about 55.2 per cent in 1995–96 to about 43.8 per cent in 2005), while urban poverty almost stagnated (28.4 per cent in 2005 compared to 29.4 per cent in 1995–96).

Table 4.5 Public food grain distribution in Bangladesh, 1989–2009

(000 metric tonnes, annual average)

Programmes	1989–92	1992–97	2001–06	2006–09
Sales channels				
Statutory Rationing	187	11	0	0
Rural Rationing	376	0	0	0
Essential Priorities	145	172	231	180
Other Priorities	232	11	18	21
Large Employees Industries	45	17	11	12
Open Market Sales	137	200	152	290
Fair Price Cards	0	0	10	0
Flour Mills	235	39	49	1
Palli Chaka (rural mills)	96	21	7	0
Other/auction	0	7	0	50
Sub-total	1,456 (63)	482 (33)	478 (34)	554 (32)
Non-sales channels				
Food-for-Work	471	444	302	225
Test Relief	153	101	132	198
Vulnerable Group Development	214	167	194	236
Gratuitous Relief	0	30	42	38
Food for Education	0	154	40	0
Vulnerable Group Feeding	0	0	111	396
Other	0	64	88	88
Sub-total	838 (37)	961 (67)	909 (66)	1181 (68)
Total	2,294 (100)	1,443 (100)	1,387 (100)	1,735 (100)

Note: *: Values in parenthesis are in per cent.
Source: Dorosh *et al.* 2004.

Over the 1984–2005 period, the absolute number of poor in the country remained almost the same, while total population increased by about 44 million. The number of rural poor declined from about 50.3 million in 1983–84 to about 45.8 million in 2005. The number of urban poor, however, increased by about 4.1 million over the same period.

Table 4.6 Incidence of poverty in Bangladesh, 1983–2005

	Headcount ratio (%)			Number of poor (million)		
	Rural	Urban	Total	Rural	Urban	Total
1983–84	59.6	50.2	58.5	50.3	5.6	55.9
1988–89	59.2	43.9	57.1	54.1	6.2	60.3
1991–92	61.2	44.9	58.8	57.6	6.3	63.9
1995–96	55.2	29.4	51.0	53.6	5.8	59.4
2000	53.0	36.6	49.8	53.4	9.3	62.7
2005	43.8	28.4	40.0	45.8	9.7	55.5

Note: The headcount ratio refers to the percentage of the population living below the upper poverty line as measured by the Cost of Basic Needs (CBN) method.
Sources: GOB 2007 and Mujeri 2000.

*The incidence of
absolute poverty has
declined from 55.7
per cent in 1985–86
to 44.3 per cent in
2000, and further to
40.4 per cent in 2005*

Access to food for most vulnerable groups

The accessibility of food encompasses both economic and physical accessibility. Access to food for the most vulnerable groups should be assessed in terms of physical accessibility. The persons who are living in chronic poverty are those who are most vulnerable nutritionally. An estimate of the nutritionally vulnerable people can be obtained from the incidence of poverty estimated by Direct Calorie Intake Method (DCIM) by BBS in different survey years (table 4.7).

The incidence of absolute poverty (in terms of percentage of total population with less than 2,122 kcal/person/day) has declined from 55.7 per cent in 1985–86 to 44.3 per cent in 2000, and further to 40.4 per cent in 2005. Although the incidence of hardcore poverty (with less than 1,805 kcal/person/day) increased during the late eighties (1988–89) and early nineties (1991–92), it then declined to 19.5 per cent, and remained almost the same thereafter (2005).[9]

Nutritional deprivation represents the most basic and acute of all deprivations. A nationally representative nutritional survey carried out by the Institute of Nutrition and Food Science (INFS) in 1981 indicated that the extent of malnutrition within the households varied substantially according to individual characteristics such as age and sex.[10] According to the INFS survey, an average rural household met 87 per cent of the calorie requirement. None of the age groups of boys and girls under the age of 20 years, however, met their requirements. Furthermore, within these age groups, the younger the child, the larger the deficiency. Lactating and pregnant mothers were deficient by as much as 30 per cent. In other words, acute maldistribution of food was observed within the household, with mothers and young children particularly vulnerable.[11]

Factors affecting food security in Bangladesh

National and household level food security in Bangladesh is affected by a number of factors including the performance of the agriculture sector, especially the incidence of natural disasters such as floods, droughts and cyclones, flow of remittances, and trade policies pursued by partner trading countries.

Table 4.7   Incidence of poverty (headcount ratio) by Direct Calorie Intake Method, 1985–2005

	National		Rural		Urban	
	No. in million	% of population	No. in million	% of population	No. in million	% of population
Poverty line 1: Absolute poverty 2,122 Kcal/person/day						
2005	56.1	40.4	41.3	39.5	14.8	43.2
2000	55.8	44.3	42.6	42.3	13.2	52.5
1995–96	55.3	47.5	45.7	47.1	9.6	49.7
1991–92	51.6	47.5	44.8	47.6	6.8	46.7
1988–89	49.7	47.8	43.4	47.8	6.3	47.6
1985–86	55.3	55.7	47.4	54.7	7.9	62.6
Poverty line 2: Hard core poverty 1,805 Kcal/person/day						
2005	27.1	19.5	18.7	17.9	8.4	24.4
2000	24.9	20.0	18.8	18.7	6.0	25.0
1995–96	29.1	25.1	23.9	24.6	5.2	27.3
1991–92	30.4	28.0	26.6	28.3	3.8	26.3
1988–89	29.5	28.4	26.0	28.6	3.5	26.4
1985–86	26.7	26.9	22.8	26.3	3.9	30.7

Sources: GOB 2001b and 2007.

Natural disasters, climate change, and food security

Natural disasters directly affect household food security status by undermining their asset base, and indirectly, through a loss of employment opportunities, an increase in health expenditure, and also an increase in necessary food expenditure. Bangladesh is a disaster prone country. Floods and cyclones damage production of food grains. Loss in domestic production is usually met through imports and increased production in the next season. Cereal production has become more resilient to natural disasters over time because of the dramatic change in the seasonal composition of production.[12] Food vulnerability is manifested in two ways: inadequate access to food throughout the year and acute food shortage on a seasonal basis. A study observed that 7 per cent of households faced acute distress in accessing food on a regular basis, and up to 30 per cent of households encountered such conditions sometimes, making the latter group as potentially highly vulnerable.[13] Besides, 12 to 15 per cent of households had chronic underconsumption of food.

Bangladesh is widely recognized as one of the countries most vulnerable to the impacts of climate change. It is apprehended that while all sectors of the economy will be affected, the impact will be very severe on the agriculture sector. Therefore, food and livelihood security is likely to be jeopardized. Production of crops and other agricultural commodities depends to a large extent on climatic conditions, therefore, changes in climatic conditions will surely affect the food production situation in the country adversely. It is predicted that a number of changes will be observed in Bangladesh due to the climate change. Rainfall patterns will change. The frequency and severity of floods, cyclones, droughts, storm surges, and heat waves will increase. Crop growing seasons will be changed in different regions of the country. Changes will also occur in water quality and quantity such as salinization.

Sea level will rise, and therefore, intrusion of salt water will increase.

A study estimated the impacts of climate change (drought, inundation and salinity) on rice production in Bangladesh by 2030 in different rice growing seasons (*aus*, *aman* and *boro*).[14] The study revealed that in a 'normal year', by 2030, rice production (with the existing technologies and production practices) is likely to be reduced by 12.19 lakh tonnes (about 4.2 per cent of current annual rice production) due to the adverse impact of climate change (table 4.8). Other studies have also indicated likely loss in crop production as a result of climate change.[15] Decrease in crop production will adversely affect the availability and consumption of food. The poor and climate change refugees will be the worst victims of climate change.

Trade policy and food security

Bangladesh as a net food importing country relies on imports to meet the deficit between demand for food grains and its domestic production. Imports are sustained through food aid received by the government, and commercial imports by both the public and private sectors. Prior to 1993, the private sector was not allowed to import food grains (rice and wheat). Currently, the private sector plays a dominant role in commercial imports. Both the quantity and share of food aid in total food grain imports has declined over time. Level of imports of food grains has fluctuated over time. Quantity of imports increased significantly in the years of natural disasters (e.g., after the floods of 1987, 1988, 1998, 2004 and 2007), but the volume of imports of food grains, particularly rice, were relatively low in

Bangladesh is widely recognized as one of the countries most vulnerable to the impacts of climate change

Table 4.8	Impact of climate change on rice production by 2030			
To be affected by	Rice area (000, hectares)	Rice production (000, tonnes)	% of total rice area	% of total rice production
Drought	6,279	703	59.45	2.43
Inundation	55	121	0.52	0.42
Salinity	2,151	395	20.37	1.37
Total	8,485	1,219	80.34	4.21

Source: Deb, Hossain and Jones 2009.

Remittance incomes from migrant workers have contributed towards ensuring food security in the country

normal years. The commercial import of rice was almost insignificant in 1991 and 2001, when the country achieved self-sufficiency. Commercial import of rice during the last fiscal year (FY2009–10) was only 77,000 metric tonnes mainly due to higher international prices and good domestic production. Import of wheat has increased substantially in recent years. Higher level of domestic demand for wheat, along with diversion of wheat area to other remunerative crops, is the underlying reason for such increases. Level of wheat import also increases substantially during the years of natural disasters.

Bangladesh's rice market is not only affected by its own production and trade policy but also by those of its trading partners, particularly India. India has been the major source of rice imports for Bangladesh. Rice imports from India have increased in the current decade because (a) it is quicker and cheaper to bring rice from India; (b) it is possible for importers to bring in small quantities of rice by road; and (c) India exports parboiled rice, which is preferred by most Bangladeshis.[16] After the floods of 1998 and 2004, Bangladesh was able to import an adequate amount of rice to offset the production loss caused by the floods. Rice prices in Bangladesh were at par with the import parity price even after the flood in 1998.[17] Bangladesh experienced dumping of rice from India in 2001–02 and 2002–03 when the Government of India provided high subsidy on rice exports.[18]

The rice market in Bangladesh followed the same trend as in the world market, with prices remaining higher by an average of 40 per cent in the 1980s, and by 20 per cent during the early 1990s. In the late 1990s, domestic prices were at the same level as in the world market. Another notable feature of the price trend is that the fluctuation of prices around the trend was less pronounced in Bangladesh than in the world market.[19] From January 2006 to April 2010, rice prices in Bangladesh were lower than in Thailand (five per cent broken rice). Rice prices in Bangladesh were usually higher than that of India

(Delhi), but showed a mixed pattern in recent years (figure 4.1). In April 2010, average wholesale price of coarse rice in Bangladesh was BTK24,722 per metric tonnes (US$357), compared to US$438 in India (Delhi) and US$477 (five per cent broken parboiled rice) in Thailand (Bangkok).

Remittances from abroad and from urban to rural areas

Remittance incomes from migrant workers have contributed towards ensuring food security in the country. Migration in Bangladesh occurs in three forms: seasonal, rural-urban and off-country (overseas).[20] Seasonal migration is predominant among the poor and urban migration is predominant among all classes, while overseas migration is predominant among the lower to upper middle classes as it involves substantial amounts of money that the poor cannot afford. Mass seasonal migration occurs twice during harvesting seasons (April–May and October–November). Rural-urban migration has increased after independence. About one-third of the migrants migrate to Dhaka city, followed by Chittagong city and the Comilla urban area.[21] Migration is critical to the livelihoods of the rural population in Bangladesh. To face the seasonal food scarcity prevailing during the time of *Monga* in the northern districts, people resort to seasonal migration to other districts such as Comilla, Kishoreganj, Sylhet, and Chittagong. *Monga* is a local term used to indicate acute deprivation caused by the erosion of purchasing power due to lack of gainful employment opportunities during the months of September to November. Remittances sent by the seasonal migrants contribute to the food security of the migrants' families.[22]

A study observed that internal migration was higher among the food-insecure households of Mymensingh and Netrakona as compared to the food-secure households.[23] Amongst the food-insecure households, 45.3 per cent households of Mymensingh and 39.7 per cent households

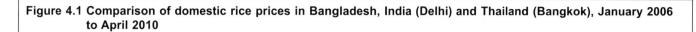

Figure 4.1 Comparison of domestic rice prices in Bangladesh, India (Delhi) and Thailand (Bangkok), January 2006 to April 2010

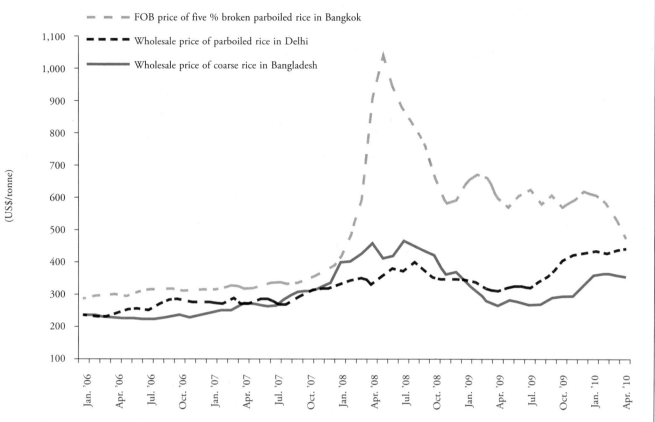

— — — FOB price of five % broken parboiled rice in Bangkok

▪ ▪ ▪ Wholesale price of parboiled rice in Delhi

——— Wholesale price of coarse rice in Bangladesh

Note: *: FOB means free on board price.

Sources: Department of Agricultural Marketing, Bangladesh; Ministry of Consumer Affairs, Food and Public Distribution, Government of India; and Thailand Rice Exporters Association for Bangkok.

of Netrakona opted for temporary migration (table 4.9). In case of food-secure households, on the other hand, only 26.6 per cent households of Mymensingh and 23.8 per cent households of Netrokona opted for temporary migration.

Studies observed that migrants remit a large portion of their income. One study[24] observed that migrants remit more than 80 per cent of their income back to Bangladesh, while another study[25] found that 51 per cent of the total income of

families is derived from remittances. The total income of households increased by 119 per cent during migration. A study reported that international remittances received by Bangladesh have reduced the incidence and severity of poverty in the country by six percentage points.[26] Another study stated that the unemployment rate has been stable due to continuous outflow of workers and inflow of remittances.[27]

Studies revealed that remittances are used for three purposes: consumption,

Table 4.9   Internal migration among food-secure and food-insecure households in Mymensingh and Netrokona, 2008

(%)

District	Food insecure			Food secure			All		
	Yes	No	All	Yes	No	All	Yes	No	All
Mymensingh	45.3	54.7	100	26.6	73.4	100	37.0	63.0	100
Netrokona	39.7	60.3	100	23.8	76.2	100	32.6	67.4	100
Mymensingh and Netrokona	41.8	58.2	100	24.5	75.5	100	34.3	65.7	100

Source: Rahman *et al.* 2009.

investment, and savings. Most of the remittances are used for food and clothing; home construction and repair; marriages and ceremonies; loan repayment; education and healthcare; and purchase of land.[28] Such consumption prevents the migrants' families from falling into poverty. As remittances are considered to be a transitory source of income, most families try to save out of this income for future needs. A study found that households who received remittances saved 50 to 75 per cent of their income compared to 5 per cent saving by households who did not receive any remittances.[29] During the severe floods of 2004, remittances sent by migrant workers were particularly useful when livelihoods were disrupted, and houses and properties destroyed.

Impact of inflation on food security

The food price hike in 2007 and 2008 had a negative impact on real income, food availability, consumption, food security, and poverty in Bangladesh. Several studies have analysed the consequences of the food price hike in the country. A study observed that 8.5 per cent of the total population, or 2.5 million households (about 1.21 crore people), were added to the poor population between January 2005 and March 2008.[30] The study made an effort to analyse the poverty impacts of the price hike and food inflation. They updated household income and poverty lines and

estimated poverty for the years 2006, 2007, and 2008. According to this study, the incidence of poverty (headcount ratio) declined from 40 per cent in 2004–05 to 39 per cent in 2006, but increased by about two percentage points in 2006–07 (from 39 to 41 per cent), and increased further by 4.3 percentage points in FY2007–08 (from 41.5 to 45.8 per cent). A study conducted by the Food and Agriculture Organization of the United Nations (FAO) quantified the impacts of the price hike on food security in Bangladesh.[31] According to this study, as a result of rising food prices and general inflation, the number of food-insecure people increased by 7.5 million and the total number of food-insecure (consuming less than 2,122 kcal/person/day) people reached 65.3 million. The study also highlighted that most of this increase occurred within the ranks of the more severely food insecure, those consuming less than 1,805 kcal/person/day. The study reported that the number of under-nourished people has increased by 6.8 million (from 27.9 to 34.7 million) following the price increase, and that more than 90 per cent of the new food insecure people are severely food-insecure.

A study also analysed the impact of the food price rise on school enrolment and dropout rates in poor and vulnerable households in selected areas of Bangladesh.[32] The study revealed that as a result of the price hike during early 2008,

Table 4.10 Changes in consumption and prices of rice, edible oil and pulses (during early 2008)

Categories of commodity	Consumption of commodity (% of households)				Average % fall in consumption*	Average % fall in consumption (for all sample)	Average % rise in price
	Fall	Unchanged	Rise	Total			
Rural							
Rice	25.1	67.7	7.2	100	21.58	3.00	50.65
Edible oil	44.0	54.8	1.2	100	36.61	13.41	94.95
Pulses	48.8	48.3	2.8	100	41.91	15.48	88.82
Urban							
Rice	18.5	73.8	7.7	100	22.79	2.00	51.85
Edible oil	37.8	60.2	2.0	100	37.82	12.69	82.04
Pulses	34.7	62.6	2.7	100	43.59	10.37	89.64

Note: *For the households who experienced fall in consumption.

Source: Raihan 2009.

Table 4.11 Types of impact on child education because of food price rise [% of households (HH) who responded 'yes']

Types of Impact	Rural	Urban
% of HH who responded 'yes' to the question 'whether there has been any impact on child education because of food price rise'	93.1	87.3
% of HH experiencing lack of nutritious food and health hazard causing interruption in education of their children	93.9	86.0
% of HH unable to meet education expenses	20.4	12.8
% of HH experiencing dropout of their children	58.2	55.6
% of HH involved their child in other works to earn money	21.2	15.5
Other	1.3	1.9

Source: Raihan 2009.

a significant number of households were forced to cut their consumption of rice, pulses and edible oil (table 4.10). The households who could maintain the level of consumption of rice, could do so only through reduced consumption of other non-rice food items and/or by reducing the non-food expenditure, i.e., expenses on their children's education. High dropout rates among the children of these households were observed because of the price hike of food items since most households could not continue to bear the expenses on their children's education. On average, 58 and 56 per cent of the households in rural and urban areas respectively experienced dropout of their children from school (table 4.11). A significant proportion of these dropout children were engaged in different jobs with the aim of contributing to their household income.

An analysis of trends in price of rice, nominal wage and rice equivalent wage for agricultural labourers revealed that an agricultural wage labourer could buy 3.5 kg of rice with their daily wage in 1990–91 which gradually increased to 5.9 kg in 2006–07 (table 4.12). In other words, the real wage increased by 4.2 per cent per year during the period 1990–91 to 2006–07. However, in 2007–08 and 2008–09, as a consequence of soaring prices, rice equivalent wage declined to about 5.0 kg per day.

A study revealed that the food price hike in early 2008 negatively impacted the food consumption and nutrition situation

in Bangladesh.[33] As a consequence of increase in the price of rice, the share of rice in total food expenditure increased from 45 per cent in 2006 to 51 per cent in 2008 in rural areas, and from about 29 per cent in 2006 to about 40 per cent in 2008 in urban areas. The increase in the share of expenditure on rice in total food expenditure was significant for the poorest groups (from 49 per cent in 2006 to 62 per cent in 2008) but only marginal for the

The food price hike in early 2008 negatively impacted the food consumption and nutrition situation in Bangladesh

Table 4.12 Average daily rice wage of agricultural labour (without food) in Bangladesh, 1990–2010

	Wholesale price of coarse rice (BTK per kilogram)	Wage rate	
		(BTK per day)	Rice wage (kilogram per day)
1990–91	10.59	37.13	3.51
1991–92	11.08	40.00	3.61
1992–93	9.42	41.50	4.41
1993–94	9.60	42.75	4.45
1994–95	12.28	44.20	3.60
1995–96	12.58	46.00	3.66
1996–97	10.87	47.00	4.32
1997–98	12.09	49.00	4.05
1998–99	13.98	52.00	3.72
1999–2000	12.36	55.00	4.45
2000–01	11.62	57.81	4.98
2001–02	12.71	61.08	4.81
2002–03	13.31	74.56	5.60
2003–04	13.07	75.42	5.77
2004–05	14.74	78.67	5.34
2005–06	15.80	89.83	5.69
2006–07	17.01	101.08	5.95
2007–08	25.00	121.67	4.96
2008–09	25.00	125.79	5.03
2009–10	22.80	129.50*	5.68

Note: *: Average for July, August and September 2009.
Source: GOB, *Monthly Statistical Bulletin* (various issues).

richest group (from 37 per cent in 2006 to 39 per cent in 2008). This indicates that the poorest people had to forgo consumption of nutritious items to cope with the increased price of rice. The key coping strategy seems to have been one where rice consumption has been further increased leaving the overall food basket even less diversified than before.

It was also observed that the food price rise and consequent food basket adjustments had negative nutritional impact on children which seems to be more pronounced for the very young (0–6 months) and older groups (24–59 months) of children (table 4.13).[34] The authors argued that the route is likely to be indirect for 0–6 months old through the impact of rising food prices on maternal nutrition for the 0–6 months old, and direct for 30–59 months old children through worsening nutritional quality of the overall household food basket. The study reported that when the researchers asked about malnutrition and rising food prices, the mothers provided an insightful story. Before the food price rise, most mothers stated that they prepared separate food for their children, especially for those who were older, consisting of milk, rice, banana and *khichuri*. With the rising food prices, they could no longer afford to do that, and the children ate from the family meal which deteriorated in terms of both quantity and quality.

Government initiatives to ensure food security in Bangladesh

The government initiatives undertaken to ensure food security over the last two decades encompass policy interventions in several areas, including those related to (a) augmenting availability largely through accelerated growth in domestic food production as well as imports whenever required; and (b) enhanced access to food through broad-based income generation as well as expansion of public distribution, especially social safety net programmes. These are briefly discussed below, followed by an account of recent initiatives of the government to ensure food security in the country.

Measures for augmenting availability of food

Measures initiated by the government for augmenting availability of food include public interventions for boosting domestic production as well as imports of food items. Major drivers of production have been the development and diffusion of improved crop varieties and more effective water management, especially expansion of irrigation infrastructure mostly shallow tubewells based on groundwater irrigation. More than 500 modern varieties of different crops have been developed in the National Agricultural Research System (NARS). Among them only a few have remained popular with farmers. Adoption of these improved varieties by replacing low-yielding traditional varieties have contributed to an increase in yield, reduction in net cost of production, and increased profitability in farming. Thus, real prices of agricultural products declined over time without hampering production incentives for the farmers.

Technological progress has been supported by both public and private investments for irrigation, flood control, and drainage. The irrigated area has expanded rapidly since the late 1980s. With the liberalization of the import of diesel engines and reduction in import duties, as well as withdrawal of restrictions on standardization of minor irrigation equipment especially shallow tubewells, these policy changes led to massive private investment in minor irrigation, which now

Measures initiated by the government for augmenting availability of food include public interventions for boosting domestic production as well as imports of food items

Table 4.13 Proportion of undernutrition by age group, 2006–08

Age group	Underweight (moderate-severe)		Stunting (moderate-severe)		Wasting (moderate-severe)	
	2006	2008	2006	2008	2006	2008
0–6 months	13.3	24.4	11.7	24.4	3.3	28.9
7–11 months	25.8	29.8	23.0	31.9	14.5	17.0
12–23 months	46.3	48.4	55.7	62.5	14.6	19.8
24–59 months	48.1	55.5	53.8	62.9	14.4	21.1
All age group	42.4	47.9	47.5	55.4	13.5	21.1
Sample size	661	435	661	435	661	435

Source: Sulaiman *et al.* 2009.

accounts for over 70 per cent of the total irrigated area. Subsequently, a water market has emerged that provides irrigation services to adjoining plots in the command area, as a result of which the small and marginal farmers who cannot afford to invest in irrigation equipment can now have access to irrigation for cultivation of irrigated *boro* rice in the dry season.[35] However, the government retains control on the management of deep tubewells. Some subsidy for irrigation is provided through the provision of electricity and diesel, as power for irrigation has become a major input in the dry-season rice cultivation.

The government had also implemented policy reforms in case of other inputs such as seed and fertilizer. The seed market in Bangladesh has a dual structure in which major crops such as rice, wheat, jute, potato and sugarcane are classified as notified crops. For these crops, variety development, evaluation, maintenance, multiplication, quality control and distribution are done by different public agencies. The private sector's role in the seed business has been restricted to the distribution of non-notified crops, mainly brand name hybrid vegetable seed. In 1999, the government allowed the private sector to import seeds of hybrid rice. Recently, some non-governmental organizations (NGOs) signed a Memorandum of Agreement (MOA) with the Bangladesh Rice Research Institute (BRRI) to obtain breeder seeds so that they can produce the certified seeds of rice for distribution. As a result, the marketing of seeds of high-yielding varieties of rice has substantially increased.

Fertilizer, irrigation, and improved seeds are three essential inputs whose procurement and distribution had once been under the sole control of the Bangladesh Agricultural Development Corporation (BADC), a semi-government organization. Policy reforms since the early 1980s, aimed at reducing government interventions as well as subsidies, have completely transformed the market for these inputs.[36] Changes in privatizing the marketing system of fertilizers began in 1978 and were pursued vigorously in the early 1980s. Beginning in July 1987, private dealers were allowed to procure fertilizer in bulk at higher discount rates from factories as well as from the large BADC supply centres known as transport discount points (TDP). By 1992, BADC withdrew from wholesale trade, allowing the private sector to procure, import (except urea) and distribute fertilizer in domestic markets. Subsidies in potash and phosphate (which were mostly imported) were also eliminated in 1992. However, fertilizer subsidies were reintroduced in 1996, following an acute fertilizer crisis in the domestic market during the 1995 *boro* season. The government virtually overtook the wholesale distribution from the private sector and started operating a buffer stock in order to stabilize fertilizer prices. More recently, the government has introduced heavy subsidy to non-urea fertilizers such as triple supper phosphate (TSP) and muriate of potash (MP) to ensure a more balanced use of chemical fertilizers, vitally needed to maintain soil fertility.

The above policies and initiatives by the government contributed substantially to the expansion of the market for agricultural inputs, stabilization of input prices, and adoption of improved technologies, especially in rice production in Bangladesh.

Bangladesh is a net importer of both rice and wheat even in normal years. It is also a net importer of pulses, edible oils, spices, fruits, sugar, milk and milk products. Most of the rice and wheat is imported by the private sector in recent years. The import of rice declines in normal years but increases substantially in years of floods and cyclones. Import of wheat has increased in recent years due to (a) decrease in domestic production (b) substantial reduction in food aid, and (c) increase in demand for products made from wheat flour in urban areas. Imports of pulses, edible oils, spices, and sugar have been on the rise at a rapid rate to meet the growing demand-supply gap. The import of edible oils, for example, has increased from 1.53 lakh tonnes in 1990–91 to 4.73

Policies and initiatives by the government contributed substantially to the expansion of the market for agricultural inputs, stabilization of input prices, and adoption of improved technologies

lakh tonnes in 2004–05, and further to 8.65 lakh tonnes in 2008–09. A similar trend is observed in the case of wheat and pulses. The volatility of prices in the world market for these basic necessities that is transmitted to the domestic market impacts the food security of low-income households. The government should, therefore, adopt policies for import substitution of many of these crops through promotion of crop diversification.

Measures for enhancing access to food

Bangladesh possesses significant experience in providing assistance to the poor through social safety net programmes. Although some of the programmes started as early as the mid–1970s, the administrative structure and the implementation mechanisms have gone through substantive changes over the years. The most notable changes include transforming relief programmes, converting ration price subsidies to targeted food distribution, and engaging other stakeholders, such as NGOs and microfinance organizations, in the implementation of various safety net programmes.

Bangladesh has a comprehensive portfolio of both food and cash-based social safety net programmes. In fact, currently, there are 58 such programmes. The safety net programmes can be categorised in accordance with the specific objective that each programme is designed to achieve. For example, the programme may be designed to develop infrastructure, provide education incentives to the poor, mitigate disaster consequences, or provide livelihood support to disadvantaged groups such as the aged and the disabled. Using these categorizations, it is possible to group existing programmes in Bangladesh into five categories: infrastructure-building programmes, training programmes, education programmes, relief programmes, and programmes for other disadvantaged groups.[37]

The trend in public expenditure for different targeted programmes for the 1990–91 to 2004–05 period is provided in table 4.14. The trend shows that public expenditure on these programmes for the poor more than doubled over the 15-year period (for which data are available).[38] This is largely attributed to introduction of the 'Food-for-Work' programme since the mid-1990s and its subsequent expansion in recent years. Total public expenditure for targeted programmes, as a percentage of gross domestic product (GDP), though displayed an upward trend (barring some fluctuations) during the 1990s, declined in the recent period.[39]

Recent government initiatives

Bangladesh has always placed due emphasis on increased food production as a mean of achieving food security. Therefore, investment in agricultural research for technology generation, input delivery systems, and extension services has been given a major thrust in government programmes. For improving efficiency in the delivery of inputs, the government has encouraged pro-market distribution of seeds, fertilizers, pesticides and diesel fuel for irrigation. In addition, any shortfall in food availability has been met through imports.[40] Although food grains, until early 1990s, were imported by the public sector, the private sector has played a dominant role in importing food grains and other foods since then. The government has modified its PFDS with greater emphasis on targeted programmes. Bangladesh has also implemented a number of targeted programmes for improving dietary and nutritional status in the country. These integrated efforts have significantly contributed towards achieving comprehensive food security in Bangladesh.

In response to the soaring prices in 2007 and 2008, a number of policy measures were initiated by the Interim Government. These measures were related to market-based actions (for increasing supply, improving effectiveness of the market and reducing production risk, and facilitating domestic production); non-market based measures (for reducing import cost,

Table 4.14 Trend in public expenditure for targeted programmes in Bangladesh, 1990–2005

(BTK in crores)

Year	FFW*	GR/TR*	VGD*	VGF*	FFE*	Others	Total**	GDP	As a % of GDP
1990–91	424.80	0	387.00	0	0	0	811.81 (973.39)	110,520	0.73
1991–92	432.77	393.82	0	0	0	0	826.59 (962.49)	119,542	0.69
1992–93	373.92	267.79	0	0	0	0	641.71 (745.15)	125,369	0.51
1993–94	384.36	302.58	0	0	68.32	0	755.26 (845.09)	135,412	0.56
1994–95	751.71	346.51	0	0	193.46	2.01	1,293.69 (1,384.44)	152,518	0.85
1995–96	558.53	400.76	0	0	267.49	1.74	1,226.78 (1,226.78)	166,324	0.74
1996–97	810.81	256.10	215.27	0	329.53	15.24	1,626.95 (1,578.18)	180,701	0.90
1997–98	836.00	258.71	225.09	76.24	374.98	1.53	1,772.55 (1,633.24)	200,177	0.89
1998–99	715.58	210.23	208.90	584.81	395.43	65.88	2,180.83 (1,920.25)	219,697	0.99
1999–2000	806.00	272.00	228.00	229.00	393.57	1.00	1,929.57 (1,631.63)	237,086	0.81
2000–01	888.19	159.75	236.90	297.11	346.14	40.00	1,968.08 (1,674.96)	253,550	0.78
2001–02	681.73	196.80	234.96	126.67	387.09	43.00	1,670.24 (1,376.95)	273,200	0.61
2002–03	432.46	153.68	230.79	104.08	623.30	42.00	1,586.31 (1,251.03)	300,580	0.52
2003–04	441.49	160.56	223.73	175.82	611.42	46.00	1,659.02 (1,255.88)	332,970	0.50
2004–05	541.62	182.72	217.53	108.76	652.52	50.00	1,753.14 (1,263.07)	370,710	0.47

Notes: *: FFW means Food-for-Work, GR means Gratuitous Relief, TR means Test Relief, VGD means Vulnerable Group Development, GDF means Vulnerable Group Feeding, and FFE means Food for Education.. **: The figures in parentheses indicate the total public expenditure for targeted programmes at constant (1995–96) prices.

Sources: GOB, *Bangladesh Economic Review* (various years), 2000 and 2001a.

decreasing production cost through subsidy for inputs and supply of necessary inputs, increasing production, raising supply, and providing price support); trade policy related measures (reduction in tariff rate, ban of rice export, encouragement of import of food items through lowering local content margins); and institutional measures for reducing market volatility. Additionally, the current government has also taken a number of initiatives to ensure food security in the country. These are:

Market based actions

- To increase food availability and intensify competition in the food market in Dhaka city, the government decided to establish four new wholesale markets (in Jatrabari, Lalbagh, Mahakhali and Amin Bazar).

- The government decided to raise efficacy of the marketing system by reducing the number of market intermediaries. It also decided to activate temporary measures for reducing prices, such as Open Market Sales by the para-military force, the Bangladesh Rifles; and direct import of essential food items (rice, flour, edible oil, onion, pulses) by the Trading Corporation of Bangladesh (TCB) under the Food Directorate. The amount of food grain distributed (either free or at a subsidized price) through the PFDS has increased from 1,137 thousand metric tonnes in 2005–06 to 1,562 thousand metric tonnes in 2007–08, and further to 2,160 thousand metric tonnes in 2008–09.

Non-market based measures

- The Bangladesh Bank directed all commercial banks to provide credit on softer terms to new importers of food items in order to encourage imports and increase competition among importers of food items.
- The government increased subsidy on diesel used in irrigation directly to the farmers amounting to BTK2,500 million in FY2007–08, and 20 per cent subsidy for electricity used in irrigation. In FY2009–10, the government continued subsidy for electricity and also provided BTK7,500 million as subsidy for diesel used in irrigation. Special efforts were made to ensure electricity for irrigation during the production of dry season rice (*boro* rice) cultivation through diversion of electricity from urban to rural areas. In view of the early drought situation in the wet season of 2009 in the Barind region, the Ministry of Agriculture provided free electricity (up to 100 units) to victims of drought for timely transplanting of *aman* rice. The government also increased the amount of fertilizer subsidy in FY2007–08 and FY2008–09 to absorb the increased cost of imported fertilizers by the government rather than pass it on to the farmers in the form of higher farm level prices. To promote increased supply of fertilizer from domestic production, the government allocated BTK680 million (19 per cent of total allocation for public sector operated fertilizer factories) for repairing of two fertilizer mills (Zia and Jamuna Fertilizer Company) in the FY2007–08 budget. In FY2009–10, subsidy for agricultural inputs were BTK49,500 million (including BTK7,500 million as subsidy for diesel used in irrigation). To ensure

availability and affordability of all types of fertilizers and to promote balanced use of fertilizers, the government has brought non-urea fertilizers under subsidy and reduced the administered price of fertilizers substantially in 2009. It has also changed the fertilizer distribution system.

- The Bangladesh Bank directed the commercial banks and the specialized banks to increase the supply of agricultural credit to meet the working capital needs of the farmers. The amount of agricultural credit distributed by the public and private commercial banks has increased from BTK54,960 million in FY2005–06 to BTK92,840 million in FY2008–09. The Bangladesh Bank also provided BTK5,000 million to tenant farmers as collateral-free agricultural credit through the Bangladesh Rural Advancement Committee (BRAC), one of the largest NGOs in Bangladesh.
- To increase the coverage of low-income households under the safety net programmes, the government increased allocation of food under the Food-for-Work, the Vulnerable Group Feeding and other safety net and social protection programmes. To mitigate the negative impact of high prices on food security for the poor segment of society, expenditure for safety net programmes has been increased from BTK114,670 million in FY2007–08 to BTK168,000 million in FY 2009–10. The budget for FY2010–11 has allocated BTK194,970 million for social safety net programmes which is about 15 per cent of the total budget and 2.5 per cent of the GDP.
- A new programme titled '100 Days Employment Generation Scheme' was introduced in the 2008–09 budget with an allocation of BTK20,000 million to generate 200 million person days of employment for the ultra-poor and marginal farmers in rural areas. The programme targeted severe poverty-stricken areas such as the *Monga* (seasonal food insecure) affected areas in the Northwest, areas prone to river

To mitigate the negative impact of high prices on food security for the poor segment of society, expenditure for safety net programmes has increased

erosion, and *Char* areas (newly emerged areas in the river bed).

- BTK10,000 million has been allocated for the Employment Generation Scheme in FY2010–11 which will be implemented in all 64 districts of the country.
- The budgets of FY2008–09 and FY2009–10 also proposed special measures to stimulate agricultural production through the provision of subsidy for agriculture and by way of reduction of duties on import of agricultural inputs and machineries.

Trade related measures

- Considering the high global price of rice and wheat, the government eliminated existing tariffs on import of rice, wheat, and other essential items (crude edible oil, lentils, onion, *motor dal* and *chola dal*) on 8 March 2007 (table 4.15). To meet the deficit in food availability from domestic production, the import of agricultural commodities was liberalized and import duties and para-tariffs on various food items were substantially reduced. The budget for FY2010–11 has reduced import duty on powdered milk.
- The provision of renewal of value added tax (VAT) registration by commercial importers on an annual basis was withdrawn.

Institutional measures

- In April 2009, the National Parliament of Bangladesh passed the Consumer Protection Act 2009. The Act has provisions to reduce harassment of consumers and to take punitive measures including fines, seizure and imprisonment, in case of violation of consumer rights. It is hoped that this will help safeguard consumer's interests which were being severely undermined due to lax supervision.
- The government established a Task Force to review prices of essential commodities regularly and suggest remedial measures to be taken by the government. An inter-ministerial monitoring committee was also set up to monitor the prices of essential commodities and make appropriate policy recommendations.

Measures related to improving health and nutrition

Bangladesh has made significant progress in health and some of the major gains have been achieved through low-cost solutions.

The aim of the government is sustainable improvement in health, nutrition, and family welfare status including women, children, and the elderly with the ultimate objective of their economic and social emancipation as well as their physical and mental well-being. In fact, the government is committed to ensure quality health, nutrition, and family welfare services which are affordable, attainable, and acceptable to its citizens. The government focuses on improving health status, expanding access to social safety net pro-grammes and encouraging affordable service delivery systems for the entire

The government is committed to ensure quality health, nutrition, and family welfare services which are affordable, attainable, and acceptable to its citizens

Table 4.15 Tariff schedule of essential imported commodities, 1991–2009

Products	Total operative tariff rate (%)					
	1991–92	1996–97	2001–02	2006–07	2007–08	2008–09
Rice	31.25	1.28	13.50	5.00	0.00	5.00
Wheat	16.44	9.46	7.50	5.00	0.00	5.00
Edible Oil (refined)	107.49	43.77	52.50	20.75	28.32	37.50
Edible Oil (crude)	67.82	35.34	36.43	0.00	0.00	5.00
Onion	31.44	33.65	30.00	5.00	0.00	25.00
Milk	52.85	56.38	52.95	72.31; 50.75	37.15	37.50
Pulses	21.44	13.49	15.00	5.00	0.00	5.00

Sources: Deb 2005, Dowla 2003 and Hossain and Deb 2009b.

population. For the poor and vulnerable, the existing facilities will be further expanded and consolidated not only to ensure access of the poor to public healthcare services but also to raise their voices and establish ownership through community participation. In this context, the National Health Policy will be re-evaluated and adjusted accordingly.[41]

Rethinking strategies and policies to promote food security in Bangladesh

Despite impressive gains in increasing domestic food grain production, problems of food and nutrition security remain. Bangladesh has yet to achieve comprehensive food security that resolves the problems of inadequate food intake and chronic malnutrition among the poor and vulnerable. Addressing these problems satisfactorily would not only require rethinking of strategies and policies to promote food security in the country but would also require decisive actions by all stakeholders—the government, the NGOs, the private sector and individual households. In fact, ensuring food security through physical availability and economic access to food would continue to be a major challenge for Bangladesh in the coming years. To meet these challenges, an integrated strategy encompassing major aspects of comprehensive food security to ensure: (a) adequacy of food supply through increased domestic production and imports; (b) access to food through public distribution and expanded safety net programmes; and (c) improved food utilization and nutrition is required. These are briefly discussed below.

Adequacy of food supply: Increased domestic production and imports

Bangladesh faces formidable challenges to feed its population in the future from an increasingly shrinking and degraded natural resource base for agriculture. Crop agriculture is heavily dominated by rice. In the past three decades, Bangladesh has experienced significant growth in food production mainly due to increasing reliance of rice on irrigated high-yielding *boro* rice. The output of other major rice crop (*aman*) has also progressed but rather slowly, due in part to its susceptibility to both flood and drought at different times.

Crop agriculture, however, faces many challenges. With millions of marginal and small farmers scattered across Bangladesh, crop diversification is still limited and natural disasters regularly damage part of the output. In many places, there are also serious problems of soil degradation and poor seed quality. The technology generation and dissemination systems are constrained by institutional weaknesses, lack of resources and unavailability of requisite skills. *Boro* rice cultivation depends heavily on groundwater irrigation which is facing severe limitations. Some further expansion of *boro* is possible, but mainly in localized pockets of the country. Moreover, water use efficiency is low and the climate variability exacts a heavy toll on output. Future climate change will further exacerbate these effects.

Against this backdrop, *boro* cultivation may be expanded in areas where surface water is more abundant. In fact, there is a general consensus to utilize surface water as far as possible to lower costs of production while optimising the use of available resources. On the other hand, because *boro* has, more or less, reached its potential under existing technology, maximising output from *aman* should be a major objective in increasing domestic production of rice.[42] But this will necessitate revamping not only the technology generation system but also technology dissemination (agricultural extension) and the marketing system.

From a longer term perspective, investments should be focused on developing an integrated water resources management plan, with a River Basin Development Approach at its core. This would ensure an integrated use of surface water and groundwater for agricultural and other purposes. The River Basin Development Approach will subsume the government's present emphasis on rejuvenation of river

Ensuring food security through physical availability and economic access to food would continue to be a major challenge for Bangladesh in the coming years

flows and will necessitate regional and bilateral cooperation for water resource development.

The agricultural research system will have to play a significant role by developing varieties which are both resistant to submergence, and drought-tolerant, as well as resistant to salinity and arsenic uptake; and suitable for deep water areas, and of shorter maturity. Some of these varieties have already been developed in the country. While these need to be popularized, more research will be needed for ecology-specific development of food products. Other priorities are cropping system development along with identifying suitable crops for problem soils.

To implement these major strategies and policies, Bangladesh needs to invest in the following areas:[43]

- Integrated water resources management, through a River Basin Development Approach.
- Technology generation system, including emphasis on biotechnology
- Technology dissemination or extension system
- Agricultural marketing services
- Soil health maintenance
- Climate change adaptation
- Provision of agricultural finances
- Modernization of the agricultural education system

As food grain production drastically falls in Bangladesh during periods of natural disasters and the supply of rice becomes scarce leading to abnormal rise in prices adversely affecting the livelihood of the poor, the private sector has been allowed to import food grains to cope with the situation. In fact, imports by the private sector now play a dominant role, in times of domestic shortages, to stabilize supplies and prices.[44] The government should follow a policy of variable tariff and subsidy with rates being fixed in the annual budgets on the basis of the assessment of the previous *aman* and *boro* harvests and the prevailing world market prices.[45] Regular monitoring of agricultural trade

policies of Bangladesh's trading partners, particularly India, will provide opportunity to the government for informed trade policy formulation and adjustments, if and when required.

Access to food: Public distribution and safety net programmes

In Bangladesh, substantial increases in rice production in the past two decades have, to a large extent, solved the food grain availability problem. The food security dialogue in the country now should increasingly focus on the other two aspects of food security—access to food through increased income support to the poor, and food utilization and nutrition. The role of the public distribution system, especially safety net programmes, in promoting food security of the poor is important in this respect.

As mentioned earlier, the size and composition of PFDS has changed significantly during the past two decades. The annual volume of food grain distribution under PFDS declined from 2.3 million metric tonnes in the early 1990s to about 1.7 million tonnes in the second half of the current decade. What is more significant, this has been accompanied by a perceptible shift in the composition (from monetised channels to non-monetized channels) of food grains distributed. Most evidence suggests that the shift from monetised (sales) to targeted programmes significantly improved the overall efficiency of the PFDS.[46]

However, proper management of public stock is essential for the improved effectiveness of the PFDS. The government has to maintain rolling stocks to cater to the routine needs of the PFDS, including safety net programmes and Open Market Sales, as well as minimum buffer stocks for emergency distribution in times of natural disasters. This calls for careful planning and management of the amount of grains to be stocked and distributed, and for the establishment of storage facilities and the improved monitoring of existing storage quality.

Proper management of public stock is essential for the improved effectiveness of the PFDS

Bangladesh's progress in economic growth has contributed to modest reduction in the poverty rate, at around 1.5 percentage points annually, since the early 1990s. This progress in poverty reduction is, however, of little comfort since the overall incidence of poverty persists at a high level. According to the 2005 estimates of food poverty, one-fourth of the country's population cannot afford an adequate diet. Chronically underfed and highly vulnerable, this segment of the population remains largely without assets (other than their own labour power) to cushion lean season hunger or the crushing blows of illness, flooding, and other calamities. The need for targeted safety net interventions to improve the food security and livelihoods of the extreme poor, therefore, remains strong.

Bangladesh possesses significant experience in providing assistance to the poor through social safety net programmes. Although some of the programmes started as early as mid-1970s, the administrative structure and the implementation mechanism have gone through substantive changes over the years. The most notable changes include transforming relief programmes to development programmes, converting ration price subsidies to targeted food distribution and engaging other stakeholders—such as NGOs and microfinance institutions—in the implementation of various safety net programmes.

Nevertheless, important challenges and issues remain. The existing safety net programmes cover only a fraction of the poor and they must be strengthened if they are to adequately address poverty or mitigate the vulnerability to food security in a sustainable way. Secondly, most safety net programmes in Bangladesh address economic vulnerability. The demographically vulnerable, including children, the elderly and those who are not able to perform intense physical labour involved in cash or food-based public works programmes, are even more in need of a safety net. A broader social protection system is required for them—programmes that involve providing allowances to elderly and disabled people. Thirdly, there is also a lack of safety nets available to the urban poor. Between 2000 and 2005 the total number of urban poor increased by 4.3 million. The rapid urbanization of Bangladesh calls for a range of measures to tackle urban food insecurity, thus, a strong safety net or social protection system for the urban poor has become imperative.[47]

Improved food utilization and nutrition

Measures for improved food utilization for better nutritional outcome have assumed special significance in Bangladesh. Long-term nutritional trends are encouraging, suggesting that breakthroughs can be made in tackling the complex problem of child and maternal malnutrition. Steady reductions have been observed in case of stunting and low maternal Body Mass Index between 1996 and 2007, but improvements in underweight have slowed recently and wasting has even increased.[48] Data on trends in micronutrient deficiencies are not available; therefore, ensuring availability of nationally representative data on micronutrient deficiencies among women and children should be a high priority.

Bangladesh has had policies to address maternal and child malnutrition for quite some time now. Notable among these are the National Nutrition Policy and National Strategy for Infant and Young Feeding in Bangladesh. The major policy instruments for direct interventions such as food supplementation and counselling for improved feeding of infants and young children is the National Nutrition Programme (NNP). Other health and nutrition interventions are implemented through the public health system and private healthcare providers. Interventions to improve infants and young child feeding are currently implemented with varying intensity and scale as well as by different stakeholders across Bangladesh.

The status of many health sector interventions is reasonably high in Bangladesh. However, sustaining an already high coverage of certain interventions, and in fact, enhancing them to attain 90–100 per cent coverage can help substantially. A review of the status of a range of key interventions for child nutrition in Bangladesh shows that for many key inputs, the coverage levels are well below 50 per cent. A core set of interventions and a call to scale these up in Bangladesh is also highlighted in a study titled, *Reducing the Burden of Malnutrition in Bangladesh*.[49] These should be vigorously pursued for attaining better nutritional outcomes in the country.

Of some concern in relation to nutrition outcomes is the poor status of sanitation, both from the perspective of sanitation behaviour and access to facilities. Only 25 per cent of households have access to improved sanitation, even though more than 95 per cent of households have access to improved sources of water. A mid-term review of the Health, Nutrition, and Population Sector Programme (HNPSP) in early 2008 highlighted a number of issues that need to be addressed in order to achieve health and nutritional objectives of the Sector programmes.[50]

As mentioned earlier, considerable intra-household disparity and discrimination persists in food consumption. It may be emphasized here that increasing food availability and household access to food alone will not be adequate to satisfactorily address the malnutrition problem. Nutritional issues have to be addressed more directly and comprehensively. Comprehensive programmes involving nutrition education, food fortification, improvement in water quality, sanitation and public health should be undertaken. Moreover, awareness of nutrition should be created through mass communication. The government should demonstrate greater commitment to ensure quality and safe food to the people.

The government should demonstrate greater commitment to ensure quality and safe food to the people

Chapter 5

Gender Dimension of Food Security

Is there a gender dimension to food security? Women, particularly rural women in South Asia, spend an over-whelming part of their lives in producing, preparing, and feeding their families. But is there any recognition of this role of women in the family and the community? And, more importantly, is this fact reflected in the national income accounts of the country? If the answer to these questions is in the negative, then there is a case for this chapter.

However, it is estimated that women are responsible for more than half of the world's food production. In South Asia a significant proportion of the total employed female labour force (70 per cent) works in agriculture.[1] Women in South Asia are active participants in agricultural work and participate in many tasks related to crop production such as sowing, transplanting, weeding, harvesting, and also contribute to post-harvest food processing, threshing, drying, grinding, husking and storage.[2] Women perform most of these activities as unpaid labourers on family farms or as paid labourers on other farms. They also play an important role in livestock management. In Nepal, for example, women have the sole responsibility of collecting fodder for buffalo while in Pakistan women provide the majority of the labour for feeding and milking cattle.[3]

Women also devote a significant proportion of their time to collecting water and firewood, preparing food, cleaning the house, and taking care of the young and old. In South Asia, a working class village woman is estimated to work up to 16 hours a day.[4] In one microenterprise project run by the Self-Employed Women's Association (SEWA) in Gujarat, India, women had to spend a greater amount of time collecting water

during the summer months than the time they were able to spend on paid activities. According to one study, reducing the time for water collection by one hour a day alone would enable these women to earn an additional US$100 a year.[5]

Despite these significant contributions to ensuring production and availability of food both at the national and household level, women's key role as food producers and providers is often overlooked and undervalued. In addition, women's contributions as producers of food are limited by constraints to their access to land, credit, and other inputs.

The second dimension of food security is access that is primarily dependent on economic resources available to a household for adequate food consumption. As several studies have shown, access to nutritious food and thereby the level of food security, is affected not only by the level of household income and welfare but more importantly by who earns that income. Most of these studies find that women are more likely than men to spend a significant proportion of their incomes on household nutrition, especially that of children.[6]

Access is also determined by the legal, political and, social structures that allow control over resources which can be used to acquire food for a nutritious diet. It is these structures that restrict women more than men in most developing countries, including those of South Asia, to equal access to paid employment, particularly in the agricultural sector. In Bangladesh, for example, it has been estimated that 24 per cent of rural men and only 3 per cent of rural women work in wage employment. In Nepal, the gender gap in rural wage employment is slightly lower, with around 13 per cent of women and 22 per cent of men employed in paid work.[7] Even when

Women are responsible for more than half of the world's food production

women are engaged in paid employment activities they are mostly employed in low wage earning, seasonal and part-time work. This in turn limits their ability to ensure adequate nutritional and food security for their households.

While adequate availability of food is necessary in achieving the goal of food security, it is not sufficient. Food security cannot be ensured without an adequate utilization of food through a proper absorption of essential micronutrients such as vitamin A, iron and iodine. Food utilization is also dependent upon access to non-food inputs such as education, clean water, environmental hygiene, sanitation and healthcare. While many of these factors are exogenous to the household, women's ability to manage and care for household members through proper nutrition, cleanliness, maintenance of the sick, the elderly, and children are the core of all human activities. The attention given by women to meeting the physical, mental and emotional needs of children is an essential component of good nutrition. While this role of women is crucial to ensuring adequate food security and well-being of the household and community, it remains unappreciated and difficult to quantify.

Another aspect of utilization is distribution of food according to the nutritional needs of individuals according to their sex, age, and life cycles. However, many of these needs are rooted in cultural and social norms rather than on dietary needs. In South Asia, especially among poorer households, evidence shows that women often eat last and least.[8]

Ensuring that each of the above dimensions of food security remains stable requires not only an understanding of the role of women for food security at the household and national level but also a realization of the several constraints to their ability to work efficiently as agricultural producers. Limits to women's ability to maximize yields in turn results in lower than possible yields for countries and the world. It also means that the number of hungry and undernourished

in the world—currently at around one billion people—continues to remain high, and targets mentioned in the Millennium Development Goals (MDGs) and World Food Summit remain elusive.

Given the above lines of argument supported by numerous studies, it can be said that all women, but in particular rural women in agriculture, not only contribute towards every dimension of food security for the household and at the national level, but in fact can be instrumental in steering future gains towards greater food security and reduction in hunger goals.[9] The role that South Asian rural women play as producers of food and the constraints that limit their potential for greater food production and thereby greater food security is discussed below.

Women as food producers

Women in rural South Asia are involved in multiple agriculture-related activities and supply their labour (both paid and unpaid) to a number of agricultural tasks at different stages of the production cycle, from sowing, transplanting, weeding, harvesting to post-harvest activities such as threshing, winnowing, drying, grinding, husking and storage (see table 5.1). Women are also responsible for livestock management and for maintenance of natural resources for their families and communities.[10]

Women's share of the total agricultural labour force in South Asia has remained between 30–40 per cent over the years. However, while the South Asian average may have remained steady, there has been considerable increase in the share of the female labour force in the total agricultural labour force in Pakistan and Bangladesh. The rate has almost tripled in Pakistan since 1980, to 30 per cent, and women now exceed 50 per cent of the total agricultural labour force in Bangladesh.[11] Much of women's work in the household, as subsistence farmers, as unpaid agricultural workers or family helpers is not reflected in official statistics. However, in recent years there have been efforts to expand definitions of economic activity that has led to some reductions in the statistical invisibility of women in South Asia. In Pakistan, for instance, with the adoption of the United Nations (UN) definition of the system of national accounts boundary, women's participation in the workforce has increased from 13.7 to 39.2 per cent and in Bangladesh from 18.1 to 50.6 per cent.[12]

As table 5.2 shows, the share of female agricultural workers, as a percentage of total economically active women, in most South Asian countries has remained quite high over the years. In Nepal and Bhutan, almost all working women are involved in the agricultural sector (see table 5.2). The only exception is Maldives where only 14.3 per cent of economically active women work in agriculture and relatively more women are involved in industries. Women's time-use in agriculture varies with the type of crop, the stage of the production cycle, the type of activity and the age, ethnicity and socio-economic status of women.

Given the complexity of work in rural households where no clear boundaries exist between tasks that fall under agricultural activities and those that can be classified as household chores, women in fact work not only more than what is depicted in official estimates but also more than men. Time-use surveys cover all agricultural activities and attempt to provide a more comprehensive account of how men and women allocate their time to different activities. In Punjab, Pakistan, it was found that women perform more than 13 major activities in the rural areas and spend more than 9 hours a day working on these multiple tasks. Almost 25 per cent of their time is spent on livestock-related activities that are routinely classified as household chores.[13] Estimates for India suggest that women contribute 32 per cent of their time to agricultural activities. However, there is a substantial within-country variation in time allocation in India, with women spending less than 10 per cent of their time in agricultural activities in West Bengal to more than

40 per cent in Rajasthan.[14] In both West Bengal and Rajasthan in India, younger women spend a greater proportion of their time in agricultural activities as compared to older women.[15]

This role of women in agriculture and rural livelihoods has increased over the years as more men continue to migrate to urban areas and households are then headed by women. Even in households headed by men, women continue to contribute a significant portion of their time to agriculture-related activities. While traditionally agricultural activities were more gender-segregated, a shortage of agricultural labour has meant that women have even taken over tasks previously performed by men. In Sri Lanka, for example, it is estimated that women perform 70 per cent of all agricultural activities.[16]

Table 5.1 South Asian rural women and their work

	Production-related activities
Bangladesh	Post-harvesting, cow fattening and milking, goat farming, backyard poultry rearing, agriculture, horticulture, food processing, fishnet making, etc.
Bhutan	Agriculture, kitchen gardens and livestock.
India	Agriculture, livestock, weeding, transplanting, harvesting and post-harvesting work, also land preparation in times of acute labour shortages.
Maldives	Subsistence agriculture, practiced as home gardens in small plots, and seed selection.
Nepal	Subsistence farming.
Pakistan	Agricultural production of crops, vegetables, livestock, cotton picking, etc.
Sri Lanka	Agricultural activities like slash and burn cultivation, rice paddies, transplanting, post-harvesting activities, home gardens, etc.

Source: Revathi 2005.

Table 5.2 Share of economically active women in South Asian agriculture, 1980–2010

			(%)
	1980	1995	2010
India	82.6	71.5	61.8
Pakistan	87.7	68.7	56.9
Bangladesh	80.9	69.9	57.4
Nepal	98.0	98.0	97.8
Sri Lanka	58.0	48.6	41.6
Bhutan	97.3	96.4	97.2
Maldives	40.0	21.1	14.3

Source: FAO 2011e.

While women participate in almost all activities related to crop production, there are certain stages in the production cycle when there is greater female participation than in others. In the initial stages of preparation of the field it is largely the men who are in charge while in the later stages of crop production that include harvesting cotton, weeding, transplanting rice and post-harvest work involving drying, storage, threshing and winnowing it is the women who are mainly responsible.[17]

Traditionally certain activities continue to be women's work—parboiling of paddy and cinnamon in Sri Lanka, manual weeding in rice fields in India, and cotton picking in Pakistan. In the case of Punjab province in Pakistan it was found that women played a significant role in weeding, seed cleaning and preparation, whereas land preparation, fertilizer application, threshing and marketing activities were largely undertaken by men. Both men and women were equally involved in harvest and post-harvest activities (see figure 5.1).

Women in South Asia also have the primary responsibility for caring, feeding and managing livestock. Livestock management is an area in which women are given greater recognition. It not only generates a source of income for poor households but also provides fertilizers for plants, draft power for farms, food for humans and biomass fuel for energy.[18] Women perform a range of activities from grazing and feeding animals, collecting fodder, cleaning animals, milking cattle, making cow dung patties for fuel, collecting manure for organic fertilizers, and processing and marketing animal products. In Pakistan, women perform most of the tasks related to livestock management and supply most of the labour. It is estimated that women's contribution to the livestock sector of the economy is as high as 70 per cent.[19] A study of Punjab province in Pakistan shows that women perform most of the activities related to livestock, while grazing animals is the core responsibility of men; women also graze animals near their homes as cultural norms restrict women from travelling too far on their own (see figure 5.2). Women were also found to be largely in control of income earned from livestock while in other agricultural activities income sources are mostly controlled by men.[20]

In Bangladesh too, women are exclusively responsible for feeding and caring for livestock. In Nepal, while both men and women are involved in grazing and milking of animals, and fodder collection,

In Pakistan women's contribution to the livestock sector of the economy is as high as 70 per cent

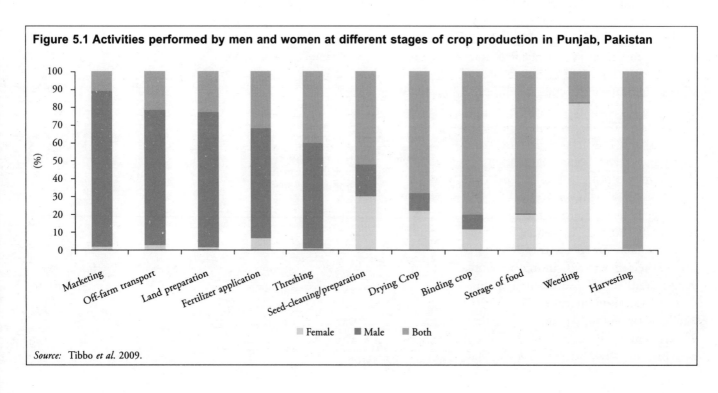

Figure 5.1 Activities performed by men and women at different stages of crop production in Punjab, Pakistan

Source: Tibbo *et al.* 2009.

women are exclusively responsible for detecting and caring for sick animals. In India, while there is considerable variation in the tasks performed across regions, it is primarily the women who are responsible for all household responsibilities related to livestock, such as milking, feeding, and cleaning of animals and their sheds while men are largely responsible for fodder production and market-related activities.

Despite significant participation and contribution of women in South Asia to rural livelihoods as food producers and providers, they are severely limited in their access to critical productive resources and services. The lack of, or restricted access to, land, credit, other inputs and extension services, limits women's ability to achieve optimal levels of food production. Limitations on women's access to these resources also results in lower food production for the country.

Gender gap in access to land

Land ownership in rural areas is critical for households that depend on agriculture for their livelihoods. In South Asia, land ownership is not merely an economic factor of production but an important source of power, status, and decision-making within the community. Yet for most women in South Asia the irony is that they rarely ever own the land that they cultivate.

Landholdings are also important for accessing credit and other agricultural support services. A study in Bangladesh identified the lack of access to land as one of the major factors for exclusion from credit services of non-governmental organizations (NGOs).[21] The gender gap in land ownership in South Asia is very wide; women are not only less likely to own land but even when they do, the size of the landholding is small. In other instances, even when women hold the legal entitlement to land they are denied control over it, and the resources that it generates. In Pakistan and Bangladesh, inequality in access to land among men and women is particularly severe: the average size of landholdings of male-headed households in both countries is twice as large as those in female-headed households.[22] As a result of small landholdings women face numerous problems in accessing

Despite significant participation and contribution of women as food producers and providers, they are severely limited in their access to critical productive resources and services

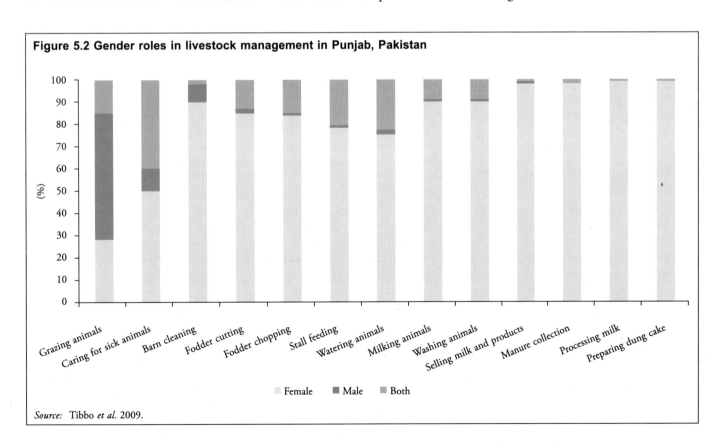

Figure 5.2 Gender roles in livestock management in Punjab, Pakistan

Source: Tibbo *et al.* 2009.

agricultural support services thereby reducing their productivity.

In India, women's access to land is becoming even more constrained as male competition for scarce land intensifies overtime. In addition, the growing migration of men makes it critical to address the issue of land rights for women in India. As more men move away from agriculture to urban areas or towards non-farm activities in rural areas, women are faced with the primary responsibility for farming but without rights to the land that they cultivate (see box 5.1).[23]

There is a conflict among legal, social/customary and actual practices that govern the access to, and inheritance of, land in South Asia

There is a conflict among legal, social/customary and actual practices that govern the access to, and inheritance of, land in South Asia. In the case of women, custom prevails over legal rights, and access to land is largely dominated by inheritance norms that are traditionally patrilineal (see box 5.2). There is the exception of some Indian states and Bhutan where matrilineal systems of inheritance prevail and land is inherited by the female line. In Pakistan, for example, it was found that women owned less than 3 per cent of plots even though 67 per cent of the villages surveyed confirmed a woman's legal right to inherit land.[24] In Nepal, inheritance laws are particularly gender-biased: only unmarried daughters above the age of 35 can inherit land, a condition that would exclude most women. Also in Nepal under the *Maluki Ain* laws, women must get the prior consent of male family members before selling their inherited property.[25]

In one study which surveyed seven Indian states, it was found that of the 470 women whose fathers owned land, only 13 per cent inherited land. This ranged from 18 per cent daughters inheriting land in

---

Box 5.1   Food sovereignty for women in Kerala: The case of Kudumbashree

Food security cannot be achieved without a change in the social and cultural structures that govern the production and consumption of food in particular and society at large. This is in fact the concept of food sovereignty that strives towards a fundamental shift in these relations. This shift is happening in Kerala, India where some 250,000 Kudumbashree women across Kerala have developed an innovative approach to solving the food security crisis. They have formed farming collectives to lease land jointly and cultivate it to not only meet their own consumption needs but also to sell to local markets.

The initiative is being run across 14 districts of Kerala, farming on some 25,000 hectares of land. The basic aim is not only to increase the participation of women in agriculture but also to ensure that as producers, women have control over decisions regarding the distribution and consumption of food.

Kudumbashree has a three-tiered structure, with the Neighbourhood Group (NHG) being the first level. The NHGs consist of 10–20 women and are led by elected representatives. These groups have regular weekly meetings to discuss issues related to their community. The NHG is key to transforming women's perceptions of themselves as 'housewives' towards active members of the community. The members of the farming collectives are then drawn from the NHGs. Decisions regarding the distribution of surplus food like how much of the collective's surplus is to be sold, how much is to be consumed, which member needs more food support, how profits are to be used, are all made collectively.

The NHGs are then federated into a single zone known as the Area Development Society (ADS) that is governed by elected office bearers who represent the NHGs. The ADSs are further federated at the level of the panchayat/municipality to form a Community Development Society (CDS). A key feature of Kudumbashree CDS is to work with the local self government to disseminate information of government programmes to the community and also to convey the needs of the community to the government.

For many women this is a critical step from their previous role as farm labourers to producers. It has also led to a substantial increase in their earnings, which in one district of Kerala were as low as INR45–65 and have now increased to INR125. Kudumbashree has also opened doors of social inclusion for many of the Dalit women who now work as farmers alongside women from other castes.

The success of the Kudumbashree collective farming experience draws on the enthusiasm of these women farmers who are eager to experiment with new crops, organic methods, and new connections to their local markets. One of the main reasons for its success is the fact that these women were already working as labourers on farms. Moving towards independent production has given them greater control over their own time and labour and also a hope to achieve more. The collective nature of the work has also given women farmers a sense of alliance and solidarity.

Source: Reed 2010.

Box 5.2 Regional dynamics in women's entitlement to land[29]

Bangladesh

In the matriarchal Garo community, husbands live in the wife's house and engage in household work. The wife not only owns the property of the household but also attains the property and assets hitherto owned by her husband. Women of this community are the most sought after in terms of marriage and often end up being punished for marrying outside of the community or even abused by their husbands, who use these women as a means of acquiring land and wealth.

India

Traditionally, among matrilineal communities post-marital residence is matrilocal and daughters have stronger claims on land, as in Kerala and Meghalaya. In contrast, in patrilineal communities, post-marital residence is patrilocal and often in another village. In addition, in the north, close-kin marriage is forbidden among most communities and there are social taboos against parents asking married daughters for help during economic crisis.

In present day India, many upper-caste Hindus of the northwest consider endowing or bequeathing a daughter with land as losing it to the family. There is less opposition in south and northeast India where in-village and close-kin marriages are allowed, and parents can, if they need to, seek support from married daughters.

Nepal

Under the Hindu belief system, family property is retained in the male ancestral line; he has the title to the land even though the land belongs to the entire family. Higher caste families often restrict their women indoors and hire women from the lower castes to perform duties in the fields, and other tasks outside the house, such as collecting water and fuel.

Women only have exclusive control on *daijo* (the small plots of land and other immovable property that are sometimes given to a woman by her family when she marries) and *pewa* (anything that is given to her as personal property).

In some minority communities, women may and do own land and control assets.

However, usually the women who hold a tenancy right to land, or who own land, are expected to hold it in trust for their sons.

Pakistan

Traditionally, women have usufructuary rights over land, that is, 'the right to the use, and to take the fruits of land for life only.' Furthermore, women, as members of the village community, have grazing rights and the right to collect firewood and fodder on communal lands. Access to water sources for domestic use, drinking and livestock is also a customary right available to women. Although these rights are recognized in all the provinces, they have no legal status. Interestingly, the right of residence in the fathers' or husbands' land for a single, widowed, or divorced female is recognized in the country, but again the legal status of such a right is hard to determine.

In Khyber Pakhtunkhwa, usufructuary rights are recognized in the natal family and at the husband's house. Women can also own land as *rawaji malika*, when a groom transfers some property to the woman as part of the marriage contract that he either has or is due to inherit. In these cases, men manage and decide about the land but cannot sell it. However, often this is a transaction on paper only.

In Punjab, women have customary access right to the village common land—*shamlat dah*—for cultivation and pasture. This includes uncultivated land, the inhabited village site, and the vacant space—*goradeh*—reserved for expansion of the village.

In Sindh, women may manage land only through an agent, *kamdar*, and only on behalf of a very young son, if there is no male member in the family. Here, a woman's dowry is considered to be a compensation for her inheritance. Women's lack of knowledge is often used to deny their rights by saying that the Holy Quran does not give women the right to own land (which is completely contrary to the rules of inheritance clearly set down in the Quran). Women work on the land and look after livestock; in many instances, payment for wage work is received by the men on behalf of the women.

The practice of *haq bakhshwana* (giving up rights) whereby girls are either never married, or 'married' to the Holy Quran (again, contrary to Islamic injunctions), is common in the southern parts of Punjab and of Sindh, and aims at preventing property from going out of the family. Similarly, cousin marriages and *watta satta* marriages (whereby one set of brother and sister are married to one another pair of siblings) are also used to prevent break up of property.

Sri Lanka

Customs and traditional practices vary across ethnic and religious groups.

Northern and Eastern Tamil and Muslim women as well as Sinhalese women in the East live within a patriarchal structure. Women generally make decisions on household matters, education of children, and health. Men make other major decisions such as buying and selling of assets. Traditionally women engage in household work and income generation within the home and contribute to the household economy by working in family farms.

Among the Sinhalese, in a *diga* marriage, the woman moves out to live virilocally with her husband and the children take the father's name. In a *binna* marriage, the husband moves to the wife's house and jointly manages the land she inherits. A *diga*-married daughter, who forfeits her share of inheritance upon marriage, can re-establish her rights if she returns to her parents' home while the father is still alive and establishes herself in *binna*. If she returns after the death of the father, the heirs must acknowledge her marriage as *binna*.

The customary law *Tesawalami* governs inheritance of property and matrimonial rights of Tamil women in Jaffna. Under *Tesawalami*, a woman can own property individually; can acquire property during marriage; and can keep the dowry she receives. Control of her property, however, is in the hands of her guardian; the guardianship of a woman passing from the father to the husband. A wife cannot invest in the property, mortgage, lease, or sell it without the prior permission of her husband. Furthermore, she cannot enter into contracts without his consent.

Source: FAO 2011c.

South India to only 8 per cent in North India. In the case of widows, the study found that only 51 per cent of widows inherited land.[26]

Degradation of communal lands and depletion of natural resources has multiplied the problems of rural women in South Asia. Forests and common areas of villages belong to everyone, including women. Rural production depends heavily on natural resources from these lands that are needed to produce crops, vegetables, and for food processing. Women rely on wood for fuel from forests, medicinal plants, and forest products for food production. These common areas provide fuel, fodder, and food for poor households. Natural resource degradation, privatization and state appropriation have all had a negative impact on women in rural households.[27]

In the northern areas of Pakistan while forest cover has reduced dramatically there has been an increase in agricultural activity and livestock farming. This has led to an increase in the workload of women.[28]

Given that land ownership is a symbol of wealth, status, and power in South Asia, a lack of land ownership for women reflects their poor status in society. It excludes them from accessing agricultural extension services, it limits their access to credit, and it exposes them to risks in case of divorce or being widowed. Having even a small landholding can have a great impact on the welfare of poor women and their families. Studies show that women with land in Bangladesh were offered higher wages to work on other fields.[30]

Having land is of paramount importance to women, if they are to successfully earn in the agricultural sector. Moreover, it is an important asset on which they can seek credit and extension services. In an era of agricultural trade liberalization, good quality land which is able to yield adequate crops is not just essential; it is critical for empowerment, poverty reduction, and food security.

The burden of low wages and unpaid work

Work in rural areas consists of farming, livestock management, self-employment in trade, small enterprises providing goods and services, and both paid and unpaid labour for these activities. In the rural context both men and women's workload changes according to seasons and many times during the year they may remain unemployed or underemployed. Also, in rural areas the divisions between domestic and market work are not always clear, especially for women. Caring for animals, for example, is very often seen as domestic work that women perform and remains unaccounted for, and unpaid. Women's reproductive activities, including caring for the young and old are not only unaccounted for and unpaid but also place extra pressure on them in terms of time used, and limits their livelihood options for taking up paid employment elsewhere. Similarly, women's responsibility for preparing food for their families, including fetching firewood and water, consume much of women's time and energy, yet remain unpaid.

In South Asia, women are more likely to be unpaid for working on their family farms and businesses than in any other region. According to estimates for 2007, almost 59 per cent of the total female labour force in South Asia works as contributing family workers compared to 36 per cent in Southeast Asia and the Pacific, 35 per cent in Sub-Saharan Africa, and 7 per cent in Latin America.[31] Within South Asia, nearly 77 per cent of rural female workers in Bangladesh, 62 per cent in Pakistan and 16 per cent in Sri Lanka work in unpaid family activities.[32] Only 3 per cent of rural women in Bangladesh are estimated to work for wage employment as compared to 24 per cent of rural men.[33] In Sri Lanka, however, there are more women than men who work for wages in the agricultural sector: 68 per cent women compared to 60 per cent men.[34]

Of all the employed women in South Asia, it is estimated that more that two-thirds are employed in agriculture. Compared to other sectors agricultural remuneration in the region is the lowest and women are often paid far less when compared to men, or are often not paid at all if they work on family farms or enterprises. In household level surveys conducted in 66 countries by the World Bank in 2000, up to 64 per cent of the rural female population was classified as 'non-active or not reported' (see table 5.3).[35] This is a reflection of the fact that much of women's work in South Asia is informal, unaccounted, and unpaid. Also, in most South Asian cultures socio-economic status of households also determines women's employment for wages in rural areas. It is women from poorer households who are more likely to be employed for wages while women from better-off households are more likely to be involved in home-based or family work that is often unpaid.[36]

Compared to other regions, gender disparity in employment status in rural areas is more marked in South Asia. Whereas in Sub-Saharan Africa female self-employment is almost at par with male self-employment in agriculture (around 54 per cent of adult rural women compared with around 57 per cent of adult rural men), the gender gap in South Asia is much wider with only 13 per cent of adult women being self-employed compared with 33 per cent men. The largest share of self-employed women in agriculture among South Asian countries is in Nepal where 29 per cent of women are self-employed.[37] Similarly, the gender gap in non-agricultural sectors in rural areas, where wages are better compared to agriculture, is also larger in South Asia than in any other region. According to a survey, while around 10 per cent of rural adult women and 16 per cent of rural adult men in Sub-Saharan Africa are employed in non-agricultural work, in South Asia less than 6 per cent of rural women work in non-agricultural sectors compared to 27 per cent of men.[38] The survey also found that while most men working in the agricultural sector in South Asia were self-employed, women in agriculture were somewhat equally distributed between self-employed and wage work (see table 5.3). The percentage of women engaged in wage employment in the agricultural sector is relatively higher in South Asia than in other regions. This may to some extent be the result of poorer property rights in land and assets, along with greater landlessness.[39]

While gender disaggregated data for remuneration in the agricultural sector is limited, a number of studies reveal that most women who are employed for wages in the agricultural sector in South Asia are paid less than men. Estimates suggest that women's wages in rural areas across South Asia range from half to two-thirds of men's wages. In one study of Bangladesh for example, it was found that 80 per cent of women and 40 per cent of men in rural areas were employed in low wage-earning jobs.[40] In studies of agricultural wages it was found that gender gaps in wages varied across countries and also across occupations. The greatest gender gap in wages in agriculture was found in Pakistan where women earned only half of what men earned (see table 5.4).[41]

In another study comparing gender-specific wage rates for agricultural and non-agricultural activities across 600 villages in 20 states of India it was found that even for the same activities in the agricultural sector women were paid up to

Most women who are employed for wages in the agricultural sector in South Asia are paid less than men

Table 5.3	Employment in South Asia's rural areas by gender and employment status (% of adult population), 2000	
Employment status	Female	Male
Agriculture	24.1	54.9
Self-employed	12.7	33.1
Wage earner	11.4	21.8
Non-agriculture	5.6	27.2
Self-employed	2.9	11.8
Wage earner	2.7	15.4
Non-active or not reported	64.3	14.6
Total	94.0	96.7
Residual	6.0	3.3

Source: FAO, IFAD and ILO 2010.

Table 5.4	Measuring the gaps in rural wages in South Asia			
	Sector	Type of employment	Wage unit	Women's wages as % of men
Bangladesh	Agriculture (fry catchers and sorters)	Wage	Daily	64
India	Agriculture	Casual wage	Daily	69
	Agriculture	Regular wage	Daily	79
	Non-agriculture	Casual wage	Daily	65
	Non-agriculture	Regular wage	Daily	57
Pakistan	Agriculture (sugar)	Wage	Daily	50

Source: FAO, IFAD and ILO 2010.

30 per cent less than men and 50 per cent less for non-agricultural work. Even in activities largely perceived to be women's work (cotton picking, tea leaf plucking) where female labour is preferred over male labour, gender disparities, though less pronounced, continue to benefit men (see figure 5.3).[42]

Disparities in agricultural wages between men and women is less pronounced in Sri Lanka, however, there are regional variations in the wage structure. The growth of agriculture in Anuradhapura and Polonnaruwa has not only led to increases in female participation in agricultural activities but also in female wages that are up to 89 per cent of male earnings in these regions. However, in regions like Puttalai,

Kandy, Kegalle and Moneragala, women receive less than 50 per cent of what men earn.[43]

The disparity in wages between men and women in South Asia is in violation of the International Labour Organization (ILO) Convention 100 that has been ratified by Sri Lanka, India, Bangladesh, Pakistan, and Nepal and calls for 'equal remuneration for men and women workers for work of equal value.'[44] The gender disparities found in agricultural wages are not the result of female inefficiency but in fact reflect the larger social, economic, and cultural position of women in South Asian society. A study in India in fact found women to be more efficient than men in potato seed farming where the picking rate for men was 1.6 per minute while for women it was much higher at 5.2 per minute.[45]

Despite the low wages and disparity in wages, women's incomes are critical to the survival of poor households. Several studies point to the contribution of women's income to improving household food security and nutritional levels, especially those of children. Most of these studies point to the differences in patterns of spending between men and women. While

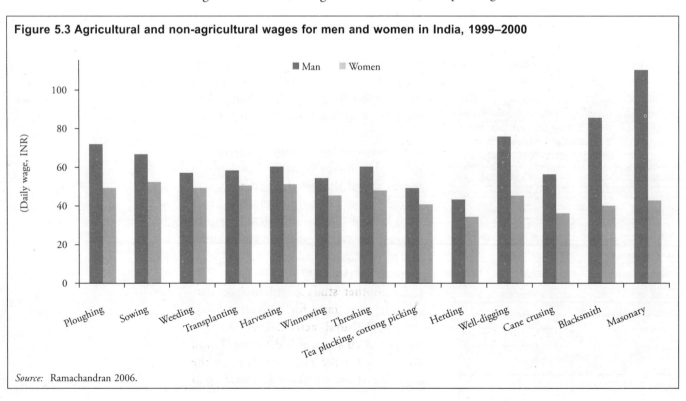

Figure 5.3 Agricultural and non-agricultural wages for men and women in India, 1999–2000

Source: Ramachandran 2006.

women tend to spend a larger proportion of their incomes on food and healthcare for children, men are more likely to spend a larger share of their incomes on personal expenditures.[46]

Access to credit, extension services, and technology

Despite the increase in women's role in agriculture and an increase in the number of households headed by women in South Asia, women's access to credit, agricultural extension services, and technology is limited. There are a number of barriers that restrict women's access to credit and other financial services. As women rarely own the land that they cultivate, they lack the necessary collateral for obtaining loans. A study in Bangladesh identified lack of access to land as the major factor for exclusion from accessing credit.[47] The nature of women's work in agriculture that includes largely subsistence farming also excludes women from accessing credit. In addition, poor levels of education and financial literacy of women, compared to men, also makes it more difficult for them to access financial services. There is also the added burden of social and cultural norms that restrict women's mobility. Thus, unless financial and credit services are brought closer to women, it is very difficult for them to travel far to access these.

However, the success of microcredit institutions across South Asia has been effective in providing capital to rural men and women. Many of these institutions in Bangladesh, India, Nepal, and Pakistan specifically target rural women. The results, however, have been mixed. While some studies report an improvement in women's livelihoods and potential for change in social relations, there are other instances where there has been an increase in social conflict in the community, violence against women by men, a tendency of men to control the actual access to loans and only use women as the front person to obtain the necessary credit.

Extension services include a wide range of services that are provided by experts to farmers that help them in improving their productivity. Extension services in South Asia have benefitted men more than women. Most of the extension services are provided by men: in India only one half per cent of extension professionals were women and in Bangladesh this percentage was 3.6.[48] Cultural and social norms in rural South Asia restrict women's communication with men thus effectively excluding them from accessing such services.

Extension services are also inherently gender-biased as most are directed towards information on cash crops, export crops, and not towards food crops and livestock. The way in which extension services are sometimes delivered can also lead to the exclusion of women. As women have lower levels of education than men, services involving a lot of written material may make it difficult for women to benefit. Also, women's domestic roles and duties also limit the time women can devote to accessing such services even when these are available.[49]

Technological innovations are also critical to improve agricultural productivity. Innovations in machinery, seeds, fertilizers, pest control methods, etc., are crucial to increasing yields. However, gender gaps to access improved technologies limit women's ability to benefit from such developments. Also, as most technological advances and research are targeted towards improvement of cash crops, there is little focus on technology that would benefit the production of female intensive activities like farming of vegetables, fruits, and pulses.

The gender gap in use of improved technologies is most pronounced in South Asia. Comparing fertilizer use by male- and female-headed households, it was found that in Bangladesh only 21 per cent of female-headed households and around 54 per cent of male-headed households used fertilizers. For Nepal, the percentages were 51 per cent for female-headed households and 63 per cent for

Women tend to spend a larger proportion of their incomes on food and healthcare for children

male-headed households. In Pakistan, only 15 per cent of female-headed households and 40 per cent of male-headed households used fertilizers.[50]

Regarding the use of mechanical equipment, it was found that only around one per cent of female-headed households in Bangladesh used such equipment while around five per cent of male-headed households did so. In Nepal, around three per cent of female-headed households and around eight per cent of male-headed households used mechanical equipment.

As the *State of Food and Agriculture Report 2010–11* points out, the use of purchased inputs depends on the availability of complementary assets such as land, credit, education, and labour.'[51] Women in South Asia have limited access to each of these, thereby excluding them from benefiting from technological advances in agriculture.

Women as consumers

Globally, hunger affects around one billion people of whom two-thirds live in just seven countries of the world: Bangladesh, China, Democratic Republic of Congo, Ethiopia, India, Indonesia and Pakistan. Over 40 per cent live in India and China alone.[52] Of these many are women and children. Table 5.5 shows the trends in the numbers of undernourished people in South Asian countries from 1990–2007.

The high levels of malnourishment, especially among women and children in South Asia, exist despite the region having made considerable progress in the production of food grains. The 'Asian enigma' as it is referred to in some literature,

where undernourishment prevails in the presence of sufficient availability of food, needs to be understood in the context of social, legal and cultural structures that dictate the lives of women in South Asia.[53] As the Food and Agriculture Organization of the United Nations (FAO) points out, 'South Asian countries struggle under the burden of persisting rural gender inequality although women directly contribute to food production as cultivators, labourers, and family workers in the agriculture sector. Rural women continue to struggle with dual responsibilities of economic production and domestic labour, and most are confronted by poverty, illiteracy, high health risks, inadequate access to productive resources, health and sanitation services and denial of market access in the profitable food sectors.'[54]

Despite women's immense contribution as producers of food both at the national and household levels in South Asia, as consumers of food they are often the last and least to be fed. Most women in South Asia lack a diet that is nutritionally adequate thus exposing women to risks of poor health, especially reproductive health that in turn leads to high levels of anaemia and maternal deaths. In a study of 11 villages in Punjab, India, it was found that while girls were given a diet high in cereals, boys were given more milk and fats along with cereals. The study also found that cultural factors had a greater impact on the gender bias in nutrition rather than economic hardship. Similar studies in Pakistan and Bangladesh also confirm a gender bias in feeding and healthcare in favour of male children and men.[55]

In a study of tribal villages in four Indian states it was found that in order to cope with seasonal food shortages, too, it was women who reduced their food consumption and resorted to skipping meals in order to ensure the food security of other male household members and children.[56] This culture of sacrifice among women is also common in other South Asian countries where women tend to eat last in order to ensure that other members of the family have been adequately fed. In

Rural women continue to struggle with dual responsibilities of economic production and domestic labour

Table 5.5 Number of undernourished people in South Asia, 1990–2007

(millions)

	1990–92	1995–97	2000–02	2005–07
Bangladesh	44.4	54.2	42.3	41.7
India	172.4	162.7	200.6	237.7
Nepal	4.2	4.4	4.6	4.5
Pakistan	29.6	26.9	36.1	43.4
Sri Lanka	4.8	4.5	3.9	3.8

Source: FAO 2010e.

a study of pregnant women in Bangladesh, it was found that the structure of the family, whether it was nuclear or joint, also had an impact on pregnant women's nutrition. In nuclear families where women were themselves responsible for household food distribution, they were more likely to take care of their husband and children's nutritional needs over their own. However, in joint families where the mother-in-law was also present it was found that pregnant women's nutritional needs were better fulfilled even if they still ate last.[57]

While it is difficult to assess whether the nutritional requirements of each individual within the household are being adequately met, levels of malnutrition, low weight, anaemia and maternal, infant and child mortality ratio indicators are useful to gauge the extent of food insecurity faced by women and subsequently passed on to children.

The nutritional deficiencies faced by South Asian women result in the world's highest percentages of women suffering from acute energy deficiencies and low levels of Body Mass Index (BMI) in South Asia (see figure 5.4). BMI levels of 18.5 per cent indicate that an individual is underweight and therefore malnourished, while levels lower than this are indicative not only of low weight but also of severe health risks that may even expose an individual to premature death. As figure 5.4 shows the percentage of women with BMI levels lower than 18.5 per cent is highest in India at 35.6 per cent followed by Pakistan where the percentage is 31.6 per cent.

Poor levels of health and nutrition have direct consequences for women's own reproductive health and also that of their children. Anaemia among pregnant women in South Asia is largely the result of poor dietary intake. Almost half of all South Asian women suffer from anaemia during pregnancy. The percentage is highest in the Maldives where an estimated 55.4 per cent of pregnant women are anaemic. In other South Asian countries too the levels are high: India (49.1 per cent), Pakistan (39.1 per cent), Bangladesh (47 per cent), Nepal (42.4 per cent) and Bhutan (49.6 per cent). The percentage is lower only in Sri Lanka where an estimated 29.3 per cent of pregnant women are anaemic.[58]

Maternal mortality ratios are also a good indicator for measuring the extent of food insecurity and lack of healthcare that women receive during pregnancies. As figure 5.5 shows, during the period between 2000 and 2008 there has been significant improvement in reducing maternal mortality ratios in all the South Asian countries, however they are still not on track in reducing maternal mortality by three-quarters by 2015, as envisaged in the MDGs.

In addition to the impact of food security on women's own health and nutritional outcomes, the inter-generational impact on children in terms of low birth weight of infants, infant mortality, child malnutrition

The nutritional deficiencies faced by South Asian women result in the world's highest percentages of women suffering from acute energy deficiencies and low levels of Body Mass Index

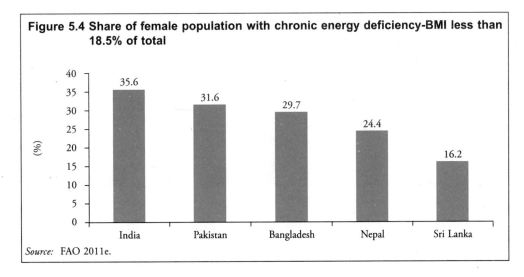

Figure 5.4 Share of female population with chronic energy deficiency-BMI less than 18.5% of total

Source: FAO 2011e.

and mortality is also severe. The incidence of low birth weight among infants is the highest in South Asia, where an estimated 27.2 per cent of the infants born each year have low birth weight. Among the South Asian countries, Pakistan has the highest percentage of low birth weight babies at 31.6 per cent. Globally it is estimated that there are 18 million low birth weight babies born each year of which 9.3 million are born in South Asia alone. Babies born with low birth weight is a reflection of mother's poor nutritional status. These newborns have lower chances of survival and healthy growth as indicated by high rates of infant and child mortality in South Asia.[59]

Policies to ensure food security for women in South Asia

Women in South Asia are vital to ensuring food security for their households. In this context, it is important to analyse how effective social protection policies in South Asia have been in reducing the risks and vulnerabilities faced by women and, as a result, improving their access to food for the entire household. A number of studies now recognize that as the risks and vulnerabilities faced by men and women are different and at times specific

to their gender, or exacerbated as a result of their gender, it is important that social protection policies are also gender sensitive. What this means is that social protection programmes must be designed with an understanding of the differentiated risks and vulnerabilities of women and men.[60] A number of social protection policies have been found to be effective in improving women's condition and promoting food security. These are policies that promote women's economic opportunities through public works programmes, enhance nutritional and food security through food transfers, increase women's access to assets through direct asset transfers, and reduce poverty and improve access to food through direct cash transfers.[61]

Enhancing women's participation in public works programme is an effective way to address the difficulties faced by women in employment. In India, the Mahatma Gandhi National Rural Employment Guarantee Act (MGNREGA) that reaches approximately 45 million households aims to achieve a change in rural livelihoods and agricultural productivity through public works. The programme specifically targets the problems faced by rural women by ensuring that at least one-third of all workers in each state are women, provides

The inter-generational impact of food security on children is also severe. The incidence of low birth weight among infants is the highest in South Asia

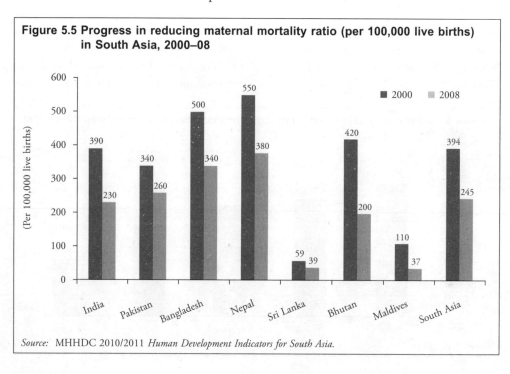

Figure 5.5 Progress in reducing maternal mortality ratio (per 100,000 live births) in South Asia, 2000–08

Source: MHHDC 2010/2011 *Human Development Indicators for South Asia.*

equal wages, care facilities for children, and facilitates that single women are able to work closer to their homes. In order to ensure female control over their incomes, it recommends that local governments allow individual accounts and also joint accounts where household members are co-signatories. MGNREGA has been successful in increasing women's access to incomes and has thus led to improvements in household food consumption.[62]

Cash transfers have been found to be extremely effective in reducing hunger and food insecurity of poor households. These are also seen as important policy tools to improve women's access to income and thereby to better food and health security of households, especially children. The Chars Livelihood Programme (CLP) in Bangladesh was found to lead to significant improvements in children's health. It was found that children of women who were registered earlier for the cash and asset transfer programme were less stunted and underweight than those who were registered later. A cash for work programme without any additional nutritional support showed marked improvements in both women and children's growth in only 10 weeks.[63]

Conditional cash transfers in Bangladesh through the Female Secondary School Assistance Programme have also led to increase in the secondary school certificate pass rates of girls who were receiving the stipend. From 39 per cent in 2001, the rate increased to 63 per cent in 2008. Improved education of girls is critical to altering gender relations, both within and outside the home. It enhances women's livelihood options and improves their incomes and livelihoods. In Nepal, too, conditional cash transfers are made to households to ensure that children, especially girls, are sent to school. Such schemes not only enhance a household's access to food but also ensure improved gender outcomes in education.[64]

The Benazir Income Support Programme (BISP) in Pakistan is also an example of a direct cash transfer programme that aims to reduce food insecurity of poor households headed by women. The BISP provides cash transfers of PKR1,000 a month to female-headed households who earn less than PKR6,000 a month. The amount is estimated to provide for 20–25 days of flour consumption for a household with 5–6 members. Under the BISP, in order for women to become eligible for cash transfers they must possess the computerized national identification cards. The payments are delivered at the homes of BISP beneficiaries.

Addressing the specific challenges faced by women in accessing social services, employment opportunities and supportive legal and institutional measures are critical to help households move out of poverty and improve their food security.

Cash transfers are important policy tools to improve women's access to income and thereby to better food and health security of households.

Chapter 6

Impact of Climate Change on Food Security in South Asia

Climate change has the potential to be the most significant challenge to humanity in the near future. It is not only an environmental issue but also one that affects our very existence because of its direct link to agriculture and food security.

The most painful reality of climate change is that it is the poorer countries that stand to suffer the most, and it is the poorest in the poor countries that have the least capacity to withstand the effects of climate change. At a time when South Asia is already seized with serious problems of poverty and inflation and its various ramifications, climate change can only further aggravate the situation. Therefore, it is imperative that action is taken on the food and agriculture sector—the most vulnerable sector to be affected by climate change.

Across South Asia a large proportion of the population depends on agriculture for their livelihood and over the centuries, farming practices have developed as a response to local climatic conditions. However, although most of South Asia receives monsoon rains every year, rainfall in the semi-arid and sub-humid regions is highly variable and unpredictable and influences agricultural productivity accordingly. Currently, about 500 million people in South Asia need to be lifted out of poverty and this already formidable challenge is made even more difficult because, along with local environmental repercussions of intensive agricultural practices, global warming has also started to affect food production. In addition, the environmental challenges due to climate change, such as water shortages and storms, also threaten future social stability with the likelihood of civil upheavals and political conflicts in the region.

Climate change: Concerns and perspectives

Climate change affects food production directly through changes in agro-ecological conditions and indirectly through changes in agricultural productivity and distribution of food. The frequency and severity of events such as cyclones, floods, hailstorms and droughts can hamper crop yields and local food supplies.

According to the fourth Assessment Report of the Intergovernmental Panel on Climate Change, future projections of climate change indicate that South Asia is very likely to get warmer during this century.[1] The availability of fresh water is projected to decrease, and coastal areas will be at the greatest risk to rising sea levels and the flooding of rivers. The rise in sea level in Bangladesh is expected to impact over 13 million people with a 16 per cent loss of rice production.

The World Bank has listed 12 countries that are most vulnerable to climate change. The list includes five out of seven countries in South Asia. The five main threats arising from climate change highlighted by the World Bank are: droughts, floods, storms, rising sea levels, and greater uncertainty in agriculture.

Floods due to climate change could have dire consequences for Bangladesh, India, Pakistan, and Sri Lanka. Bangladesh heads this list of countries most at risk of flooding, as glacial melt from the Himalayan ranges increases river water in the Ganges and Brahmaputra rivers. These rivers and their hundreds of tributaries, flood 30 to 70 per cent of Bangladesh each year, as the water makes its way to the Bay of Bengal in the south. Bangladesh, along with most low-lying island states, is also highly vulnerable to flooding from rising sea levels and storms.

The most painful reality of climate change is that it is the poorer countries that stand to suffer the most

India is one of the 12 countries most at risk from droughts. Due to climate change, greater uncertainty in agriculture and food security issues could hamper future growth rates in India and Pakistan.

Climate change impacts in South Asia can be roughly divided into two groups: a) biophysical impacts include physiological effects on crops, pastures, forests, and livestock; changes in land, soil, and water resources; shifts in spatial and temporal distribution of impacts; increased weed and pest challenges; sea level rise and changes to ocean salinity; and sea temperature rise causing fish to inhabit different ranges; and b) socio-economic impacts include decline in yields and production, increased number of people at risk of hunger and food insecurity, and migration and civil unrest.

The agricultural sector, including crops and livestock, forestry, and fisheries need to prepare for the impacts of global climate change. Some specific options for climate change mitigation and adaptation for the agriculture sector, such as sustainable land and forest management include efficient water use, changing crop varieties, altering the timing or location of cropping, improving pest control, and weed management practices.

What climate change means for food security in South Asia

Agriculture in South Asia is dependent on the ecosystem that is synchronized with the monsoon rain system. Any unexpected change in climatic conditions could bring devastation to millions of farming families in South Asia. Systematic analysis of any signs that show deviation from long-term trends in precipitation and temperatures is required. Meanwhile, disaster preparedness for devastation caused by floods, storms, cyclones, avalanches and landslides needs to be accelerated in climatically vulnerable areas. The cropping and livestock systems will need to be made more flexible in case of climate change related prolonged droughts or regular flooding. The farm to market infrastructure and transport system will need to be in sync with these changing crops and livestock breeds.

South Asia has a diverse ecosystem consisting of high mountains with glaciers; plain areas with agriculture that are dependent on monsoon rains and related irrigation systems; a massive coastal ecosystem with fishery resources; and vast desert land. With climate change, the monsoon rain system could lead to untimely rains or floods. Climate change related warming could melt the Hindukush, Karakoram and Himalaya (HKH) glaciers on an accelerated rate resulting in glacial lake outburst floods (GLOFs). The coastal areas could face cyclones, degradation, and increased sand erosion due to sea level rise. Desertification could accelerate in the arid areas due to further reductions in rains.

Glacier melt—reduced river flows and GLOFs

The rivers of South Asia obtain their water from the glaciers, snow and rains of the Himalayas which could be affected by a change in global climate. As a consequence of global warming, more devastating river flooding is expected, due to the rapid melting of snow.[2] According to some estimates, the rivers will be hit by increasing temperatures and intense rainfall in summers with some possibility of decreasing snow projections in the winters, resulting in river water shrinkage of 8.4 per cent by 2050.[3] This means an exacerbation of the already serious problems of flooding and poor drainage in the river basins over the next 50 years, followed by a 30–40 per cent drop in river flows in 100 years time.[4]

Bhutan is undergoing the most dramatic effects of climate change in the region as its mountain glaciers are retreating rapidly.[5] Melting of some of Bhutan's glaciers has significant consequences not only for Bhutan but also for South Asia. These mountains are considered the 'water towers of the world' and disappearing glaciers mean a loss of one of the world's

Any unexpected change in climatic conditions could bring devastation to millions of farming families in South Asia

larger reserves of fresh water for millions of South Asians. This could also enhance the risk of GLOFs. Bhutan frequently experiences seasonal GLOF, resulting in destruction of life and property, damaging large agricultural lands and infrastructure.

Due to these fast changing glacier lakes, Bhutan was among the first few countries to prepare and submit a National Adaptation Programme of Action (NAPA) under the United Nations (UN) Framework Convention on Climate Change. Along with the Pacific Ocean Small Island States, Bhutan was among the first few countries to access funds from the Least Developed Countries Fund (LDCF) to start implementing measures to reduce environmental risks.

Monsoon rain system—reduced, untimely rains, or floods

One of the factors affecting the global climate system is the temporary shift in the Pacific Ocean currents by El Nino, which has caused the ocean to release large amounts of heat into the atmosphere. El Nino strongly influences the weather pattern of South Asia; the increased sea temperature over the western Pacific reduces cloud formation over the Indian Ocean thereby decreasing summer monsoon rains and resulting in severe droughts. El Nino influenced South Asia's monsoon rainfall in 1918 and then in 1982–83 and 1997–98. Most recently, it reduced the region's summer rain in 2009 and its effects continued till early 2010.

Another factor affecting the global climate system and influencing monsoon rains in South Asia is the Russian heat wave. According to climate scientists, huge South Asian monsoon floods and Russia's intense heat wave are linked and fit the description of weather trends in global warming and climate change. Russia's heat wave generates a heating pattern that increases the monsoon's intensity in and above the Indian Ocean thereby increasing monsoon rains in the region. This factor explains the heavier monsoon rains the region received between 1981 and 2000.

Excessive rain in Pakistan towards the end of 2010 and the resulting flooding signifies the vulnerability of people due to the adverse effect of climate change on the global climate system.

Thus, the natural ecosystems that agriculture depends on are severely affected by changes in the disruption of precipitation and temperatures expected with climate change. Climate change, as explained above, undoubtedly worsens the living conditions of millions of farmers, fishermen and forest dependent communities in South Asia. Their economic, food, health, and physical security is likely to suffer through higher incidences of crop damage and loss of livestock from floods and droughts. The disruption of global weather patterns has serious consequences for agriculture, food security, and energy consumption.

Coastal ecosystems—threats to marine and inland fisheries

Globally, there is increasing concern over the consequences of climate change for food security and livelihoods. The fisheries sector is crucial for millions of the world's poorest people, as more than 500 million depend on fisheries and aquaculture as a source of protein and income. For 400 million of the poorest, fish provides half or more of their animal protein and dietary minerals.[6] Nearly 1.5 billion consumers worldwide rely on fish for more than 20 per cent of their dietary animal protein needs.[7]

Millions of fishermen, fish farmers and coastal inhabitants will experience less stable livelihoods due to changes in the availability and quality of fish as a result of climate change. Vulnerable fishing and coastal communities in South Asia will bear the brunt of regional impacts of climate change. Many of these fishing and coastal communities subsist in precarious conditions because of poverty and underdevelopment. This is further exacerbated by overexploitation of fishery resources and degraded ecosystems.

The natural ecosystems that agriculture depends on are severely affected by changes in the disruption of precipitation and temperatures expected with climate change

Fisheries are an already vulnerable sector facing widespread and often profound changes due to climate variability. Marine fisheries are already facing multiple challenges due to overfishing and habitat loss. Small island developing states including the Maldives depend on fisheries and aquaculture for at least 50 per cent of their animal protein intake. These island states are in a particularly vulnerable position. The fisheries of islands and atolls of the Maldives could be adversely affected by the climate change. The negative effects on the coral reefs, mangroves and seagrass could change the reef fish population.

Climate change could also threaten the food supply and livelihoods of some of the world's poorest populations involved with inland fisheries. Nearly 65 per cent of aquaculture is inland and concentrated mostly in the tropical and subtropical regions of Asia.

Sea level rise over the next decades could increase upstream salinity affecting fish farms, as most of the Asian fish farms are often in the delta areas of major rivers at the mid to upper levels of tidal ranges.

The increasing sea temperature has profound adverse effects on both the coastal environment and the vulnerable coastal communities in the province of Sindh in Pakistan. The coastal districts of Badin and Thatta are experiencing declining fish stocks and the fast disappearance of commercially important marine species of fish.[8]

The climate change related natural disasters caused by global warming makes fish harvesting less profitable; it increases costs of rebuilding fishing fleets, shortens the duration of fish harvesting at sea, increases risk of accidents, and reduces viability of fish harvesting. It significantly impacts livelihoods of the poor living in coastal zones, such as the three districts along the south and southeastern coast of Bangladesh: Laxmipur, Chittagong, and Noakhali.[9]

Climate change is likely to drastically worsen the situation of the coastal communities in the South Asian region, if immediate and effective adaptation and mitigation measures are not put in place. With mounting evidence of the impacts of climate change on aquatic ecosystems, the resulting impacts on fishery livelihoods are likely to be significant.

Desertification—reduced water for agriculture

Desertification is a global phenomenon of land degradation, which reduces the natural potential of the ecosystems. It has a direct impact on people in terms of depletion of natural resources resulting in vulnerability to food shortages and deterioration of the environment through natural disasters like prolonged drought.[10]

In the drylands, water scarcity limits the production of crops, forage and wood. Human activities and climate change persistently degrade the dryland ecosystem and convert it into desert. Ongoing desertification threatens South Asia's poorest population. It affects food security, triggers internal and international migration, starts resource-based conflicts and causes civil unrest. Desertification is one of the greatest environmental challenges and a major barrier to meeting basic human needs in drylands.

About one-third to a quarter of the 328 million hectares of land in India is going through land degradation, including desertification in drylands. There is a tremendous pressure on land-based natural resources, resulting in water and wind erosion.[11] Very high human and livestock demand for food, fodder, and fuelwood in the form of deforestation and overgrazing are accelerating the process of desertification. Northern and western Indian states of Rajasthan, Gujarat, and Maharashtra are the hardest hit.

The Thar desert, that spreads over a large part of south-west India (Rajasthan, Haryana, Punjab, and Gujarat states) and south-east Pakistan (Sindh and Punjab), is also prone to desertification. The region faces frequent droughts, exacerbating wind and water erosion. The main reasons are destruction of vegetative cover in the sandy terrain for fuel and fodder and overgrazing

Climate change is likely to drastically worsen the situation of the coastal communities in the South Asian region

by a huge animal population. Mining and other related industries also cause land degradation destroying the desert ecosystem.

Livestock in both India and Pakistan are increasing at a rate of two per cent per annum mounting a tremendous pressure on the limited land resources. There has been a steady decline in the quality of common property resources used as grazing lands and pastures as a result of increase in livestock population.

Climate change adaptation and mitigation measures for food security

Greater uncertainty in agriculture due to climate change induced impacts on land, soil, and water resources can have physiological effects on crops, pastures, forests, and livestock. Shifts in the spatial and temporal distribution of the prevailing weather system, could also increase weed and pest challenges. The socio-economic impacts of decline in yields and production could increase the number of people at risk of hunger and food insecurity.

For adaptation to climatic change, there is a need for an environmentally sustainable agricultural system under conditions of growing intensity of cultivation in South Asia. Innovative technologies are needed to improve agricultural productivity, particularly the technologies geared towards adapting to increasing climatic variation such as, new crop varieties that are drought and frost resistant; irrigation technologies based on water efficiency in agriculture, as a means to adapt to water shortages in the future; drip irrigation; organic farming; etc.

Climate change adaptation in agriculture

Climate change-induced glacial lake outburst floods (GLOFs), avalanches and snow storms: In a regional cooperative effort, the South Asian countries of Bhutan, Nepal, Pakistan and India, under the UN Regional Climate Risk Reduction Project (RCRRP), an initiative of the International Research Institute for Climate and Society

(IRI), have identified three main impacts of climate change in the region:

a) Increase in avalanches and snow storms at high altitudes. More than 80 per cent of the land area in Nepal is mountainous and still tectonically active.[12] Snowstorms, avalanches and landslides are becoming more intense in the heart of the Himalayas near the village of Lukla, Nepal. Similar storms are happening with increasing frequency in the Indian states of Himachal Pradesh, Uttarakhand and Ladakh.

b) The thawing of slopes, thereby increasing glacial lakes and leading to GLOF hazards. GLOFs are common in the Himalayan region. The *Dudh Kosi* river near the Phakding in Nepal's Khumbu region below Mount Everest experienced GLOF.[13] The cascading impacts of a GLOF incident need to be scientifically assessed, as systematic empirical data could establish anthropological evidence. For the Regional GLOF Risk Reduction Initiative, the regional members from RCRRP promoted community-based approaches for GLOF risk mitigation and articulated the need for interaction with various stakeholders in the Hindu Kush Himalayan mountain terrain region.

c) Retreat of snow cover affecting run-offs, resulting in inadequate water supply to the downstream communities leading to severe droughts. Due to climate change, rising temperatures and drought have resulted in reduced agricultural productivity. During the summer of 2010, crop failure due to drought had severely impacted farmers in the western hill region of Nepal, stretching along the border with India into the eastern part of the Terai region. Meanwhile, floods and landslides devastated the mid-western region.

In light of these findings Nepal is finalizing a NAPA. One of its main

For adaptation to climatic change, there is a need for an environmentally sustainable agricultural system

features is to incorporate the climate changes into national agricultural policies. To adapt to and mitigate higher frequency of water-related climate shocks and hydrometeorological hazards that could devastate agricultural productivity, investment under NAPA will be focused on water management. As Nepal needs to reduce its vulnerability to both droughts and floods, investment will be for a strategic balance between large-scale hydropower infrastructure investments and small-scale local storage systems.[14] This new dimension for future investments will build resilience to climate change and upgrade water management resulting in improved rainfed agriculture.

Nepal is undertaking efforts to improve rainfed agriculture as more than 80 per cent of arable land is still under rainfed agriculture, supporting about 70 per cent of the population.[15] Traditionally, farmers were growing crops like rice, potatoes, wheat, and maize in these areas.

Since January 2010, the Food and Agriculture Organization of the United Nations (FAO) is supporting farmers in 10 most food-insecure districts with improved varieties of cereal seeds to boost the productivity of farmers. FAO is also introducing new agricultural technologies for a rice intensification system that requires less water and is appropriate for areas with rainfed agriculture. These new crop strains of drought tolerant rice for rainfed mountain areas should have a much better chance to adapt to climate change.[16]

India has also implemented innovation for sustainable agriculture in the form of artificial glaciers in its Ladakh region. Until the 1960s, Ladakh was self-sufficient in its food supply for its 300,000 population. However, increasingly less glacial activity and reduced snow melt from the Himalayas is affecting the farmers dependent on these factors. Water and food security concerns in this region are further complicated as the glaciers are receding rapidly and winters are getting shorter and warmer. In addition, the timings of irrigation needs and water availability do not coincide. The

solution to these concerns was provided by adopting simple agricultural innovations; the most popular are the artificial glacier lakes. These artificial lakes collect and store glacial melt on the sides of hills. Initially, with the aim of providing water to farmers during the sowing season in April, an embankment system was designed that collects and stores glacial melt on the sides of hills that are shadowed from the sun. The ice starts to melt in April, when it is planting time; the water is released to villages through a network of canals. Availability of this irrigation water in early spring enables farmers to harvest two crops in a year, which was not possible earlier. In this region, nine artificial glaciers are in place, with four more scheduled for mid-2011.[17]

Bhutan—mountain terrain, cattle, herdsmen, and rangeland management: Bhutan's agriculture and rangeland is increasingly exposed to new climate change related ecological challenges in the recent years that have implications for its economic growth and impact on poverty. This has resulted in a need to adapt to climate change. Investments in water management in rainfed agriculture should form a cornerstone of any country's strategy for adapting to climate change, particularly in a county like Bhutan with mountain agriculture and rangeland, where rainfed agriculture and livestock play such an important economic role.

The Government of Bhutan has taken the initiative to develop a national adaptation plan for climate change to reduce the vulnerability of the local population living in the region by developing a regional framework for mitigation of the adverse consequences of such climate change.

Citizens of the eastern Himalayan countries of Bangladesh, Bhutan, India, and Nepal, on their part, got together in August 2010 to forge an alliance to work in developing medium- and long-term strategies focusing on the southern slopes of the eastern Himalayan region.[18] As the livelihoods of these people are connected to the waters from the Himalayas, even with the ongoing controversy regarding the speed at which the Himalayan glaciers are melting, the region needs to prepare for the consequences of climate change.[19]

Crop and cattle management in drought prone areas of India: For India, more than half the country's 1.2 billion people depend on agriculture for a living, although agriculture represents only 18 per cent of the total national income. During 2001–02, India experienced an 'all-India drought', with 49 per cent rainfall deficiency in July 2001, and 19 per cent deficiency in 2002.

The state of Rajasthan was severely affected with 60–70 per cent below normal rainfall. The other states that faced 30–40 per cent below normal rainfall were: Chhattisgarh, Gujarat, Madhya Pradesh, Orissa, Himachal Pradesh, Maharashtra and Uttaranchal, where thousands of villages were affected, and nearly a million hectares of crop area and millions of livestock and cattle perished.[20]

During 2009, India was affected by the worst drought in 37 years, affecting *kharif* production in 317 districts.[21] Regionally, the effects were more devastating, the monsoon of 2009 came about 12 weeks late in Andhra Pradesh, causing widespread damage to cereal and lentil crops with stunted growth on small rainfed farms. The summer rainfall was down 25 per cent; roughly half of the rural districts were declared drought zones. As production fell, prices rose for staple crops like rice.

The drought led to focused attention on the problems facing Indian agriculture with water resources coming under greater pressure as the population continues to expand. Many agriculture analysts are calling for a second Green Revolution to sharply improve grain output, which addresses the complicated problems presented by global warming and rapidly diminishing groundwater supplies. For increasing production, any further introduction of high-yielding seeds and fertilizers could be counter-productive due to already increased acidification of soil and deteriorating groundwater quality. Today, the challenge is even more pronounced and needs a nationwide coordinated effort to improve irrigation, and conserve rainwater and groundwater.[22]

Climate change and livestock

Trends show that future farm incomes in South Asia are climate sensitive, and will be severely threatened in the event of extreme climate change. Farmers could tolerate mild or moderate climate change through various adaptation measures, including switching among crops and livestock species, or between crops and livestock. Under certain climatic conditions, livestock species may provide more flexibility to some farmers and could help offset losses in crop income.

As temperatures rise, farmers will raise more livestock and switch species. However, if rainfall increases, they will own less livestock, and crop most of the land where water has become available. Climate change adaptation for livestock includes:

- Shifting to higher elevation zones in very hot and dry weather.
- Varying species choice across the different agro-ecological zones. For example, in a mild and moist climate, sheep ownership could increase at high elevation and mid-elevation areas, and in lowland humid regions.
- Moving away from chicken, sheep, beef, and dairy cattle towards goats and camels as temperatures rise.
- Investing in beef and dairy cattle and sheep, with additional focus on high-yielding goats and chickens as rainfall increases.

Livestock management should also include: modifying herd composition; varying species and breeds; and adapting grazing management practices to reduce soil erosion.

Under certain climatic conditions, livestock species may provide more flexibility to some farmers and could help offset losses in crop income

Climate change adaptation and mitigation for agriculture in arid areas

As global warming sets in, it is advisable to apply conservation agriculture. This includes minimum disturbance of soil, in combination with maintenance of year-round crop cover with crop rotation, increasing the proportion of leguminous crops to boost soil nitrogen.

Keeping in view the emerging climate change impacts, there is a need to design special research programmes for developing new crop plasmas for conditions like drought, flood, and increased salinity. Adopting new crops will become a necessity as irrigation water per unit of land reduces. Crop rotation and change in crop varieties, along with re-adjustment at the time of planting and harvesting; altering the location of cropping and a more efficient water use, with improved pest control and weed management practices; and introducing water efficient integrated soil-fertility management systems that cater to the nutritional needs of the crop—are some of the areas that need research in South Asia.

Since South Asian countries are at a greater threat to suffer from natural disasters like floods, cyclones, etc., climate change related mitigation strategies should also incorporate disaster preparedness. These should focus on providing immediate assistance due to loss of livelihood, and rehabilitation for quick recovery to normal life (see box 6.1).

Climate change adaptation in fisheries

Climate change also affects the marine ecosystem and fishery production systems of coastal and inland river areas in South Asia. Fisheries, coastal resources, and habitats are directly affected by pollution, sediment run-off and coastal development projects. With continued population growth in this region and impending climate change threats exacerbate the problem, and in many cases could lead to overfishing and loss or damage to marine habitats. South Asian countries have undertaken several initiatives to adapt to climate change.

The integrated coastal management (ICM) in Sri Lanka: ICM is practiced as a solution to climate change adaptation for fisheries management and conservation in the coastal areas of Sri Lanka.[23] ICM

Since South Asian countries are at a greater threat to suffer from natural disasters, climate change related mitigation strategies should also incorporate disaster preparedness

---

Box 6.1 Floods and restoration of degraded lands in Pakistan

Irrigated agriculture provides Pakistan with economic stability and export earnings. The monsoon system brings every year eagerly awaited waters for the summer crops. But most years it also brings along storms, floods, and disaster. To ensure stability and progress for the irrigated agriculture in Pakistan, several measures need to be adopted including: (i) flood-related disaster preparedness to reduce damages to life and property; and (ii) a plan for a quick recovery in the form of restoration of degraded lands with high production potential.

Floods and related disasters are detrimental to local environment. A policy revision is necessary to place land restoration and flood prevention as a top priority within disaster management in Pakistan. The flood-related land degradation brings greater uncertainty to agriculture in Pakistan. It has a physiological effect on crops, pastures, forests, and live-stock. Changes in land, soil, and water resources also have socio-economic impacts due to the decline in yields and production, increasing the number of people at risk of hunger and food insecurity.

Changing crop varieties in the lands with high production potential could minimize flood-related damages. Special research programmes are needed for developing new plasmas for salinity and flood submersion. This should also focus on improving soil drainage to reduce salinity in the aftermath of floods.

In Pakistan, the need is to scale up pro-poor climate change adaptation to ensure food security. There is a need to prioritize policies and investments in climate change adaptation to promote resilient agriculture and food security using emerging agriculture research and technologies.

and environmentally friendly aquaculture practices in Sri Lanka will ensure ecological management of fisheries for food security. ICM is a framework for coastal ecosystem management. It is a form of land use planning targeted at coastal areas, which provides the framework for management of the coastal and marine environment. ICM focuses primarily on managing coastal development for residential and recreations purposes. Marine and coastal protected areas (MCPAs) framework is more effective as part of an ICM.

Biodiversity conservation and maintaining ecological processes is the key component of the MCPAs. Activities taking place outside the boundaries of MCPAs could affect the fragile ecosystems. These include industry, agriculture, aquaculture, urban construction, port development and shipping. ICM practice is currently being developed throughout the South Asia region. Local level ICM activities with other South Asian countries, for example Bangladesh, are underway in Sri Lanka for developing proposals for national level programmes.

The Maldives' Mangroves for the Future (MFF) and the National Strategy and Action Plan (NSAP) are related to the sustainable use and management of coastal ecosystems and adaptation to climate change in the context of ICM. The NSAP provides an opportunity for implementation of ICM for selected ecosystems and supports the sustainable development vision.

Marine aquatic systems adaptation to climate change in Bangladesh: The coastline of Bangladesh is a complex ecology which is affected by natural hazards like cyclones, coastal flooding, tidal surges and rising salinity in coastal agricultural areas. Vulncrabilities in the coastal zone to fisheries are increasing with accentuations of sea level rise caused by climate change. Similarly, environmental degradation due to exploitation of mangroves has had adverse effects on fisheries. The marine fisheries of Bangladesh are affected by overfishing, and pollution of estuaries and the coastal sea waters. This is further exacerbated by the destruction of marine habitat, especially wetlands and sea-grasses. The Government of Bangladesh is utilizing recent scientific research findings and indigenous knowledge to develop policies for sustainable coastal zone management.[24]

The Bangladesh Rice Research Institute has achieved a breakthrough in developing high-yielding salinity tolerant crops for irrigated, and for rainfed conditions. Bangladesh has taken protective measures to protect resources with massive coastal afforestation and freshwater reservoirs, due to growing concern regarding coastal ecosystem damages.

Coastal Resource Management for Improving Livelihoods Project in Bangladesh has shown positive results for fisheries and cropping adaptability in the interface between fresh and saline waters of the estuary. In more saline water environments, the project successfully improved rice-aquaculture integration in rice-shrimp systems. Salinity-tolerant rice varieties and genetically improved farm freshwater prawns were grown together in rice fields.[25]

The Maldives—A leader in planning for climate change for small island nations: For Maldives climate vulnerability to local-level ocean and risk to fisheries is highlighted by the fact that the Maldives consists of a series of low lying islands. The islands of the Maldives depend entirely on the coastal and marine ecosystems including coral reefs, seagrass beds, lagoons, beaches, and small areas of mangrove as the asset base of the national economy. Tourism is the largest contributor to gross domestic product (GDP), and the second largest industry is fisheries. Both are based wholly on the health and attractiveness of the Maldives' coastal and marine ecosystems.

Some of the key challenges facing the Maldives are: climate-related hazards, such as accelerated sea level rise, sea surface temperature rise, and changes in monsoon patterns. The Maldives is globally recognized for its leadership among small island nations in planning for climate

The Bangladesh Rice Research Institute has achieved a breakthrough in developing high-yielding salinity tolerant crops for irrigated, and for rainfed conditions

change. One of the main objectives of the NAPA is to prepare for the adverse effects of climate change. Also, coastal zone management has become a part of national policy to support and strengthen adaptation to impacts of climate change.

The Maldives' MFF and the NSAP reflect these considerations as climate change related actions are mainstreamed in strategic actions. The Maldives NSAP has been developed to contribute and complement existing environmental emergencies for Integrated Coastal Zone Management (ICZM) and the National Development Plan (NDP).[26]

Conclusion

The nexus of climate change and food security presents a vital combination of issues and challenges for South Asia, but the current policies remain far behind what is needed to deal with the challenge. South Asia is among the areas expected to face severe impacts of climate change. Devastating flooding in 2007 along the Ganges and Brahmaputra rivers affected over 13 million people in Bangladesh. Flooding in Pakistan in 2010 severely affected 20 million people. India has suffered a drastic drop in groundwater levels due to overexploitation, heavy rainfall, devastating flooding, and severe droughts. Sea level rise is a threat to low lying areas of Bangladesh and Sri Lanka.

South Asia is highly vulnerable to the impact of climate change because of its reliance on agriculture and forestry with a concentration of large populations along exposed coastlines and rivers. Millions of South Asians live in fast-growing cities along the coast.

There is a need to develop a system of networking and collaboration among relevant research organizations involved in research on the adaptation to climate change in South Asia. For climate change impacts, adaptation, and policy response in the South Asian countries, a regional approach is needed to focus on the food security of the vulnerable people in South Asia.

There is a need to develop a system of networking and collaboration among relevant research organizations involved in research on the adaptation to climate change in South Asia

Chapter 7

Global Commitments to Food Security

Global initiatives to ensure food security

In 1945, the Food and Agriculture Organization of the United Nations (FAO) was created for the purpose of 'raising the levels of nutrition and standards of living of the peoples; securing improvements in the efficiency of the production and distribution of all food and agricultural products, and bettering the condition of rural populations.'[1] For the following twenty-five years, many proposals, strategies and institutional innovations were put forward to fight poverty and hunger in developing countries. Yet poverty persisted, the number of hungry people in the world increased, and the world faced an impending food crisis. Against this background, the World Food Conference was held in Rome in November 1974 to seriously address the food security concerns of the world. The Conference recommended the evolution of a world food security system based on global arrangements for early warning, increased food stock and food aid, and for increasing food production in developing countries. The World Food Summits of 1996, 2002, and 2009 made further commitments to address the rising food security concerns of the world. The Millennium Development Goals (MDGs) of the United Nations in 2000 adopted the reduction of hungry people in each country as the number one goal. The World Trade Organization (WTO) brought agricultural trade under its purview so that developing countries could benefit from such trade. With this background of global commitments to food security, we briefly review below how far the global community has been able to assist developing countries to achieve their food security goal.

The World Food Summits and the Millennium Summit: Progress made so far

The World Food Summit in 1996 set the goal of halving the number of under-nourished people in the world between 1990–92 and 2015. The objective was reinforced during the World Food Summits of 2002 and 2009. A further commitment was made at the Millennium Summit held in 2000 to reduce the proportion of hungry people, and underweight children under-five, by half between 1990 and 2015 (MDG goal 1).

Figure 7.1 shows the progress towards achieving the hunger reduction targets of MDGs and the World Food Summit. A comparison of South Asia with developing countries and other developing regions of

Many proposals, strategies and institutional innovations were put forward to fight poverty and hunger. Yet poverty persisted, the number of hungry people in the world increased, and the world faced an impending food crisis

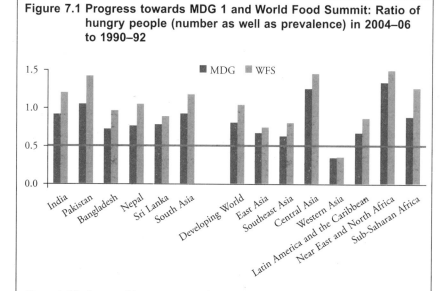

Figure 7.1 Progress towards MDG 1 and World Food Summit: Ratio of hungry people (number as well as prevalence) in 2004–06 to 1990–92

Notes: *: The horizontal line, intersecting the bars, shows the value of 0.7 which indicates three cases. First, if any bar is exactly equivalent to this line it means that the particular country/region has achieved the MDG 1 / World Food Summit target till 2004–06. Second, if any bar is lower than this line, it means that the particular country/region has performed better even than the MDG 1 / World Food Summit target till 2004–06. Third, if any bar is higher than this line, it means that the particular country/region has not performed satisfactorily towards achieving the MDG 1 / World Food Summit target till 2004–06. **: Data for South Asia is the weighted average value of seven countries, India, Pakistan, Bangladesh, Nepal, Sri Lanka, Bhutan and Maldives.

Source: FAO 2011b and MHHDC staff computations.

Table 7.1   Trends in proportion and number of undernourished people in South Asia, 1990–2007

	Proportion of undernourished (%)		Number of undernourished (millions)	
	1990–1992	2005–2007	1990–1992	2005–2007
India	24	21	210.2	237.7
Pakistan	22	26	25.7	43.4
Bangladesh	36	27	41.6	41.7
Nepal	21	16	4.0	4.5
Sri Lanka	27	19	4.6	3.8
South Asia*	25	22	286.1	331.1

Note: *: Data for South Asia is the weighted average value of seven countries, India, Pakistan, Bangladesh, Nepal, Sri Lanka, Bhutan and Maldives.

Sources: FAO 2011b and MHHDC 2010/2011 *Human Development Indicators for South Asia.*

the world shows how East Asia, Southeast Asia, Western Asia, and the Near East and North Africa are progressing towards achieving MDG 1.

Within South Asia the situation varies: the situation is worse in Pakistan as the proportion of undernourished increased between 1990–92 and 2005–07 (see table 7.1 and figure 7.1). In Bangladesh, the proportion of undernourished initially reduced due to various government initiatives such as an increase in food availability through increased domestic food production as well as imports, and an improvement in access to food through income generation and social safety net programmes. However, this was before the emergence of the current food and

financial crises which have made the achievement of MDG 1 more difficult even for Bangladesh.

Ironically, the number of hungry people in the world decreased during the 1970s, 1980s, and mid-1990s—the period before the WTO and global commitments in the MDGs and World Food Summits (see figure 7.2). But after the mid-1990s, the number of hungry people has gone up in the world. In 2009, more than a billion people were estimated to be hungry due to food, financial, and economic crises. The number was expected to go up in 2010 and beyond due to the continuing food price crisis. Despite the reversal of the global food crisis after June 2008, food prices were still very high in South Asia. This was mostly attributable to hoarding and speculation by private sector traders who were influenced by the global financial speculation in commodity markets.

The situation of hunger among infants and pre-school children is even more disturbing. Figure 7.3 shows that South Asia does not only have the highest proportion of undernourished children in the world, it also has shown poor progress in reducing this proportion between 1990 and 2008. Overall, the prevalence of childhood malnutrition in all South Asian countries, except Bhutan, is higher than in Sub-Saharan Africa (see figures 7.3 and 7.4).

Besides global commitments, some regional level initiatives have also been taken in South Asia to address the issue of food security. In 1988, the SAARC Food Security Reserve was set up to address the problem of food insecurity in the region. However, it could not achieve the desired results due to the complicated process of implementation, harsh conditions, and the regional balance of payments crisis.[2] In 2007, the Food Bank was established which replaced the Food Security Reserve. The Food Bank decided to hold a reserve of 241,580 metric tonnes of rice and wheat with 63.4 per cent contribution from India, 16.6 per cent from Pakistan and Bangladesh each, 1.7 per cent from Nepal and Sri Lanka each, 0.08 per cent from the Maldives, and 0.07 per cent from Bhutan.

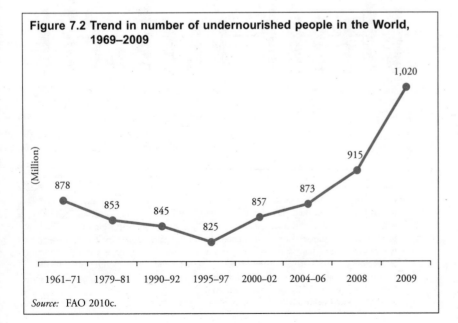

Figure 7.2 Trend in number of undernourished people in the World, 1969–2009

(Million)

878
853
845
825
857
873
915
1,020

1961–71   1979–81   1990–92   1995–97   2000–02   2004–06   2008   2009

Source: FAO 2010c.

The establishment of the Food Bank is a solution for emergency needs and crises, but in order to attain sustainable long-term food security, South Asia needs to focus on strengthening the production base, improving access, and providing safety nets to the very poor.

The crisis of global food prices and food security

Food prices in international markets have been volatile to a greater extent than ever seen before. First, the prices increased significantly from January 2007 to June 2008, then they declined dramatically during June 2008 to February 2009—a period of global financial and economic crisis. However, decreasing prices during late 2008 and early 2009 could not benefit the poor in developing countries due to their lower level of income and employment. Although the attention of the world got diverted from the food crisis to the financial and economic crisis, most analyses show that the financial crisis was very closely linked to the food crisis through the impact of financial speculation on world trade in food prices.

The high food prices in international trade in 2007–08 negatively affected the food security of both producers as well as consumers in developing countries,

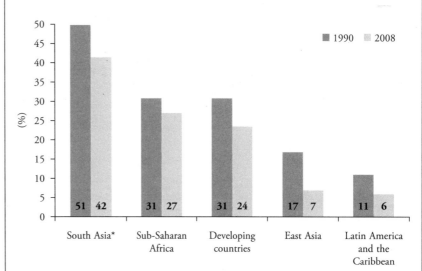

Figure 7.3 Progress towards MDG 1: Proportion of children under-five who are underweight (%), 1990–2008

Note: *: Data for South Asia is the weighted average value of seven countries, India, Pakistan, Bangladesh, Nepal, Sri Lanka, Bhutan and Maldives.
Sources: UN 2010 and MHHDC 2010/2011 *Human Development Indicators for South Asia.*

including South Asia. For instance, in Bangladesh, an additional 7.5 million people became food insecure in 2008, increasing the prevalence of hunger to 45 per cent. In Nepal, food insecure people increased from 4.2 to 6.4 million between 2007 and 2008, increasing acute malnutrition to 20 per cent in some areas, with 33 out of 75 districts being cited as chronically food insecure. And in Pakistan, in mid-2008, 51 per cent of the population was consuming inadequate food.[3]

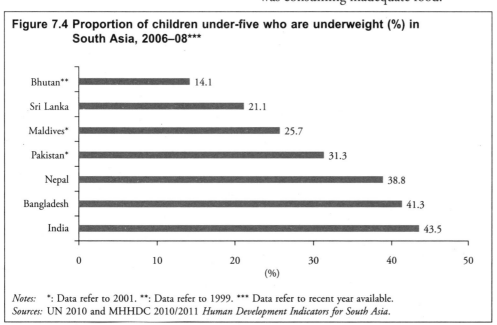

Figure 7.4 Proportion of children under-five who are underweight (%) in South Asia, 2006–08***

Notes: *: Data refer to 2001. **: Data refer to 1999. *** Data refer to recent year available.
Sources: UN 2010 and MHHDC 2010/2011 *Human Development Indicators for South Asia.*

Figure 7.5 Change in food price indices, January 2007–August 2010

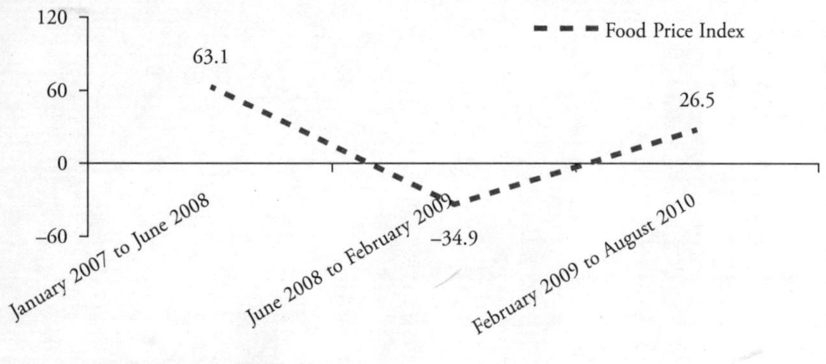

63.1

January 2007 to June 2008

June 2008 to February 2009   −34.9

February 2009 to August 2010   26.5

- - - Food Price Index

Sources: FAO 2010b and MHHDC staff computations.

The global food price increase transmitted into the domestic retail prices, negatively affecting the purchasing power of urban and rural poor. It also affected the small and marginal farmers who were outside the export-oriented agricultural sector. As a result of rise in world food prices, cultivation of world food grain increased to 2,241 million metric tonnes in 2008–09 (figure 7.7). However, almost all the increase in production was contributed by developed countries where it increased by 11 per cent compared to only 1 per cent increase in developing countries. Despite an increase in the prices of food grain in international market, its production declined in most developing countries due to two factors. First, only retail prices of food increased in developing countries

because of speculation and hoarding of food grains by private traders, while the wholesale prices or farm gate prices did not increase significantly. Second, the majority of the farmers in developing countries in general and in South Asia in particular are small and landless farmers. Most of them are net food buyers. High and fluctuating prices negatively affected their food security.

The emergence of the financial and economic crisis in September 2008 worsened the situation further. It reduced the purchasing power of poor households by impacting negatively on employment. In 2008, in South Asia, 76 per cent of the workers were engaged in vulnerable employment, characterized by inadequate income, low productivity and sub-standard working conditions. In 2009, the financial and economic crisis increased this ratio. Similarly, the crisis increased the ratio of working poor in the region. In South Asia, the proportion of working poor increased from 44 per cent in 2008 to 51 per cent in 2009.

The current rising trend of food prices as shown in figures 7.5 and 7.6 is attributed to the same factors that were responsible for the food price crisis in 2007–08, which was the result of speculation in the commodities futures markets.

While the global demand for food consumption is stable, global supply is

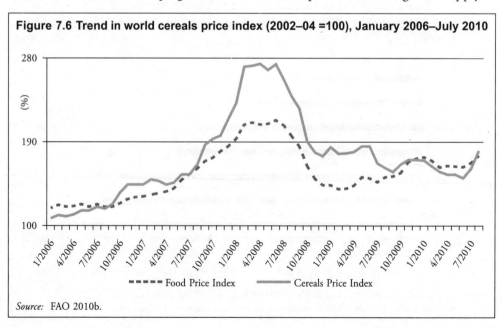

Figure 7.6 Trend in world cereals price index (2002–04 =100), January 2006–July 2010

(%)

- - - Food Price Index   —— Cereals Price Index

Source: FAO 2010b.

volatile, albeit around a stable trend. In fact, over the last few years, production has risen faster than consumption, and as a result, stock holding has gone up (see figure 7.7). It indicates that food grain prices should go down but in fact they have gone up from early 2009. Such fluctuations in food grain prices are not related to seasonal variation in real economy factors such as demand and supply, rather they are driven by financial speculations.

The rapid process of globalization has changed the global food system which in turn has affected the food as well as nutritional security of both consumers and producers in developing countries. In developing countries, the seed industry is in the process of transformation from an industry dominated by small seed companies, on-farm seed provision, and public programmes, to a large integrated business controlled by transnational corporations (TNCs).

The transformation of the global food supply chain in the form of commodity buyers has resulted in increasing control over supplies to meet the standards demanded by global retailers. Also, the food processing industry is rapidly expanding and consolidating. Global retailers and fast food chains are expanding their networks

in developing countries, including South Asia. All these developments of the process of expansion and consolidation of the global food system have resulted in an increasing trend in the concentration of food production and distribution chains in developing countries. These developments provide significant benefits to food retailers, food processors and commodity buyers, while reducing the bargaining power of small-scale food producers and consumers in developing countries.

International agricultural trade and food security[4]

In the Uruguay Round, for the first time, agriculture was brought under the effective purview of a multilateral trading system. It was believed at that time that new WTO rules would bring about a structural change in global agricultural trade, and more efficient agricultural producers would stand to benefit from the WTO agreement. As many developing countries are low cost producers of agricultural goods, it was expected that these countries would significantly benefit from a more open and less distorted global agricultural trade regime.

The rapid process of globalization has changed the global food system which in turn has affected the food as well as nutritional security of both consumers and producers in developing countries

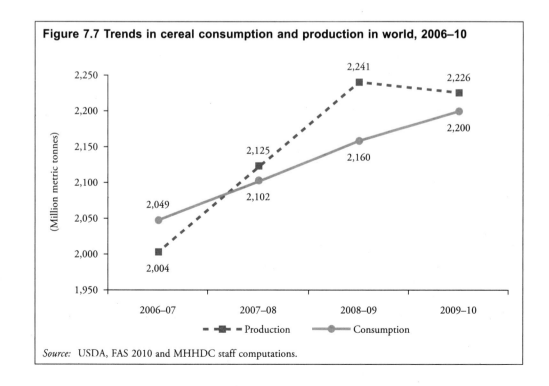

Figure 7.7 Trends in cereal consumption and production in world, 2006–10

Source: USDA, FAS 2010 and MHHDC staff computations.

However, the implementation of the Agreement on Agriculture (AOA) shows that, despite WTO rules, some developed countries still continue to heavily subsidize their agriculture sector, thereby distorting global production and trade. Data show that Organization for Economic Cooperation and Development (OECD) countries pay more than US$300 billion as subsidies to their farm sector. To put this figure into perspective, total global agricultural export is around US$600 billion. As a result of continued distortion, none of the perceived benefits occurred to developing countries. But, on the other hand, opening up of their agricultural sector has exposed the vulnerable section of these countries to market distortions of international commodity trade.

Developed-country farm subsidies hurt farmers in poor countries in a number of ways. First, it restricts their market access in developed countries. In these countries, a high percentage of subsidies are given to farmers through market price support. This basically means that the government pays the farmer an assured price which is higher than the market clearing price. However, such high prices may attract imports. Therefore, to maintain high prices for their subsidized products in their domestic markets, developed countries have to erect high market access barriers (through high tariffs, quotas, or other non-tariff measures) in their own countries. As a result, low cost producers from developing countries are kept out of these markets.

Secondly, as subsidies raise domestic prices of agricultural goods, they encourage farmers to produce more. The surplus production is then dumped into the international market at a cheaper price. Again, subsidies are used to cover the difference between domestic prices and international prices.[5] Excess supply and dumping of agricultural goods drive down their prices in the international markets. The farmers of developing countries suffer from such undercutting not only by losing markets in the export markets but these cheap imports also threaten their domestic production base. This can potentially have disastrous implications for the vulnerable section of the population in developing countries.

In fact, a set of studies[6] done under the 'Import Surge Project' of the FAO has shown that import surges for agricultural products in developing countries have occurred more frequently in the post–1994 period.[7] Under the same project, Sharma[8] has listed a number of case studies where import surges have negatively affected domestic production. For example, in Sri Lanka, vegetable-producing sub-sectors like onions and potatoes have suffered from import surges. In 1999, an import surge of onions and potatoes resulted in a decline in the cultivated area of these crops and affected the livelihood of approximately 300,000 persons involved in their production and marketing.

What is even more ironical is that the subsidies given to farmers in developed countries hardly help the poorer section of the population in those countries. To justify high levels of farm subsidies, it is sometimes argued that agricultural support in developed countries protects the interests of vulnerable communities and serves the objective of rural development in those countries. However, there is little evidence to support this justification. The *WTO Annual Report of 2003* shows that, contrary to popular belief, subsidies in most developed countries are not targeted towards the poor farmers.[9] In fact, in most OECD countries, a very high proportion of subsidies go to the top 25 per cent of farmers. The *Human Development Report 2005* finds that the farm subsidy system in developed countries is extremely inequitable.[10] According to the figures quoted in the report, more than three-quarters of the European Union (EU's) Common Agricultural Policy (CAP) support goes to top 10 per cent of subsidy recipients. The distribution is also skewed in the US where the top five per cent get over half the total subsidies.[11]

Agreement on Trade-Related Intellectual Property Rights (TRIPS)

After the establishment of the WTO in 1995, developing countries, including South Asia, were required to comply with the TRIPS Agreement—the WTO's agreement on intellectual property rights (IPRs). The Agreement requires WTO member countries to register for patents for all inventions, whether processes or products, in all fields of technology. For plant varieties, all member countries are required to provide protection either by *patents* or by a *sui generis system* for protection of plant breeders.

Globally, various actions have been taken to ensure the protection of farmers' rights. South Asian countries are members of various conventions formulated to address the issue of farmers' rights. In 1992, the Convention on Biological Diversity was concluded in part to address the issue of inequitable sharing of the benefits arising from the use of genetic resources among patent holders as well as farmers and local communities. However, implementation of the Convention is still controversial, especially its relation to the TRIPS Agreement. Similarly, the International Treaty on Plant Genetic Resources for Food and Agriculture was adopted in 2001. The objective was the conservation and sustainable use of plant genetic resources for food and agriculture, and the fair and equitable distribution of the benefits among plant breeders and farmers. However, the Treaty does not make the protection of farmer's rights a global responsibility. It makes the national governments responsible for protecting these rights.

The commercialization of the seed industry and the emergence of genetically modified crops have led to increased demand for plant variety protection. There has been a shift from seeing agricultural research as a freely available public good to a monopoly of plant breeders and patent holders. The granting of IPRs in the form of patents or plant breeders' rights is justified to encourage further research and development (R&D) in plant breeding.

However, this process has created a number of concerns for farming communities in developing countries, especially for small-scale and marginal farmers. In South Asia, a vast majority of farmers use locally produced on-farm seeds either produced by themselves or by other farmers. According to a study, 80 to 90 per cent of the farmers in South Asia and Sub-Saharan Africa do not use commercially produced seeds.[12] Women farmers are the key producers of on-farm seeds by cultivating a number of seed varieties.

The use of seeds produced by farmers has many advantages such as: independence of farmers from the expensive commercial seeds, lowering the cost of production; development of locally suitable seeds, and diversification of crops; geographical compatibility with local environments; and resilience to local pests or diseases.

The irony of today's technological development in the agricultural sector is that the main focus of the research is not oriented towards the needs of food security in developing countries. Private companies, and national and international research institutes, are promoting seed varieties for an industrial model of agriculture which is in contrast to the needs of marginal farmers and local systems.

Do farm subsidies help the poor food-importing countries?

There is also a school of thought which argues that rich-world subsidies are a net boon to poor countries because they provide cheap food to the masses. While it is indeed true that in the short run, subsidies contribute to the food security of net food-importing countries, one should be more careful about its longer term implications. There are reasons to believe that the continued subsidization of agricultural goods in developed countries may actually harm the interest of all developing countries in the medium and long term. This happens because:

The irony of today's technological development is the promotion of an industrial model of agriculture which is in contrast to the needs of marginal farmers and local systems

Opening up of agricultural trade is threatening the food security and livelihood security of millions of small farmers who are engaged in subsistence farming

1. Agricultural subsidies lead to artificially competitive products. They hamper the development of agriculture in developing and least developed countries, as farmers find it difficult to compete with these cheap products both in domestic and international markets. This can gradually erode the domestic production base of agriculture and make a country totally dependent on imported food. In such a situation, the food security of these countries becomes totally reliant on the domestic macroeconomic policies followed in the developed countries.

2. Also, reliance on trade to bridge the shortfall between production and consumption is not free from risks. The risks include uncertainty of supplies and world market price instability. Access to the global market in terms of food security requires access to foreign exchange. Further, when needed, food may not be readily available in the international market if there is a simultaneous shortfall in the major supplying markets, leading to a steep rise in prices.

3. Moreover, subsidized exports depress world prices and lead to substantial declines in domestic farmers' income. As food security also incorporates economic access to food, any decline in agricultural income can adversely affect the food security situation of a country.

Because of these reasons, it is somewhat misleading to claim that farm subsidies, which impoverish millions of farmers in developing countries, are actually beneficial for the poor because they bring down the prices of food in the short-run. Such arguments, in fact, are extremely harmful in multilateral negotiations as they can create a division among the developing countries.

To conclude, it is quite obvious that unless trade distortions in this sector are brought down, developing countries do not stand to gain much from the opening up of this sector. On the other hand, opening up of agricultural trade is threatening the food security and livelihood security of millions of small farmers who are engaged in subsistence farming. It must be kept in mind that a very high proportion of farmers in developing countries are small farmers who take to farming not as a commercial proposition, as in the case of developed countries, but because they do not have any other alternative means of livelihood and the land is passed down to them from generations. Here agriculture is a way of life in the rural areas and not a business venture. Naturally these small farmers stand grave risks of losing their livelihood and food security if they are exposed to unfair international competition. Therefore, it is highly unlikely that the agriculture sector in developing countries will benefit much from trade liberalization.

Conclusion and policy recommendations

The food security status of developing countries, particularly South Asia, has deteriorated further in recent years despite global institutions and commitments. Today, about one billion people are hungry worldwide. Despite being an agrarian economy, South Asia has the largest number of undernourished people in the world. However, the current food security situation in South Asia cannot be attributed to lack of progress by global institutions. The situation is directly a result of failure of domestic policies to strengthen the agricultural production base, and empower the poor through job creation and accelerated human development. However, there is still a need to take various regional and international level steps to improve food security in South Asia. For example,

1. International institutions of governance should ensure that their political, economic, and trade policies do not negatively affect the food security of developing countries.
2. A balanced conclusion to the Doha Round is needed to allow developing countries to use various safeguard

mechanisms in case of price and output volatility.

3. There is also a need to improve the international supervisory mechanisms for TNCs to ensure food security of developing countries.

4. South Asian governments should improve the efficiency and capacity of the SAARC Food Bank. There is also an urgent need to encourage intraregional trade in agriculture.

5. There is a need to improve governance at the national, regional, and global levels. National governments should encourage the creation of grain reserves to prevent any volatile increase in prices and to discourage speculation. Also, the entry of financial companies into commodity markets needs to be banned to reduce speculation.

The entry of financial companies into commodity markets needs to be banned to reduce speculation

Background Papers

Gupta, S. 'Food Security in India: Status and Policy'.

Malik, U. 'Food Security in Pakistan'.

Mallick, S. 'Climate Change and Food Security in South Asia'.

Maqbool, N. 'Globalization and Food Security in South Asia'.

Masood, A. 'Food Security: A Conceptual Framework'.

Murad, S. 'Women and Food Security in South Asia'.

Shahabuddin, Q., and U. K. Deb. 'Food Security and Human Development in Bangladesh'.

Notes

Chapter 1

1. FAO 2003 and 2006.
2. FAO 2008a.
3. Hall 1998.
4. World Bank 1986.
5. FAO 2001.
6. FAO 2003.
7. FAO 2009c.
8. FAO 2010e.
9. Bingxin *et al.* 2010.
10. The MDER is the amount of energy needed for light activity and to maintain a minimum acceptable weight for attained height. It varies by country and from year to year depending on the gender and age structure of the population. FAO 2010e.
11. FAO 2011b.
12. FAO 2006.
13. Undernourishment refers to the condition of people whose dietary energy consumption is continuously below a minimum dietary energy requirement (MDER) for maintaining a healthy life and carrying out a light physical activity. FAO 2011b.
14. EC-FAO 2008.
15. Ibid.
16. World Bank 2010.
17. Brinkman and Hendrix 2010.
18. Ibid.
19. IFPRI 2002.
20. Dev 2009.
21. SDPI, SDC and WFP-P 2010.
22. Ibid.
23. Dev 2009.
24. FAO 2003.
25. *Lankapuvath* 2011.
26. FAO 2003.
27. Downes 2004.
28. FAO 2010e.
29. FAO 2011e.
30. Seddon and Adhikari 2003.
31. Ibid.
32. World Bank 2011e.
33. CIMMYT 2010.
34. IFPRI 2009.
35. World Bank 2010.
36. Dev 2009.
37. World Bank 2008.
38. Dev 2009.
39. Ibid.
40. WFP, UNICEF and GOB 2009.
41. FAO 2010e.
42. Cook and Jeng 2009.
43. Alderman *et al.* 2006.
44. World Bank 2010.
45. Hamelin *et al.* 1999.
46. Cook and Jeng 2009.
47. Reid 2000.
48. Allouche 2011.
49. Brinkman and Hendrix 2011.
50. *India Daily* 2008.
51. *Dawn* 2009.
52. Brinkman and Hendrix 2011.
53. Pradhan 2008.
54. SDPI, SDC and WFP-P 2010.

Chapter 2

1. GOI 2007a.
2. GOI, *Economic Survey of India* (various issues)
3. GOI 2006b.
4. FAO 2011a.
5. GOI 2008.
6. Deaton and Dreze 2008.
7. GOI 2007a.
8. Kumar, A.K.S. 2007.
9. The land legislation aimed to create capitalist landlords and rich peasants and was not 'land to the tiller'.
10. The government's expenditure, including subsidies to agricultural inputs, credit, inputs like seeds, fertilizers, etc., irrigation, power and other infrastructural facilities were cornered by the agrarian elite in the well-endowed regions.
11. Swaminathan 2008.
12. GOI 2005.
13. Swaminathan 2008.
14. GOP 2005.
15. Khera 2006.
16. Rajivan 2001.
17. Ibid.
18. GOI 2010.
19. GOI 2006a.

Chapter 3

1. GOP 2009c.
2. MHHDC 2010/2011 *Human Development Indicators for South Asia*.
3. MHHDC 2003.
4. GOP 2010c.
5. Ibid.
6. Ibid.
7. Ibid.
8. Ahmed 2009.
9. MHHDC and UNDP forthcoming.
10. World Bank 2010.
11. GOP 2010a.
12. Ibid.

13. 1973 and 1979 were the exceptions when global oil price shocks resulted in double-digit inflation.
14. GOP 2009b.
15. Ibid.
16. WWF 2007.
17. GOP 2010b.
18. USAID 2010c.
19. GOP 2010c.
20. Ibid.
21. Iqbal 2010.
22. GOP 2010c.
23. GOP forthcoming.
24. GOP 2009c.
25. Ibid.
26. Ibid.
27. Kardar 2008.
28. USAID 2010b.
29. Ibid.
30. USAID 2010a.
31. SDPI, SDC and WFP-P 2010.
32. USAID 2010a.
33. Ibid.
34. Ibid.
35. Ibid
36. GOP 2009c.
37. GOP 2006.
38. UN 2008.
39. WFP-P 2010.
40. World bank 2011d.
41. GOP 2010b.
42. UN 2008.
43. MHHDC 2010/2011 *Human Development Indicators for South Asia*.
44. UN 2008.
45. GOP, UNICEF and PIDE 2004.
46. MHHDC 2010/2011 *Human Development Indicators*.
47. UN 2008.

Chapter 4

1. Since the area under early-monsoon low-yielding *aus* rice (April to July) has been reduced from 3.5 to 1.1 million hectares; the loss of production due to drought (late arrival of monsoon) is now substantially lower than before. Similarly, the area under deep-water *aman* rice (March to November) has been reduced from 2.2 to 0.7 million hectares thereby considerably reducing crop losses due to floods. The *boro* rice area, on the other hand, has expanded from 0.5 million hectares in the early 1970s to nearly 4.5 million hectares in 2008.
2. Hossain and Deb 2009a.
3. Bangladesh does not export any other food item except shrimp and aromatic rice.
4. Hossain and Deb 2009.
5. The growth of population declined slowly from about 3.0 per cent in the 1960s to 2.4 per cent in the 1980s, but then sharply to 1.4 per cent in the 1990s.
6. The use of deflator for measuring the real wage is also problematic.
7. Workers engaged in the urban informal sector such as rickshaw pullers and petty traders were also able to adjust their real income somewhat by asking for higher fares and marketing margin. The worst affected were the workers in the urban labour markets such as those engaged in the low-wage garment industry and low-paid employees in the services sector, since their wages remained fixed. The recent downward movement in coarse rice prices, however, has improved the situation.
8. These include, among others, rural infrastructure development, boosting primary school enrolment rates and human capital development.
9. One, however, gets a contrasting picture in the rural and urban areas in this respect. While the number of food-insecure and vulnerable people declined by 4.1 million in the rural areas, this has increased by 4.5 million in urban areas over the last two decades (between 1985–86 and 2005).
10. Chowdhury 1993.
11. A nutrition survey carried out by the Bangladesh Institute of Development Studies (BIDS) in 1990–91 also reported similar findings of maldistribution of food within the household. The findings indicated that none of the boys and girls under the age of 20 years met the calorie requirements. The younger they were, the higher was the deficiency. The girls were in more disadvantaged situation than boys in this respect.
12. Hossain and Deb 2009a.
13. Murshid *et al.* 2008.
14. Deb, Hossain and Jones 2009.
15. CEGIS 2006, Sultana *et al.* 2008 and Yu *et al.* 2010.
16. Deb, Hossain and Jones 2009.
17. Dorosh *et al.* 2003.
18. Hossain and Deb 2003.
19. Hossain and Deb 2010 forthcoming.
20. Ali 2005.
21. Hossain 2001.
22. CPD 2006.
23. Rahman *et al.* 2009.
24. Mahmud and Osmani 1980.
25. Siddiqui and Abrar 2001.
26. Adams and Page 2005.
27. Afsar *et al.* 2002.
28. Afsar *et al.* 2002 and Siddiqui and Abrar 2001.
29. Mahmood 1991.
30. Hossain and Deb 2009b.
31. FAO 2008b.
32. Raihan 2009.
33. Sulaiman *et al.* 2009.
34. Ibid.
35. Hossain and Deb 2010 and forthcoming.
36. Hossain 1996.
37. Ahmed *et al.* 2010.

38. Strictly speaking, although data are available for more recent years, these are not comparable due to definitional changes of the programmes.

39. The budgetary allocation of the government for safety net programmes however, has increased in recent years—from BTK114,674 million in 2007–08 to BTK138,453 million in 2008–09 and further to BTK159,720 million in 2009–10. The allocation increased substantially in the last two years mainly due to the introduction of 100-day Employment Generation Programme in September 2008 created to mitigate the impact of 2007–08 food price crisis and the recently introduced Employment Generation of Hard Core Poor Programme. Ibid.

40. Mandal *et al.* 2007.

41. GOB 2009a.

42. It is possible to increase area under high-yielding *aman* rice, particularly in the coastal belt. *Aman* rice has lower unit cost of production and higher profitability compared to *boro* rice and is competitive internationally. Deb, Khaled, Amin and Nabi 2009.

43. Asaduzzaman *et al.* 2010.

44. However, the recent escalation in food prices has demonstrated that a liberalized trade regime cannot guarantee stable supplies and prices. In fact, the international market can no longer be relied as a source of food grains when there is a shortage in the domestic market. A shift in strategy from self-reliance to self-sufficiency in food has thus become imperative for a food importing country like Bangladesh.

45. Hossain and Deb 2003.

46. Dorosh *et al.* 2004.

47. Ahmed *et al.* 2010.

48. Using the National Centre for Health Statistics (NCHS) reference standards for anthropometry, which are the same as those used in Millennium Development Goals (MDGs) target, it has been observed that the proportion of underweight children has dropped from 60 per cent in 1996 to 46 per cent in 2007. Stunting has shown a steady decline as well with severe stunting also declining from 28 to 16 per cent in a matter of one decade between 1996–97 and 2007. The declines in stunting are particularly encouraging given the long-term impact of stunting on later cognition schooling and other development outcomes. However, given the stalling of the trend in underweight, accelerating efforts to improve nutrition will be essential to achieve the MDGs target of 33 per cent child underweight by 2015. Sen *et al.* 2010.

49. Ahmed and Ahmed 2009. Interventions that are particularly important to address are early and exclusive breastfeeding, age-appropriate complimentary feeding, ensuring diet quality through diversified diets and additional food/micronutrients supplements as needed, treatment of acute malnutrition when needed and improved maternal nutrition, and sanitation interventions.

50. Sen *et al.* 2010.

Chapter 5

1. FAO 2011e.
2. MHHDC 2003.
3. Karl 2009.
4. MHHDC 2003.
5. FAO, IFAD and ILO 2010.
6. Quisumbing *et al.* 1995.
7. FAO 2011e.
8. FAO 2011d.
9. Quisumbing *et al.* 1995.
10. MHHDC 2003.
11. FAO 2011e.
12. MHHDC 2004.
13. Tibbo *et al.* 2009.
14. FAO 2011e.
15. Ibid.
16. MHHDC 2003.
17. Ibid.
18. Ibid.
19. Tibbo *et al.* 2009.
20. Ibid.
21. Ramachandran 2006.
22. FAO 2011e.
23. Bina 2003 cited in FAO, IFAD and ILO 2010.
24. FAO, IFAD and ILO 2010.
25. MHHDC 2003.
26. Ramachandran 2006.
27. Revathi 2005.
28. Ibid.
29. For further reading, please see box 7.2 in *Human Development in South Asia 2002: Agriculture and Rural Development.* MHHDC 2003.
30. Ramachandran 2006.
31. FAO, IFAD and ILO 2010.
32. MHHDC 2004.
33. FAO 2011e.
34. MHHDC 2004.
35. FAO, IFAD and ILO 2010.
36. Ramachandran 2006.
37. Ibid.
38. FAO, IFAD and ILO 2010.
39. Ibid.
40. FAO 2011e.
41. FAO, IFAD and ILO 2010.
42. Ramachandran 2006.
43. Ibid.
44. MHHDC 2004.
45. Ibid.
46. Quisumbing *et al.* 1995.
47. Ramachandran 2006.
48. MHHDC 2004.
49. FAO 2011e.
50. Ibid.
51. Ibid.
52. FAO 2010e.
53. Ramachandran 2006.

54. Revathi 2005.
55. Ramachandran 2006.
56. Ibid.
57. Ramachandran 2006 and UNESCAP 2009.
58. World Bank 2011d.
59. MHHDC 2010/2011 *Human Development Indicators for South Asia*.
60. Thakur *et al.* 2009.
61. Holmes and Jones 2010.
62. Holmes *et al.* 2010.
63. DFID 2011.
64. Ibid.

Chapter 6

1. World Bank 2011e.
2. Utrecht University 2010.
3. Barley 2010.
4. World Bank 2005.
5. Namgyel 2010.
6. FAO 2009b.
7. Badjeck *et al.* 2009.
8. ADB 2004.
9. Tietze *et al.* 2000.
10. Caritas, India 2010.
11. Red Orbit 2009.
12. Shrestha 1997.
13. Dixit 2010.
14. Rockstrom *et al.* 2008.
15. ADB 1989.
16. *IRIN News, UN-OCHA* 2010.
17. Pudasaini 2010.
18. *Bhutan Observer* 2010.
19. Banerjee and Collins 2010.
20. CSE, India 2010.

21. PTI News Agency 2010.
22. Narain 2003.
23. GOS 2006.
24. Rahman 2010.
25. CPWF 2010.
26. MFF 2010.

Chapter 7

1. As quoted in Aziz 1975.
2. Mittal and Sethi 2009.
3. Kohler and Toole 2009.
4. The following discussion is drawn on *Human Development in South Asia 2009: Trade and Human Development*, pp. 11–17. MHHDC 2010.
5. A report by Institute of Agriculture and Trade Policy (IATP) points out that the US data of 2002 show that wheat was exported at an average price of 43 per cent below cost of production; Soybeans were exported at an average price of 25 per cent below cost of production; Corn was exported at an average price of 13 per cent below cost of production; Cotton was exported at an average price of 61 per cent below cost of production and Rice was exported at an average price of 35 per cent below cost of production. See IATP 2004.
6. FAO 2009a.
7. Nigris 2005.
8. Sharma 2005.
9. WTO 2003.
10. UNDP 2005.
11. Ibid., p. 130.
12. 3D 2009.

References

Adams, R. H., and J. Page. 2005. Do International Migration and Remittances Reduce Poverty in Developing Countries? *World Development* 33(10): 1645–69.

ADB (Asian Development Bank). 1989. *Rainfed Agriculture in Asia and the Pacific*. Manila: ADB.

———. 2004. Sindh Coastal and Inland Community Development Project: Pakistan. http://pid.adb.org/pid/TaView.htm?projNo=37188&seqNo=01&typeCd=2 (accessed December 2010).

———. 2010. *Key Indicators for Asia and the Pacific 2010*. Manila: ADB.

———. 2011. Statistical Database System. https://sdbs.adb.org/sdbs/index.jsp (accessed April 2011).

Afsar R., M. Yunus, and A.B.M.S. Islam. 2002. *Are Migrants after the "Golden Deer"? A Study on Cost-Benefit Analysis of Overseas Migration by the Bangladeshi Labour*. Dhaka: International Organization for Migration, Regional Office for South Asia.

Ahmed. F. 2009. Food Security in Pakistan. *Pakistan Journal of Agriculture Sciences* 46(2).

Ahmed, M., and U. Farooq. 2010. The State of Food Security in Pakistan: Future Challenges and Coping Strategies. Paper presented at the Pakistan Society for Development Economics (PSDE) 26th Annual Conference on 'Fiscal Decentralization: Empowering the Provinces and Strengthening the Federation', 28–30 December, Islamabad. Islamabad: PSDE.

Ahmed, A.U., P. Dorosh, Q. Shahabuddin, and R.A. Talukder. 2010. Income Growth, Safety Nets, and Public Food Distribution. Paper presented at the Bangladesh Food Security Investment Forum 2010, 26–27 May 2010, organized by Ministry of Food and Disaster Management.

Ahmed, T., and A.M.S. Ahmed. 2009. Reducing the Burden of Malnutrition in Bangladesh. *British Medical Journal* 339.

Alderman, H., J. Hoddinott and B. Kinsey. 2006. Long Term Consequences of Early Childhood Malnutrition. *Oxford Economic Papers* 58: 450–75.

Ali, A. 2005. Livelihood and Food Security in Rural Bangladesh: The Role of Social Capital. PhD Thesis submitted to the Wageningen University. http://edepot.wur.nl/121729 (accessed November 2010).

Allouche, J. 2011. The Sustainability and Resilience of Global Water and Food Systems: Political Analysis of the Interplay between Security, Resource Scarcity, Political Systems and Global Trade. *Food Policy* 36: S3–S8.

Asaduzzaman, M., C. Ringler, J. Thurlow and S. Alam. 2010. Investing in Crop Agriculture in Bangladesh for Higher Growth and Productivity, and Adaptation to Climate Change. Paper prepared for the Bangladesh Food Security Investment Forum. http://www.bids.org.bd/ifpri/investing6.pdf (accessed December 2010).

Aziz, S. 1975. *Hunger, Politics and Markets: The Real Issues in the Food Crisis*. New York: New York University Press.

Badjeck, M.C., E.H. Allison, A.S. Halls and N.K. Dulvy. 2009. Impacts of Climate Variability and Change on Fishery-Based Livelihoods. *Marine Policy* 34(3): 375–83.

Banerjee, B., and G. Collins. 2010. Anatomy of IPCC's Mistake on Himalayan Glaciers and Year 2035: Undoing 'The Curse' of a Chain of Errors. The Yale Forum on Climate Change and the Media, 4 February. http://www.yaleclimatemediaforum.org/2010/02/anatomy-of-ipccs-himalayan-glacier-year–2035-mess (accessed September 2010).

Barley, S. 2010. Himalayan Ice is Stable, But Asia Faces Drought. *New Scientist* 10 June. http://www.newscientist.com/article/dn19029-himalayan-ice-is-stable-but-asia-faces-drought.html (accessed April 2011).

Bhutan Observer. 2010. Himalayan Countries Discuss Roadmap to Adapt to Climate Change. 22 August.

BICC (Bonne International Centre for Conversion). 2011. The Global Militarization Index. http://www.bicc.de/our-work/gmi.html (accessed April 2011).

Bina, A. 2003. Gender and Land Rights Revisited: Exploring New Prospects via the State, Family and Market. *Journal of Agrarian Change* 3(1): 184–224.

Bingxin, Y., L. You and S. Fan. 2010. Toward a Typology of Food Security in Developing Countries. International Food Policy Research Institute (IFPRI) Discussion Paper No. 945. http://www.ifpri.org/sites/default/files/publications/ifpridp00945.pdf (accessed April 2011).

Brinkman, H.J., and C.S. Hendrix. 2010. Food Insecurity and Conflict: Applying the WDR Framework. Background Paper for the World Development Report 2011. Washington, D.C.: World Bank.

Caritas, India. 2010. Desertification in India. http://www.caritas.org/activities/climate_

change/desertification_in_india.html (accessed September 2010).

CBGA (Centre for Budget and Governance Accountability). 2010. *Response to the Union Budget 2010–11: Which Way Now?* New Delhi: CBGA.

CEGIS (Centre for Environmental and Geographic Information Services). 2006. *Impact of Sea Level Rise on Land Use Suitability and Adaptation Options*. Dhaka: CEGIS.

Chowdhury, O.H. 1993. 'Review of Rural Nutrition'. In *Growth and Development in Rural Bangladesh: A Critical Review*, eds. Asaduzzaman, M., and K. Westergaard. Dhaka: University Press Limited.

CIMMYT (International Maize and Wheat Improvement Centre). 2010. CIMMYT and the Government of India to Launch a Second Green Revolution in India. http://www.cimmyt.org/ru/component/content/article/172-media-resources/780-cimmyt-and-the-government-of-india-to-launch-a-second-green-revolution-in-south-asia (accessed April 2011).

Cook, J., and K. Jeng. 2009. *Child Food Insecurity: The Economic Impact on Our Nation*. Chicago: Feeding America.

CPD (Centre for Policy Dialogue). 2006. *Regional Cooperation in South Asia: A Review of Bangladesh's Development 2004*. Dhaka: University Press Limited (UPL).

CPWF (CGIAR Challenge Program on Water and Food). 2010. PN10—Coastal Resource Management for Improving Livelihoods. https://sites.google.com/a/cpwf.info/phase1/phase–1-projects-overview/pn10—coastal-resource-management-for-improving-livelihoods (accessed February 2011).

CRED (Centre for Research on the Epidemiology of Disasters). 2011. EM-DAT: The International Disaster Database. http://www.emdat.be/database (accessed April 2011).

CSE (Centre for Science and Environment), India. 2010. What is Drought? http://www.rainwaterharvesting.org/crisis/Drought.htm (accessed September 2010).

Dawn. 2009. Karachi: Rice Dealer Testifies in Stampede Deaths Case. 18 September.

Deaton, A., and J. Drèze 2008. Nutrition in India: Facts and Interpretations. http://wws-roxen.princeton.edu/chwpapers/papers/deaton_dreze_india_nutrition.pdf (accessed December 2010).

Deb, U.K. 2005. Trade Liberalization and Bangladesh Agriculture: Impacts on Cropping Pattern, Resource Use Efficiency and Effective Incentives. A Report prepared at the Centre for Policy Dialogue (CPD) under Research Programme IV of the South Asia Network of Economic Research Institutes (SANEI). Mimeo.

Deb, U.K., M. Hossain and S. Jones. 2009. Rethinking Food Security Strategy in Bangladesh: Self-Sufficiency or Self-Reliance. Research Monograph No. 3. Dhaka: Department for International Development (DFID).

Deb, U.K., N. Khaled, M.A. Amin, and A. Nabi. 2009. Climate Change and Rice Production in Bangladesh: Implications for R&D Strategy. Paper presented at the Special Conference on 'Climate Change and Bangladesh Development Strategy: Domestic Tasks and International Cooperation', 2 January, Institute of Cost and Management Accountants of Bangladesh, Nilkhet, Dhaka. Dhaka: Bangladesh Paribesh Andolan (BAPA) and Bangladesh Environment Network (BEN).

Dev, S.M. 2009. Rising Food Prices and Financial Crisis in India: Impact on Women and Children and Ways for Tackling the Problem. Paper prepared for the United Nations Children's Fund (UNICEF) Social Policy Programme. http://www.unglobalpulse.org/sites/all/files/reports/Rising%20Food%20Prices%20in%20India%20UNICEF%20Final.pdf (accessed April 2011).

DFID (Department for International Development). 2011. Cash Transfers Evidence Paper. http://www.dfid.gov.uk/r4d/PDF/Articles/Evidence_Paper-FINAL-CLEARAcknowledgement.pdf (accessed May 2011).

Dixit, K. 2010. From Nepal to Maldives, Eyewitness Sees Impact of Warming, Melting Glaciers: Bursting Glacial Lakes, Storm Surges and Drought Among the Dangers. *Solve Climate News* 18 March.

Dorosh, P., Q. Shahabudin and N. Farid. 2004. 'Price Stabilization and Food Stock Policy'. In *The 1998 Floods and Beyond: Towards Comprehensive Food Security in Bangladesh*, eds. Dorosh, P., C.D. Ninno and Q. Shahabuddin. Dhaka: University Press Limited and International Food Policy Research Institute.

Dorosh, P., C.D. Ninno and Q. Shahabuddin. 2003. *The 1998 Flood and Beyond: Moving Towards a Comprehensive Food Security in Bangladesh*. Dhaka: University Press Limited and International Food Policy Research Institute.

Dowlah, C.A.F. 2003. 'Bangladesh'. In *Agriculture, Trade, and the WTO in South Asia*, ed. Ingco, M.D. Washington, D.C.: World Bank.

Downes, G. 2004. TRIPs and Food Security: Implications of the WTO's TRIPs Agreement for Food Security in the Developing World. *British Food Journal* 106(5): 366–79.

EC-FAO (European Commission-Food and Agriculture Organization of the United Nations). 2008. Food Security Information for Action: What is Food Security? http://www.foodsec.org/DL/course/shortcourseFC/en/lesson.asp?lessoncode=0411 (accessed February 2011).

FAO (Food and Agriculture Organization of the United Nations). 2001. *The State of Food Insecurity in the World 2001: When People Live with Hunger and Fear Starvation*. Rome: FAO.

———. 2003. *Trade Reforms and Food Security: Conceptualizing the Linkages*. Rome: FAO.

_____. 2006. Food Security. Policy Brief No. 2. ftp://ftp.fao.org/es/ESA/policybriefs/pb_02.pdf (accessed January 2011).

_____. 2008a. High Prices or Food Crisis? Context and Perspectives. Paper prepared for the High-Level Conference on 'Food Security: The Challenges of Climate Change and Bioenergy', 3–5 June, Rome. Rome: FAO.

_____. 2008b. FAO/WFP Crop and Food Supply Assessment Mission to Bangladesh: Special Report. http://www.fao.org/docrep/011/ai472e/ai472e00.htm (accessed December 2010).

_____. 2009a. FAO Import Surge Project. http://www.google.co.in/search?q=+site:www.fao.org+%22FAO+Import+Surge+Project%22&hl=en&lr=&safe=off&filter=0 (accessed October 2009).

_____. 2009b. Fisheries and Aquaculture: Multiple Risks from Climate Change. http://www.fao.org/news/story/en/item/38060/icode/ (accessed December 2010).

_____. 2009c. The State of Food Insecurity in the World 2009: Economic Crises: Impacts and Lessons Learned. Rome: FAO.

_____. 2010a. Country Profile: Food Security Indicators: Pakistan. http://www.fao.org/fileadmin/templates/ess/documents/food_security_statistics/country_profiles/eng/Pakistan_E.pdf (accessed April 2011).

_____. 2010b. Food Prices Indices. http://www.fao.org:80/fileadmin/templates/worldfood/Reports_and_docs/Food_price_indices_data.xls (accessed August 2010).

_____. 2010c. Hunger Statistics. http://www.fao.org/hunger/en/ (access August 2010).

_____. 2010d. Post Flood Food Security in Pakistan. Paper presented in a seminar on 'Flood Damage and Coping Strategies', 8 September, ILO office, Islamabad. Islamabad: WFP, SDC and SDPI.

_____. 2010e. The State of Food Insecurity in the World 2010: Addressing Food Insecurity in Protracted Crises. Rome: FAO.

_____. 2011a. FAOSTAT. http://faostat.fao.org/default.aspx (accessed April 2011).

_____. 2011b. Food Security Statistics. http://www.fao.org/economic/ess/ess-fs/en/ (accessed April 2011).

_____. 2011c. Gender and Land Rights Database. http://www.fao.org/gender/landrights (accessed May 2011).

_____. 2011d. Module 1: Gender and Food Security. http://siteresources.worldbank.org/INTGENAGRLIVSOUBOOK/Resources/Module1.pdf (accessed May 2011).

_____. 2011e. The State of Food and Agriculture 2010–11: Women in Agriculture: Closing the Gender Gap for Development. Rome: FAO. Available at http://www.fao.org/publications/sofa/en/ (accessed May 2011).

FAO (Food and Agriculture Organization of the United Nations), IFAD (International Fund for Agricultural Development) and ILO (International Labour Office). 2010. Gender Dimensions of Agricultural and Rural Employment: Differentiated Pathways Out of Poverty: Status, Trends and Gaps. Rome: FAO, IFAD and ILO. http://www.fao.org/docrep/013/i1638e/i1638e.pdf (accessed May 2011).

GOB (Government of Bangladesh). Various issues. Bangladesh Economic Review. Dhaka: Ministry of Finance.

_____. Various issues. Labour Force Survey. Dhaka: Bangladesh Bureau of Statistics.

_____. Various issues. Monthly Statistical Bulletin. Dhaka: Bangladesh Bureau of Statistics.

_____. 2000. Annual Report 1998/99. Dhaka: Food Planning and Monitoring Unit, Ministry of Food and Disaster Management.

_____. 2001a. Annual Report 1999/2001. Dhaka: Food Planning and Monitoring Unit, Ministry of Food and Disaster Management.

_____. 2001b. Preliminary Report of Household Income and Expenditure Survey 2000. Dhaka: Bangladesh Bureau of Statistics.

_____. 2007. Report of the Household Income and Expenditure Survey 2005. Dhaka: Bangladesh Bureau of Statistics.

_____. 2009a. National Strategy for Accelerated Poverty Reduction II (Revised) FY2009–11: Steps towards Change. Dhaka: Planning Commission.

_____. 2009b. Report on Monitoring of Employment Survey 2009. Dhaka: Bangladesh Bureau of Statistics.

GOI (Government of India). Various issues. Agricultural Statistics at a Glance. New Delhi: Ministry of Agriculture. http://agricoop.nic.in/Agristatistics.htm (access August 2010).

_____. Various issues. Annual Reports. New Delhi: Department of Food and Public Distribution, Ministry of Consumer Affairs, Food and Public Distribution.

_____. Various issues. Economic Survey of India. New Delhi: Ministry of Finance.

_____. Various issues. Employment and Unemployment Situation in India. New Delhi: National Sample Survey Organization (NSSO), Ministry of Statistics and Programme Implementation.

_____. 1991. Census of India 1991. New Delhi: Ministry of Home Affairs.

_____. 2000. National Family Health Survey (NFHS–2) 1998–99, India. Mumbai: International Institute for Population Sciences. http://www.nfhsindia.org/india2.shtml (accessed September 2010).

_____. 2001. Census of India 2001. New Delhi: Ministry of Home Affairs.

_____. 2005. Performance Evaluation of Targeted Public Distribution System (TPDS). New Delhi: Planning Commission. http://planningcommission.nic.in/reports/peoreport/peo/peo_tpds.pdf (accessed September 2010).

_____. 2006a. Employment and Unemployment Situation in India 2004–05. National Sample Survey (NSS) 61st Round, Report No. 515. New

Delhi: Ministry of Statistics and Programme Implementation.

———. 2006b. *Mid-Term Evaluation of the Tenth Plan*. New Delhi: Planning Commission.

———. 2007a. *National Family Health Survey (NFHS-3) 2005–06, India*. Mumbai: International Institute for Population Sciences.

———. 2007b. *Public Distribution System and Other Sources of Household Consumption 2004–05*. National Sample Survey (NSS) 61st Round, Report No. 510. New Delhi: Ministry of Statistics and Programme Implementation.

———. 2007c. *Report on Conditions of Work and Promotion of Livelihoods in the Unorganised Sector*. New Delhi: National Commission for Enterprises in the Unorganised Sector. http://nceuis.nic.in/Condition_of_workers_sep_2007.pdf (accessed December 2010).

———. 2008. *Household Consumer Expenditure in India 2006–07*. National Sample Survey (NSS) 63rd Round, Report No. 527. New Delhi: Ministry of Statistics and Programme Implementation.

———. 2010. *Economic Survey of India 2009–10*. New Delhi: Ministry of Finance.

GOP (Government of Pakistan). Forthcoming. *Pakistan Framework for Economic Growth*. Islamabad: Planning Commission.

———. 2003. *Pakistan Economic Survey 2002–03*. Islamabad: Ministry of Finance.

———. 2004. *Pakistan Economic Survey 2003–04*. Islamabad: Ministry of Finance.

———. 2006. *Household Income and Expenditure Survey 2005–06*. Islamabad: Federal Bureau of Statistics.

———. 2009a. *Agriculture Statistics of Pakistan 2008–09*. Islamabad: Ministry of Food and Agriculture.

———. 2009b. *Household Income and Expenditure Survey 2007–08*. Islamabad: Federal Bureau of Statistics.

———. 2009c. *Task Force on Food Security: Final Report*. Islamabad: Planning Commission.

———. 2010a. *Pakistan Labour Force Survey 2008–09*. Islamabad: Federal Bureau of Statistics.

———. 2010b. *Millennium Development Goals Report 2010: Development Amidst Crisis*. Planning Commission and Centre for Poverty Reduction and Social Policy Development. Islamabad.

———. 2010c. *Pakistan Economic Survey 2009–10*. Islamabad: Ministry of Finance.

———. 2011. *Monthly Review on Price Indices*. February 2011. Islamabad: Federal Bureau of Statistics. http://www.statpak.gov.pk/fbs/sites/default/files/price_statistics/monthly_price_indices/mpi2/cpi_detail.pdf (accessed April 2011).

GOP (Government of Pakistan), UNICEF (United Nations Children's Fund) and PIDE (Pakistan Institute of Development Economics). 2004. *National Nutrition Survey of Pakistan 2001–02*. Islamabad: GOP, UNICEF and PIDE.

GOS (Government of Sri Lanka). 2006. Gazette Extraordinary of the Democratic Socialist Republic of Sri Lanka 2006. http://www.coastal.gov.lk/czmp%20english.pdf (accessed September 2010).

Hall, D.O. 1998. Food Security: What Have Sciences to Offer? A study for International Council for Science (ICSU). http://www.icsu.org/publications/reports-and-reviews/food-security (accessed April 2011).

Hamelin, A.M., J.P. Habicht and M. Beaudry. 1999. Food Insecurity: Consequences for the Household and Broader Social Implications. *The Journal of Nutrition* 129(2s): 525S–528S.

Haq, S. 2010. Food Insecurity in Pakistan 2009. Paper presented at 13th Conference on 'Peace and Sustainable Development in South Asia: The Way Forward', 21–23 December, Sustainable Development Policy Institute (SDPI). Islamabad: SDPI.

Holmes, R., and N. Jones. 2010. Gender-Sensitive Social Protection and the MDGs. Overseas Development Institute Briefing Paper No. 61.

Holmes, R., N. Sadana, and S. Rath. 2010. *Gendered Risks, Poverty and Vulnerability in India: Case Study of the Indian Mahatma Gandhi National Rural Employment Guarantee Act (Madhya Pradesh)*. London: Overseas Development Institute and Indian Institute of Dalit Studies. Available at http://www.odi.org.uk/resources/download/5089.pdf (accessed May 2011).

Hossain, M. 1996. 'Agricultural Policies in Bangladesh: Evolution and Impact on Crop Production'. In *State, Market and Development: Essays in Honour of Rehman Sobhan*, eds. Abdullah, A., and A.R. Khan. Dhaka: University Press Limited.

Hossain, M., and A. Bayes. 2010. *Rural Economy and Livelihoods: Insights from Bangladesh*. Dhaka: AH Development Publishing House.

Hossain, M., and U.K. Deb. Forthcoming. Volatility in Rice Prices and Policy Resources in Bangladesh. In *The Rice Crisis: Markets, Policies and Food Security*, ed. David, D.D. London and Washington, D.C.: Earthscan.

———. 2003. Trade Liberalization and the Crop Sector in Bangladesh. Centre for Policy Dialogue (CPD) Occasional Paper No. 23. Dhaka: CPD.

———. 2009a. 'Food Security and Containing Price Inflation: Facts and Implications for Policy'. In *Development of Bangladesh with Equity and Justice: Immediate Tasks for the New Government*, ed. Centre for Policy Dialogue (CPD). Dhaka: CPD.

———. 2009b. Recent Food Crisis in Bangladesh: An Anatomy of Causes, Consequences and Policy Actions. Paper presented in an Asia Regional Meeting organized by International Food Policy Research Institute, July 30–31 in New Delhi, India.

————. 2010. *A Study on Crop Agriculture and Agrarian Reforms in Bangladesh: Present Status and Future Options.* Background Studies No. 6 for the Sixth Five-Year Plan (2011–2015). Dhaka: Bangladesh Institute of Development Studies.

Hossain, M.Z. 2001. Rural-Urban Migration in Bangladesh: A Micro-Level Study. Paper presented at the International Union for the Scientific Study of Population (USSP) General Conference, 20–24 August, Salvador.

IATP (Institute of Agriculture Trade Policy). 2004. United States Dumping on World Agricultural Markets. Cancun Series Paper No. 1. http://www.iatp.org/iatp/publications.cfm?accountID=451&refID=26018 (accessed April 2011).

IFPRI (International Food Policy Research Institute). 2002. Green Revolution: Curse or Blessing? http://www.ifpri.org/sites/default/files/pubs/pubs/ib/ib11.pdf (accessed April 2011).

————. 2009. Impact of Climate Change on Agriculture—Factsheets. http://www.ifpri.org/sites/default/files/20090930fsall.pdf (accessed March 2011).

————. 2010. *2010 Global Hunger Index: The Challenge of Hunger: Focus on the Crisis of Child Undernutrition.* Washington, D.C., Bonn and Dublin: IFPRI.

India Daily. 2008. Food Riots in Bangladesh, Egypt and Philippines: Many Other Nations Ready to Explode. 12 April.

Iqbal, S. 2010. Farm Sector to be Key Driver of Growth for five Years. *Dawn* 3 March.

Iqbal, M., and R. Amjad, 2011. Food Security in South Asia: Strategies and Programmes for Regional Collaboration. South Asia Network of Economic Research Institutes (SANEI) Working Paper No. 11. Dhaka: SANEI.

IRIN (Integrated Regional Information Networks) *News, UN-OCHA* (United Nations Office for the Coordination of Humanitarian Affairs). 2010. Nepal: Training Farmers to Adapt to Unpredictable Weather. 19 July.

Kardar, S. 2008. Economy: Understanding the Wheat Crisis. *Daily Times* 22 January. http://www.dailytimes.com.pk/default.asp?page=2008%5C01%5C22%5Cstory_22–1–2008_pg3_3 (accessed April 2011).

Karan, A.K., and S. Selvaraj. 2008. *Trends in Wages and Earnings in India: Increasing Wage Differentials in a Segmented Labour Market.* New Delhi: Sub Regional Office for South Asia, International Labour Organization (ILO). http://www.ilo.org/wcmsp5/groups/public/—asia/—ro-bangkok/documents/publication/wcms_098852.pdf (accessed December 2010).

Karl, M. 2009. Inseparable: The Crucial Role of Women in Food Security Revisited. Women in Action. http://www.isiswomen.org/downloads/wia/wia–2009–1/1wia09_00aFeatures_Karl.pdf (accessed May 2011).

Khalil, J.K. 2007. *Food Security with Special Reference to Pakistan.* Islamabad: Higher Education Commission, Government of Pakistan.

Khera, R. 2006. Mid-day Meals in Primary Schools. *Economic and Political Weekly* 18 November: 4742–50.

Kohler, G., and D. Toole. 2009. The Impact of Crises on Children: A Policy View from South Asia. *Global Social Policy* 9(5): 16–20.

Kumar, A.K.S. 2007. Why are Levels of Child Malnutrition Not Improving? *Economic and Political Weekly* 14 April: 1337–45.

Lankapuvath. 2011. Mahinda Chinthana Implements Mid-Day Meal to School Children. 8 January.

Mahmood, R.A. 1991. Employment of Bangladeshis Abroad and Uses of their Remittances. Bangladesh Institute of Development Studies. Mimeo.

Mahmud, W., and S.R. Osmani. 1980. Manpower Export from Bangladesh to the Middle East: A Cost Benefit Analysis. Bangladesh Institute of Development Studies. Mimeo.

Malik, A. 2009. Sugar and Political Power. *The News* 12 September. http://www.thenews.com.pk/TodaysPrintDetail.aspx?ID=198042&Cat=9&dt=9/12/2009 (accessed May 2011).

Mandal, M.A.S., M.M. Rahman, U.K. Deb, M.I. Hossain, M.R.A. Talukder, S.M.H. Uddin and M. Kamal. 2007. Bangladesh: Country Position Paper on Regional Cooperation for Food Security in the SAARC Region. Food and Agriculture Organization of the United Nations (FAO), Bangladesh Office. Mimeo.

Menon, P., A. Deolalikar, and A. Bhaskar. 2009. *India State Hunger Index: Comparisons of Hunger across States.* Washington, D.C., Bonn, and Riverside: International Food Policy Research Institute (IFPRI). http://www.ifpri.org/sites/default/files/publications/ishi08.pdf (accessed September 2010).

MFF (Mangroves for the Future). 2010. Countries: Maldives. http://www.mangrovesforthefuture.org/Countries/Maldives.html (accessed February 2011).

MHHDC (Mahbub ul Haq Human Development Centre). 2003. *Human Development in South Asia 2002: Agriculture and Rural Development.* Karachi: Oxford University Press.

————. 2004. *Human Development in South Asia 2003: The Employment Challenge.* Karachi: Oxford University Press.

————. 2010. *Human Development in South Asia 2009: Trade and Human Development.* Karachi: Oxford University Press.

MHHDC (Mahbub ul Haq Human Development Centre) and UNDP. Forthcoming. *Pakistan National Human Development Report: Human Security in Pakistan.*

Mittal, S., and D. Sethi. 2009. Food Security in South Asia: Issues and Opportunities. Indian Council for Research on International Economic Relations (ICRIER) Working Paper No. 240.

http://www.esocialsciences.com/data/articles/ Document11192009340.3889276.pdf (accessed July 2010).

MSSRF (M.S. Swaminathan Research Foundation) and WFP (World Food Programme). 2008. *Report on the State of Food Insecurity in Rural India*. Chennai: Nagaraj and Company Private Limited.

Mujeri, M.K. 2000. Poverty Trends and Agricultural Growth Linkages. Food Management and Research Support Project Working Paper No. 26. Dhaka: Ministry of Food and Disaster Management, Bangladesh.

Murshid, K.A.S., N.I. Khan, Q. Shahabuddin, M. Yunus, S. Akhter and O.H. Chowdhury. 2008. *Determinants of Food Availability and Consumption Patterns and Setting up of Nutritional Standard in Bangladesh*. Dhaka: Bangladesh Institute of Development Studies (BIDS) and Maxwell Stamp.

Namgyel, T. 2010. Climate Change Threatens Bhutan's Middle Path to Development. *Drukpa* 20 May. http://www.drukpa.bt/ bhutan/784/climate-change-threatens-bhutan%e2%80%99s-middle-path-to-development/ (accessed April 2011).

Narain, S. 2003. Harvesting the Raindrop. *New Internationalist* 354 (March).

Nigris, M.D. 2005. Defining and Quantifying the Extent of Import Surges: Data and Methodologies. FAO Import Surge Project Working Paper No. 2. Rome: FAO.

Patnaik, U. 2009. Changes in Urban Poverty in the Light of Rural Poverty: Trends under Economic Reforms, 1993–94 to 2004–05. Unpublished document.

Pradhan, S. 2008. Food Riots as Floods Swamp South Asia. *Reuters* 22 August.

PTI (Press Trust of India) News Agency, New Delhi. 2010. India Better Prepared to Tackle Drought: Agriculture Secretary. 19 March.

Pudasaini, S. 2010. Farming High in a Himalayan Desert. Science and Development Network, 22 February. http://www.scidev.net/en/features/ farming-high-in-a-himalayan-desert–2.html (accessed September 2010).

Quisumbing, A.R., L.R. Brown, H.S. Feldstein, L. Haddad and C. Pena. 1995. *Women: The Key to Food Security*. Washington, D.C.: International Food Policy Research Institute.

Rahman, M.A. 2010. Coastal Zone Management in Bangladesh. http://feppcar.org/122/coastal-zone-management-in-bangladesh (accessed September 2010).

Rahman, R.I., A. Begum and H.R. Bhuyan. 2009. *Impact of Paid Employment and Self-Employment on Income and Prospects of Food Security*. Dhaka: Bangladesh Institute of Development Studies (BIDS).

Raihan, S. 2009. Impact of Food Price Rise on School Enrolment and Dropout in the Poor and Vulnerable Households in Selected Areas of Bangladesh. Research Monograph No. 1. Dhaka:

Department for International Development (DFID).

Raihan, S., A.K.I. Haque, I.A. Khan and R. Chowdhhury. 2008. Updating Poverty Estimates in Bangladesh: A Methodological Note. *Bangladesh Economic Outlook* 1(4): 1–3.

Rajivan, A.K. 2001. 'Nutrition Security in Tamil Nadu'. In *Social and Economic Security in India*, eds. Dev, S.M., P. Antony, V. Gayathri and R.P. Mamgain. New Delhi: Institute for Human Development.

Ramachandran, N. 2006. Women and Food Security in South Asia: Current Issues and Emerging Concerns. United Nations University-World Institute for Development Economics Research (UNU-WIDER) Paper No. 2006/131. www.wider.unu.edu/publications/working-papers/research-papers/2006/en_GB/rp2006–131 (accessed May 2011).

Red Orbit. 2009. Parts of India Experiencing Desertification. 26 November. http://www. redorbit.com/news/science/1791671/parts_of_ india_experiencing_desertification/ (accessed September 2010).

Reed, A.M. 2010. Food Security as If Women Mattered: A Story from Kerala. *One World South Asia* 23 October. http://southasia.oneworld.net/ weekend/food-security-as-if-women-mattered-a-story-from-kerala (accessed May 2011).

Reid, L.L. 2001. The Consequences of Food Insecurity for Child Well-Being: An Analysis of Children's School Achievement, Psychological Well-Being, and Health. Joint Centre for Poverty Research Working Paper No. 137.

Revathi, B. 2005. *Rural Women and Food Security in Asia and the Pacific. Prospects and Paradoxes*. Bangkok: Food and Agriculture Organization of the United Nations (FAO). http://www.fao. org/docrep/008/af348e/af348e00.htm (accessed May 2011).

Rockstrom, J., N. Hatibu, T.Y. Oweis, S. Wani, J. Barron, A. Bruggeman, J. Farahani, L. Karlberg, and Z. Qiang. 2007. 'Managing Water in Rainfed Agriculture'. In *Water for Food, Water for Life: A Comprehensive Assessment of Water Management in Agriculture*, ed. David, M. London: Earthscan. pp. 315–52.

Saxena, N. C. 2008. Hunger, Undernutrition and Food Security in India. Chronic Poverty Research Centre (CPRC) Working Paper No. 44. http://www.chronicpoverty.org/uploads/ publication_files/CPRC-IIPA%2044.pdf (accessed September 2010).

SBP (State Bank of Pakistan). 2009. Banking Statistics of Pakistan 2009. http://www.sbp.org. pk/publications/anu_stats/2009.htm (accessed May 2011).

SDPI (Sustainable Development Policy Institute), SDC (Swiss Agency for Development and Cooperation) and WFP-P (World Food Programme-Pakistan). 2010. *The State of Food Security in Pakistan*. Islamabad: SDPI, SDC and WFP-P.

Seddon, D., and J. Adhikari. 2003. *Conflict and Food Security in Nepal: A Preliminary Analysis.* Kathmandu: Rural Reconstruction Nepal.

Sen, B., P. Menon and F.P. Chowdhury. 2010. Food Utilization and Nutrition Security. Paper presented in the Bangladesh Food Security Investment Forum 2010, 26–27 May, Dhaka: Ministry of Food and Disaster Management, Bangladesh.

Shah, S. 2011. Growers Forced to Sell Wheat at Low Prices. *The News* 8 April. http://www.thenews.com.pk/TodaysPrintDetail.aspx?ID=40403&Cat=3&dt=4/8/2011(accessed May 2011).

Sharma, R. 2005. Overview of Reported Cases of Import Surges from the Standpoint of Analytical Content. Import Surge Project Working Paper No. 1. Rome: FAO.

Shrestha, D.P. 1997. Assessment of Soil Erosion in the Nepalese Himalaya, a Case Study in Likhu Khola Valley, Middle Mountain Region. *Land Husbandry* 2(1): 59–80.

Siddiqui, T., and C.R. Abrar. 2001. *Migrant Worker Remittances and Microfinance in Bangladesh.* Dhaka/Geneva: International Labour Organization.

SIPRI (Stockholm International Peace Research Institute). 2011. Databases: SIPRI Military Expenditure Database. http://www.sipri.org/databases (accessed April 2011).

Sulaiman M., M. Parveen, and N.C. Das. 2009. Impact of the Food Price Hike on Nutritional Status of Women and Children. Research Monograph Series No. 38. Dhaka: Research and Evaluation Division, Bangladesh Rural Advancement Committee (BRAC).

Sultana W., M.A. Aziz and F. Ahmed. 2008. Climate Change: Impact on Crop Production and its Coping Strategies. Paper presented on 27 August at Gazipur, Bangladesh: Agronomy Division, Bangladesh Agricultural Research Institute (BARI).

Swaminathan, M. 2008. Programmes to Protect the Hungry: Lessons from India. Department of Economic and Social Affairs (DESA), United Nations Working Paper No. 70. http://www.un.org/esa/desa/papers/2008/wp70_2008.pdf (accessed September 2010).

Thakur, S.G., C. Arnold and T. Johnson. 2009. Gender and Social Protection. http://www.oecd.org/dataoecd/26/34/43280899.pdf (accessed May 2011).

Tibbo, M., M.A. Martini, B. Rischkowsky and A.A. Hassan. 2009. Gender Sensitive Research Enhances Agricultural Employment in Conservative Societies: The Case of Women Livelihoods and Dairy Goat Programme in Afghanistan and Pakistan. Paper presented at a workshop on 'Gaps, Trends and Current Research in Gender Dimensions of Agricultural and Rural Employment: Differentiated Pathways out of Poverty', 31 March–2 April, Rome. http://www.fao-ilo.org/fileadmin/user_upload/ fao_ilo/pdf/Papers/24_March/Tibbo_et_al_-_Paper_final.pdf (accessed May 2011).

Tietze, U., G. Groenewold and A. Marcoux. 2000. *Demographic Change in Coastal Fishing Communities and Its Implications for the Coastal Environment.* Rome: Food and Agriculture Organization of the United Nations (FAO).

3D (Trade—Human Rights—Equitable Economy). 2009. Seeds of Hunger: Intellectual Property Rights on Seeds and the Human Rights Response. Thread Backgrounder No. 2. http://www.3dthree.org/pdf_3D/3D_THREAD2seeds.pdf (accessed August 2010).

UIS (UNESCO Institute for Statistics). 2011. Data Centre. http://stats.uis.unesco.org/unesco/TableViewer/document.aspx?ReportId=143&IF_Language=eng (accessed April 2011).

UN (United Nations). 2008. *High Food Prices in Pakistan: Impact Assessment and Way Forward.* The UN Inter Agency Assessment Mission FAO/UNDP/UNESCO/UNICEF/WFP/WHO. Islamabad: UN.

————. 2010. *The Millennium Development Goals Report 2010.* New York: UN.

UNDP (United Nations Development Programme). 2005. *Human Development Report 2005: International Cooperation at a Crossroads: Aid, Trade and Security in an Unequal World.* New York: Oxford University Press.

UNDP (United Nations Development Program). 2010a. *Early Recovery Need Assessment.* Islamabad: UNDP.

————. 2010b. *Human Development Report 2010: The Real Wealth of Nations: Pathways to Development.* New York: Palgrave Macmillan.

UNESCAP (United Nations Economic and Social Commission for Asia and the Pacific). 2009. *Sustainable Agriculture and Food Security in Asia and the Pacific.* Bangkok: UNESCAP. http://www.unescap.org/65/documents/Theme-Study/st-escap–2535.pdf (accessed May 2011).

UNESCO (United Nations Educational, Scientific and Cultural Organization). 2011. *EFA Global Monitoring Report 2011. The Hidden Crisis: Armed Conflict and Education.* Paris: UNESCO.

UNICEF (United Nations Children's Fund). 2001. *The State of the World's Children 2002: Leadership.* New York: UNICEF.

————. 2011. *The State of the World's Children 2011: Adolescence: An Age of Opportunity.* New York: UNICEF.

UNPD (United Nations Population Division). 2011. World Population Prospects Database: The 2008 Revision. http://www.un.org/esa/population/ (accessed April 2011).

USAID (United States Agency for International Development). 2010a. Pakistan: Floods Fact sheet No. 2. August 2010. http://www.usaid.gov/our_work/humanitarian_assistance/disaster_assistance/countries/pakistan/template/fs_sr/fy2010/pakistan_fl_fs02_08–10–2010.pdf (accessed April 2011).

———. 2010b. Pakistan: Floods Fact Sheet No. 8. December 2010. http://ftp.info.usaid.gov/pk/downloads/da/12.23.10-USAID-DCHAPakistanFloodsFactSheet8-FY2011.pdf (accessed April 2011).

———. 2010c. Safe Drinking Water and Hygiene Promotion Project. http://www.safewaterpak.com (accessed April 2011).

USDA, FAS (United States Department of Agriculture, Foreign Agricultural Service). 2010. Grain: World Markets and Trade: No Global Shortage of Food Grains. 12 August. http://www.fas.usda.gov/grain/circular/2010/08–10/grainfull08–10.pdf (accessed August 2010).

Utrecht University. 2010. Climate Change Threatens Food Supply of 60 Million People in Asia. http://www.uu.nl/EN/Current/Pages/Klima atveranderingbedreigtvoedselvoorziening van 60miljoenAziaten.aspx (accessed April 2011).

WFP-P (World Food Programme-Pakistan). 2010. Pakistan Flood Impact Assessment. Islamabad: WFP-P.

World Bank. 1986. Poverty and Hunger: Issues and Options for Food Security in Developing Countries. Washington, D.C.: World Bank.

———. 2005. Pakistan Country Water Resources Assistance Strategy—Water Economy: Running Dry. Report No. 34081-PK. Washington, D.C.: World Bank.

———. 2008. Double Jeopardy: Responding to High Food and Fuel Prices. Paper prepared for the G–8 Hokkaido-Toyako Summit, 7–9 July, Toyako.

———. 2009. Project Appraisal Document for Social Safety Net Technical Assistance Project. Islamabad: World Bank.

———. 2010. World Development Indicators 2010. Washington, D.C.: World Bank.

———. 2011a. Education Statistics Database. http://databank.worldbank.org/ddp/home.do?Step=1&id=4 (accessed April 2011).

———. 2011b. Gender Statistics Database. http://databank.worldbank.org/ddp/home.do?Step=1&id=4 (accessed April 2011).

———. 2011c. Global Development Finance Database. http://databank.worldbank.org/ddp/home.do?Step=1&id=4 (accessed April 2011).

———. 2011d. Health, Nutrition and Population Statistics Database. http://databank.worldbank.org/ddp/home.do?Step=1&id=4 (accessed April 2011).

———. 2011e. South Asia and Climate Change: A Development and Environmental Issue. http://web.worldbank.org/WBSITE/EXTERNAL/COUNTRIES/SOUTHASIAEXT/0, content MDK:21469804~menuPK:2246552~pagePK:2 865106~piPK:2865128~theSitePK:223547,00.html (accessed April 2011).

———. 2011f. World Development Indicators Database. http://databank.worldbank.org/ddp/home.do?Step=1&id=4 (accessed April 2011).

WFP (World Food Programme), UNICEF (United Nations Children's Fund) and GOB (Government of Bangladesh). 2009. Bangladesh Household Food Security and Nutrition Assessment Report 2009. Dhaka: Ministry of Health and Family Welfare, Bangladesh, UNICEF and WFP.

WTO (World Trade Organization). 2003. WTO Annual Report 2003. Geneva: WTO.

WWF (World Wildlife Fund). 2007. Pakistan's Waters at Risk: Water and Health Related Issues in Pakistan and Key Recommendations. Lahore: WWF, Pakistan. http://www.wwfpak.org/pdf/water-report.pdf (accessed September 2010).

Yu, W., M. Alam, A. Hassan, A.S. Khan, A. Ruane, C. Rosenzweig, D. Major, and J. Thurlow. 2010. Climate Change Risks and Food Security in Bangladesh. London: Earthscan.

Human Development Indicators for South Asia

Contents

Table 7: Profile of Military Spending   158
- Defence expenditure
- Defence expenditure annual increase
- Defence expenditure (% of GDP)
- Defence expenditure (% of central government expenditure)
- Defence expenditure per capita
- Armed forces personnel
- Arms imports
- Global militarization index (GMI)

Table 8: Profile of Wealth and Poverty   159
- Total GDP
- GDP per capita
- GNI per capita
- GDP per capita growth
- Gross capital formation
- Gross domestic savings
- Sectoral composition of GDP
- Trade
- Tax revenue
- Exports
- Total net official development assistance received
- Total debt service
- Total external debt
- Total debt service
- Income share: ratio of the highest 20% to the lowest 20%
- Population below 1.25 $ a day
- Population below income poverty line, rural, urban
- Public expenditure on education
- Public expenditure on health

Table 9: Demographic Profile   161
- Population
- Population growth rate
- Population rural
- Population urban
- Annual growth rate of urban population
- Crude birth rate
- Crude death rate
- Total fertility rate
- Dependency ratio
- Total labour force
- Male labour force
- Female labour force
- Annual average growth in labour force
- Unemployment rate

Table 10: Profile of Food Security and Natural Resources   162
- Food production per capita index
- Food exports
- Food imports
- Cereal production
- Cereal imports
- Cereal exports
- Forest production
- Crop production index
- Land area
- Land use
- Irrigated land
- Daily dietary consumption
- Undernourished people

Table 11: Energy and Environment   163
- Energy use per capita
- Total electricity production
- Motor vehicles per kilometre of road
- The number of disaster-affected people
- Economic losses from natural disasters

Table 12: Governance   164
- Average annual rate of inflation
- Average annual growth of food prices
- Average annual growth of money supply
- Total revenue
- Total expenditure
- Budget deficit/surplus
- Tax revenue
- Tax revenue by type
- Public expenditure per capita
- Imports of goods and services
- Net inflow of FDI
- Total external debt
- Total debt service
- Total debt service

Note on Statistical Sources for Human Development Indicators

The human development data presented in these tables have been collected with considerable effort from various international and national sources. For the most part, standardized international sources have been used, particularly the UN system and the World Bank data bank. The UNDP and World Bank offices made their resources available to us for this report.

Countries in the indicator tables are arranged in descending order according to population size. Data for South Asia is the total/ weighted average value of seven countries, India, Pakistan, Bangladesh, Nepal, Sri Lanka, Bhutan, and Maldives. While most data have been taken from international sources, national sources have been used where international data have been sparse. Such data have to be used with some caution as their international comparability is still to be tested.

Several limitations remain regarding coverage, consistency, and comparability of data across time and countries. The data series presented here will be refined over time, as more accurate and comparable data become available.

In certain critical areas, reliable data are extremely scarce: for instance, for employment, income distribution, public expenditure on social services, military debt, foreign assistance for human priority areas, etc. Information regarding the activities of NGOs in social sectors remains fairly sparse.

It is time for policymakers to make a significant investment in the collection and analysis of up-to-date, reliable, and consistent indicators for social and human development. If development is to be targeted at the people, a great deal of effort must be invested in determining the true condition of these people.

It is hoped that the various gaps visible in the tables will persuade national and international agencies to invest more resources and energy in investigating human development profiles.

1. Basic Human Development Indicators

	India	Pakistan	Bangladesh	Nepal	Sri Lanka	Bhutan	Maldives	South Asia (weighted average)	Developing countries
Total estimated population (million)									
— 2000	1,043	148	141	24	19	0.6	0.27	1,376T	4,920T
— 2009	1,198	181	162	29	20	0.7	0.31	1,592T	5,596T
— 2050	1,614	335	223	49	22	1.0	0.46	2,244T	7,875T
Annual population growth rate (%)									
— 1990–2000	1.9	2.5	2.0	2.5	0.8	0.2	2.3	2.0	1.7
— 2000–09	1.6	2.2	1.6	2.1	0.8	2.4	1.4	1.6	1.4
Life expectancy at birth									
— 2000	60	64	60	61	67	60	65	61	63
— 2008	62	66	65	66	70	64	70	63	65
Adult literacy rate (% age 15 and above)									
— 2000–01[a]	61	43[b]	48	49	91	...	96	58	78
— 2005–08[a]	63	54	55	58	91	53	98	61	79
Female literacy rate (% age 15 and above)									
— 2000–01[a]	48	29[b]	41	35	89	...	96	45	72
— 2005–08[a]	51	40	50	45	89	39	98	50	73
Combined 1st, 2nd and 3rd level gross enrolment ratio (%)									
— 2000	52	...	...	56	67[c]	50	78	52	59
— 2007–09[a]	63	42	49	...	...	61	69	59	65
Infant mortality rate (per 1,000 live births)									
— 2000	68	85	66	63	17	68	43	68	60
— 2009	50	71	41	39	13	52	11	51	47
GDP growth (%)									
— 2000	4.0	4.3	5.9	6.2	6.0	7.5	4.8	4.3	5.4
— 2009	9.1	3.6	5.7	4.7	3.5	7.4	–3.0	8.0	2.7
GDP per capita (PPP[d], constant 2005 international $)									
— 2000	1,769	1,931	893	905	3,068	2,749	3,470	1,700	3,289
— 2009	2,993	2,369	1,286	1,049	4,333	4,643	4,972	2,731	4,982
Human Development Index (HDI)									
— 2000	0.440	0.416	0.390	0.375	0.584[e]	...	0.513	0.433	...
— 2010	0.519	0.490	0.469	0.428	0.658	...	0.602	0.511	...
Gender Inequality Index (2008)									
value	0.599	0.533	0.748	0.721	0.734	0.716	...	0.611	...
rank	72	59	122	112	116	110	...	...	...

Notes: a: Data refer to recent year available. b: Data refer to 1998. c: Data refer to 2002. d: PPP means purchasing power parity. e: Data refer to 1995.

Sources: Rows 1, 2: UNPD 2009 and MHHDC staff computations; Rows 3, 7: World Bank 2011d; Rows 4, 5: UIS 2011, UNESCO 2011 and World Bank 2011a; Row 6: World Bank 2011a; Rows 8, 9: World Bank 2011f; Rows 10, 11: UNDP 2010b.

2. Education Profile

	India	Pakistan	Bangladesh	Nepal	Sri Lanka	Bhutan	Maldives	South Asia (weighted average)	Developing countries
Adult literacy rate (% age 15 and above)									
— 2000–01[a]	61	43[b]	48	49	91	...	96	58	78
— 2005–08[a]	63	54	55	· 58	91	53	98	61	79
Male literacy rate (% age 15 and above)									
— 2000–01[a]	73	55[b]	54	63	92	...	96	70	84
— 2005–08[a]	75	67	60	71	92	65	98	73	85
Female literacy rate (% age 15 and above)									
— 2000–01[a]	48	29[b]	41	35	89	...	96	45	72
— 2005–08[a]	51	40	50	45	89	39	98	50	73
Youth literacy rate									
— 2000–01[a]	76.4	55.3[b]	63.6	70.1	95.6	...	98.2	73.0	85.2
— 2005–09[a]	81.1	71.1	75.5	82.0	98.0	74.4	99.3	79.6	87.0
Primary enrolment (%) gross									
— 2001	94	70	...	110	108	81	132	91	99
— 2007–09[a]	113	85	95	...	97	109	111	108	107
Primary enrolment (%) net									
— 2001	79	57	...	71[c]	100	61	97	76	81
— 2007–09[a]	90	66	86	...	95	87	96	87	87
Secondary enrolment (%) gross									
— 2000	46	27[d]	44	35	...	41	54	44	55
— 2006–09[a]	60	33	42	44	87[e]	62	84	55	63
Secondary enrolment (%) net									
— 2007–09[a]	...	33	42	...	...	48	69	37	55
Combined 1st, 2nd and 3rd level gross enrolment ratio (%)									
— 2000	52	...	...	56	67[f]	50	78	52	59
— 2007–09[a]	63	42	49	...	...	61	69	59	65
Enrolment in technical and vocational education (%)									
— 2001	0.7	2.3[d]	1.2	1.4	...	1.7	6.2	0.9	...
— 2006[a]	0.8	4.1	3.4	0.7	...	1.6	3.9[e]	1.4	...
Pupil teacher ratio (primary level)									
— 2001	40.1	34.7	...	37.0	26.3	39.5	22.5	39.2	28.9
— 2009	40.2[e]	39.7	45.8	33.3	23.1	27.7	12.7	40.4	26.5[g]
Percentage of children reaching grade 5 (% of grade 1 students)									
— 2006–08[a]	69	60	67	62	89	96	...	68	...
Researchers per million inhabitants									
— 2002–07[a]	137	152	...	59	93	...	...	137	595
R&D expenditures as a % of GDP									
— 2002–07[a]	0.80	0.67	...	...	0.17	...	...	0.77	0.96
Public expenditure on education (% of GDP)									
— 2000	4.4	1.8	2.4	3.0	3.1[b]	5.8	3.7[b]	3.9	3.8
— 2006–09[a]	3.1	2.7	2.4	4.6	...	4.8	8.1	3.0	3.9
Children not in primary schools (million)									
— 2001	19.332	8.721	...	0.847[c]	0.004	0.042	0.001	28.9T	...
— 2008–09[a]	3.852	7.300	2.024	...	0.008	0.012	0.002	13.2T	...
School life expectancy (years) primary to tertiary									
— 2006–09[a]	10.3	6.9	8.1	8.8[e]	12.7[e]	11.0	12.4	9.7	10.4
primary to secondary									
— 2006–09[a]	10.0	6.6	7.5	8.6[f]	12.5[e]	11.3	12.4	9.4	9.5

Notes: a: Data refer to most recent year available. b: Data refer to 1998. c: Data refer to 2000. d: Data refer to 2003. e: Data refer to 2004. f: Data refer to 2002. g: Data refer to 2007.

Sources: Rows 1, 2, 3: UIS 2011, UNESCO 2011 and World Bank 2011a; Row 4: UNESCO 2011 and World Bank 2011a; Rows 5–12, 15–17: World Bank 2011a; Rows 13, 14: UIS 2011 and World Bank 2010.

3. Health Profile

	India	Pakistan	Bangladesh	Nepal	Sri Lanka	Bhutan	Maldives	South Asia (weighted average)	Developing countries
Population with access to safe water (%)									
— 2000	81	88	79	83	80	91	91	82	79
— 2008	88	90	80	88	90	92	91	87	84
Population with access to sanitation (%)									
— 2000	25	37	46	23	82	62	81	29	49
— 2008	31	45	53	31	91	65	98[b]	36	54
Child immunization rate									
One-year-olds fully immunized against measles (%)									
— 2000	50	59	72	77	98	78	99	54	70
— 2009	71	80	89	79	96	98	98	74	81
One-year-olds fully immunized against DPT (%)									
— 2000	60	62	81	80	99	92	98	63	72
— 2009	66	85	94	82	97	96	98	72	81
Physicians (per 1,000 people)									
— 1998–2001[a]	0.51	0.66	0.23	0.05	0.43	0.05	0.78	0.49	…
— 2004–07[a]	0.58	0.78	0.30	0.21	0.55	0.02	0.92	0.57	…
Maternal mortality ratio (per 100,000 live births)									
— 2000	390	340	500	550	59	420	110	394	370
— 2008	230	260	340	380	39	200	37	245	290
Contraceptive prevalence rate (% of women aged 15–49)									
— 1999–2001[a]	47	28	54	39	70	31	42	46	60
— 2006–08[a]	54	30	53	48	68	35	39[b]	51	61
People with HIV/AIDS									
People Living with HIV/AIDS (Adults and Children) (000)									
— 2001	2,700	51	7.5	56	3.0	…	…	2,818T	…
— 2009	2,400	98	6.3	64	2.8	<1.0	<0.1	2,571T	29,800T
People with HIV/AIDS adults (% age 15–49)									
— 2001	0.5	0.1	…	0.5	…	…	…	0.5	1.0
— 2009	0.3	0.1	<0.1	0.4	<0.1	0.2	<0.1	0.3	0.9
Public expenditure on health (% of GDP)									
— 2000	1.3	0.6	1.1	1.3	1.8	5.3	4.1	1.2	2.4
— 2009	1.4	0.9	1.1	2.1	1.8	4.5	5.2	1.3	2.9

Notes: a: Data refer to most recent year available. b: Data refer to 2004.

Sources: Rows 1–6, 8: World Bank 2011d; Row 7: UNICEF 2011 and World Bank 2009d.

4. Human Deprivation Profile

	India	Pakistan	Bangladesh	Nepal	Sri Lanka	Bhutan	Maldives	South Asia (weighted average)	Developing countries
Population below income poverty line (%)									
Population below 1.25 $ a day (PPP) (%)									
— 2002–05[a]	42	23	50	55	14	26	...	40	25
Population below national poverty line (%)									
— 1999–05[a]	29	33	40	31	23	...	...	31	...
Population without access to safe water									
number (million)									
— 2000	198	17.8	29.6	4.2	3.8	0.05	0.02	253	1,022
— 2008	142	17.7	32.0	3.5	2.0	0.05	0.03	197	865
% of total population									
— 2000	19	12	21	17	20	9	9	18	21
— 2008	12	10	20	12	10	8	9	13	16
Population without access to sanitation									
number (million)									
— 2000	782	93.3	76.0	18.8	3.4	0.21	0.05	974	2,486
— 2008	815	97.3	75.2	19.9	1.8	0.24	0.01	1010	2,562
% of total population									
— 2000	75	63	54	77	18	38	19	71	51
— 2008	69	55	47	69	9	35	2	64	46
Illiterate adults									
number (million)									
— 2000–01[a]	270	47[b]	48	7.6	1.3	...	0.006	373T	...
— 2005–08[a]	283	51	49	7.6	1.4	0.20	0.003	393T	786T
% of total adult population									
— 2000–01[a]	39	57	53	51	9	...	4	42	22
— 2005–08[a]	37	46	45	42	9	47	2	39	21
Illiterate female adults									
number (million)									
— 2000–01[a]	175	28[b]	27	4.9	0.8	0.00	0.003	235T	...
— 2005–08[a]	184	32	27	5.1	0.9	0.12	0.002	250T	503T
% of total adult female population									
— 2000–01[a]	52	71	59	65	11	...	4	55	29
— 2005–08[a]	49	60	50	55	11	61	2	50	27
Child malnourished (weight for age) (% of children under-five)									
— 2006–08[a]	43.5	31.3[c]	41.3	38.8	21.1	14.1[d]	25.7[c]	41.5	23.5
Under-five mortality rate (per 1,000 live births)									
— 2000	92.7	107.7	89.6	85.4	20.7	106	53.3	92.9	85.9
— 2009	65.6	87.0	52.0	48.2	14.7	78.6	12.7	65.7	66.5
People with HIV/AIDS adults (% age 15–49)									
— 2001	0.5	0.1	...	0.5	...	...	...	0.5	1.0
— 2009	0.3	0.1	<0.1	0.4	<0.1	0.2	<0.1	0.3	0.9

Notes: a: Data refer to most recent year available. b: Data refer to 1998. c: Data refer to 2001. d: Data refer to 1999.

Sources: Row 1: World Bank 2011f; Rows 2, 3: UNPD 2011, World Bank 2011d and MHHDC staff computations; Rows 4, 5: UIS 2011, UNESCO 2011, World Bank 2011a and MHHDC staff computations; Rows 6, 7: World Bank 2011d; Row 8: UNICEF 2011 and World Bank 2009d.

5. Gender Disparities Profile

	India	Pakistan	Bangladesh	Nepal	Sri Lanka	Bhutan	Maldives	South Asia (weighted average)	Developing countries
Female population									
number (million)									
— 2000	502	72	69	12.2	9.4	0.28	0.13	665T	2,418T
— 2009	579	88	80	14.8	10.3	0.33	0.15	772T	2,752T
as % of male									
— 2000	93	94	97	100	101	97	97	94	97
— 2009	94	94	98	101	103	90	98	94	97
Adult female literacy (as % of male)									
— 2000–01[a]	65	52	76	56	97	...	100	65	85
— 2005–08[a]	68	60	83	64	97	60	100	68	86
Female primary school gross enrolment (as % of male)									
— 2001	85	68	...	84	99	90	98	75	92
— 2007–09[a]	97	83	104	...	100	101	95	94	96
Female primary school net enrolment (as % of male)									
— 2001	85	68	...	82[b]	100	92	99	75	93
— 2007–09[a]	96	83	108	...	101	103	98	94	97
Female 1st, 2nd and 3rd level gross enrolment ratio (as % of male)									
— 2000	78	...	...	76	103[c]	85	101	62	90
— 2007–09[a]	90	82	103	...	...	98	98	88	96
Female life expectancy (as % of male)									
— 2000	103	101	103	101	111	106	104	103	106
— 2008	105	101	103	102	111	106	104	104	106
Female economic activity rate (age 15+) (as % of male)									
— 2000	40	19	64	74	47	51	53	41	64
— 2008	41	25	70	79	46	74	75	43	65
Female professional and technical workers (as % of total)									
— 2006	...	26	12	...	46	...	...	21	...
Seats in parliament held by women (% of total)									
— 1999	8	2	9	3	5	2	6	7	12
— 2009	11	23	19	33	6	9	7	13	18
Gender Inequality Index (2008)									
value	0.599	0.533	0.748	0.721	0.734	0.716	...	0.611	...
rank	72	59	122	112	116	110	...	...	...
Female unemployment rate (%)									
— 2000	4.1	15.8	3.3	10.7[d]	11.4	...	2.7	5.5	...
— 2004–09[a]	5.1	8.7	7.0	...	8.1	3.3	23.8	5.6	...

Notes: a: Data refer to most recent year available. b: Data refer to 2000. c: Data refer to 2002. d: Data refer to 2001.

Sources: Row 1: UNPD 2011 and MHHDC staff computations; Row 2: UIS 2011, UNESCO 2011, World Bank 2011a and MHHDC staff computations; Rows 3, 4, 5: World Bank 2011a and MHHDC staff computations; Row 6: World Bank 2011d; Row 7: World Bank 2011f and MHHDC staff computations; Rows 8, 9, 11: World Bank 2011b; Row 10: UNDP 2010b.

6. Child Survival and Development Profile

	India	Pakistan	Bangladesh	Nepal	Sri Lanka	Bhutan	Maldives	South Asia (weighted average)	Developing countries
Population under 18									
number (million)									
— 2000	400	68	62	10.9	6.1	1.03	0.15	549T	1,883T
— 2009	447	79	61	12.7	5.9	0.26	0.11	606T	1,971T
% of total population									
— 2000	38	46	44	45	33	...	54	40	38
— 2009	37	44	38	43	29	37	36	38	35
Population under-five									
number (million)									
— 2000	116	22	19	3.6	1.6	0.33	0.05	163T	547T
— 2009	126	24	16	3.5	1.8	0.07	0.03	172T	569T
% of total population									
— 2000	11	15	13	15	8	...	17	12	11
— 2009	11	13	10	12	9	10	9	11	10
Infant mortality rate (per 1,000 live births)									
— 2000	68	85	66	63	17	68	43	68	60
— 2009	50	71	41	39	13	52	11	51	47
Under-five mortality rate (per 1,000 Live births)									
— 2000	92.7	107.7	89.6	85.4	20.7	106	53.3	92.9	85.9
— 2009	65.6	87.0	52.0	48.2	14.7	78.6	12.7	65.7	66.5
One-year-olds fully immunized against tuberculosis (%)									
— 2000	73	67	95	84	99	97	99	75	81
— 2008	87	90	98	87	99	99	99	89	90
One-year-olds fully immunized against measles (%)									
— 2000	50	59	72	77	98	78	99	54	70
— 2009	71	80	89	79	96	98	98	74	81
One-year-olds fully immunized against polio (%)									
— 2000	60	61	83	72	99	98	98	63	72
— 2008	67	81	95	82	98	96	98	72	82
Births attended by trained health personnel (%)									
— 2000–01[a]	43	23	12	13	96	24	70	37	59
— 2006–09[a]	53	39	24	19	99	71	84[b]	48	63
Low birthweight infants (%)									
— 2006–08[a]	27.6	31.6	21.6	21.2	17.6	15.0[c]	22.2[d]	27.2	15.3
Children (aged 5–14) in the labour force (% age group 5–14)									
— 2000–09[a]	12	...	13	34	8	19	...	13	16

Notes: a: Data refer to most recent year available. b: Data refer to 2004. c: Data refer to 1999. d: Data refer to 2001.

Sources: Rows 1, 2: UNICEF 2001, 2011, UNPD 2011 and MHHDC staff computations; Rows 3–9: World Bank 2011d; Row 10: UNICEF 2011.

7. Profile of Military Spending

	India	Pakistan	Bangladesh	Nepal	Sri Lanka	Bhutan	Maldives	South Asia (weighted average)	Developing countries
Defence expenditure at 2009 prices (million US$)									
— 2000	21,798	3,839	842	82	1,421	...	...	27,982T	...
— 2009	35,819	5,039	1024	210	1480	...	...	43,572T	...
Defence expenditure annual increase (%)									
— 1990–2000	3.9	0.8	6.0	3.3	12.9	...	...	3.8	...
— 2000–09	5.7	3.1	2.2	11.1	0.5	...	...	5.0	...
Defence expenditure (% of GDP)									
— 2000	3.1	4.0	1.4	1.0	5.0	...	...	3.0	2.1
— 2009	2.7	3.0	1.1	1.6	3.5	...	...	2.6	2.1
Defence expenditure (% of central government expenditure)									
— 2000	19.5	23.4	14.9[a]	12.3[b]	21.9	...	...	19.4	15.0[c]
— 2009	16.6	18.0	10.0	12.8[d]	18.5[e]	...	...	16.0	12.2[e]
Defence expenditure per capita at 2009 prices (US$)									
— 2000	20.9	25.9	6.0	3.3	75.7	...	...	20.3	...
— 2009	29.9	27.9	6.3	7.2	73.1	...	...	27.4	...
Armed forces personnel number (000)									
— 2000	2,372	900	137	90	204	6	5	3,714T	22,965T
— 2009	2,626	921	221	158	223	...	...	4,149T	22,195T
as % of total labour force									
— 2000	0.6	2.2	0.2	0.9	2.6	3.3	5.6	0.8	1.0
— 2009	0.6	1.6	0.3	1.2	2.7	...	...	0.7	0.8
Arms imports at 1990 prices (million US$)									
— 2000	911	158	205	11[a]	274	...	...	1,559T	8,925T
— 2008	2,116	1,146	12[e]	5[d]	64[e]	...	10[f]	3,353T	10,889T
Global militarization index (GMI)[g]									
Index									
— 2000	526	648	400	401	628	...	...	526	...
— 2009	514	556	379	458	609	...	...	505	...
Rank									
— 2000 (out of 139 countries)	87	43	122	119	50	...	...	...	...
— 2009 (out of 147 countries)	79	63	128	99	38	...	...	...	...

Notes: a: Data refer to 2001. b: Data refer to 2004. c: Data refer to 2002. d: Data refer to 2005. e: Data refer to 2008. f: Data refer to 2006. g: The GMI represents the relative weight and importance of the military apparatus of a state in relation to society as a whole. Militarization is defined, in a narrow sense, as the resources (expenditure, personnel, heavy weapons) available to a state's armed forces. For further information please see www.bicc.de.

Sources: Rows 1, 2: SIPRI 2011 and MHHDC staff computations; Rows 3, 4, 6, 7: World Bank 2011f; Row 5: SIPRI 2011, UNPD 2011 and MHHDC staff computations; Row 8: BICC 2011.

8. Profile of Wealth and Poverty

	India	Pakistan	Bangladesh	Nepal	Sri Lanka	Bhutan	Maldives	South Asia (weighted average)	Developing countries
Total GDP (billion US$)									
— 2000	460.2	74.0	47.1	5.5	16.3	0.4	0.6	604.1T	5,859.1T
— 2009	1,377.3	162.0	89.4	12.5	42.0	1.3	1.5	1,686.0T	16,657.6T
GDP per capita (PPP[a], constant 2005 international $)									
— 2000	1,769	1,931	893	905	3,068	2,749	3,470	1,700	3,289
— 2009	2,993	2,369	1,286	1,049	4,333	4,643	4,972	2,731	4,982
GNI per capita (US$)									
— 2000	450	490	350	220	880	730	2,150	446	1,128
— 2009	1,220	1,000	580	440	1,990	2,020	3,970	1,126	2,968
GDP per capita growth (%)									
— 2000	2.3	1.8	4.0	3.7	5.4	4.5	3.1	2.5	3.9
— 2009	7.7	1.4	4.3	2.8	2.8	5.8	−4.4	6.5	1.4
Gross capital formation (% of GDP)									
— 2000	24.2	17.2	23.0	24.3	28.0	48.2	26.3	23.4	23.8
— 2009	36.5	19.0	24.4	29.7	24.5	53.9	53.5[b]	33.0	27.9
Gross domestic savings (% of GDP)									
— 2000	23.2	16.0	17.8	15.2	17.4	26.9	44.2	21.7	25.2
— 2009	32.0	11.4	17.2	8.0	18.0	63.6	18.8[b]	27.5	28.4
Sectoral composition of GDP									
Agriculture value added (% of GDP)									
— 2000	23.4	25.9	25.5	40.8	19.9	28.4	8.8	24.1T	12.1
— 2009	17.8	21.6	18.7	33.8	12.6	17.6	5.0	18.5	10.0
Industry value added (% of GDP)									
— 2000	26.2	23.3	25.3	22.1	27.3	35.3	15.0	25.7	35.1
— 2009	27.0	24.3	28.7	15.9	29.7	45.0	17.4	26.7	34.7
Services value added (% of GDP)									
— 2000	50.5	50.7	49.2	37.0	52.8	36.3	76.2	50.2	52.8
— 2009	55.3	54.2	52.6	50.2	57.7	37.4	77.5	54.8	55.2
Trade (% of GDP)									
— 2000	27.4	28.1	33.2	55.7	88.6	81.8	161.1	29.5	52.5
— 2009	43.6	33.2	46.0	53.1	49.2	106.3	161.3	43.0	53.3
Tax revenue (% of GDP)									
— 2000	9.0	10.1	7.6[c]	8.7	14.5	10.3	13.8	9.0	10.9
— 2009	9.8	9.3	8.6	12.2	13.3[d]	9.1	14.1	9.7	14.0[d]
Exports of goods and services (% of GDP)									
— 2000	13.2	13.4	14.0	23.3	39.0	30.5	89.5	13.9	27.0
— 2009	19.6	12.8	19.4	15.7	21.4	58.0	67.0	18.8	26.9
Total net official development assistance received									
amount (million US$)									
— 2000	1,372.7	700.4	1,171.7	386.0	274.5	53.1	19.2	3,977.6T	49,233.6T
— 2009	2,393.0	2,780.6	1,226.9	854.6	703.8	125.4	33.3	8,117.6T	127,093.2T
% of GDP									
— 2000	0.3	0.9	2.5	7.0	1.7	12.4	3.1	0.7	0.8
— 2009	0.2	1.7	1.4	6.8	1.7	9.8	2.3	0.5	0.8

Continued

	India	Pakistan	Bangladesh	Nepal	Sri Lanka	Bhutan	Maldives	South Asia (weighted average)	Developing countries
Total debt service (% of exports of goods, services and income)									
— 2000	17.5	27.9	10.5	7.5	12.1	5.1ᵉ	4.2	17.6	20.9
— 2009	5.9	15.0	5.6	10.4	15.6	11.4	8.3	7.1	11.3
Total external debt (billions US$)									
— 2000	100.2	32.7	15.5	2.9	9.1	0.2	0.2	160.9T	2,122.1T
— 2009	237.7	53.7	23.8	3.7	17.2	0.8	0.8	337.7T	3,545.1T
Total debt service (% of GDP)									
— 2000	2.4	3.9	1.6	1.9	4.8	1.6	3.2	2.6	5.9
— 2009	1.2	2.1	1.1	1.4	3.4	5.9	4.7	1.3	3.2
Income share: ratio of the highest 20% to the lowest 20%									
— 2003–07ᶠ	5.6	4.7	4.4	8.9	6.9	9.9	6.8	5.5	…
Population below 1.25 $ a day (PPP) (%)									
— 2002–05ᶠ	42	23	50	55	14	26	…	40	25
Population below income poverty line (%)									
Urban population below income poverty line (%)									
— 1999–05ᶠ	24.7	24.2	28.4	9.6	24.7	…	…	24.7	…
Rural population below income poverty line (%)									
— 1999–05ᶠ	30.2	35.9	43.8	34.6	7.9	…	…	32.0	…
Public expenditure on education (% of GDP)									
— 2000	4.4	1.8	2.4	3.0	3.1ᵍ	5.8	3.7ᵍ	3.9	3.8
— 2006–09ᶠ	3.1	2.7	2.4	4.6	…	4.8	8.1	3.0	3.9
Public expenditure on health (% of GDP)									
— 2000	1.3	0.6	1.1	1.3	1.8	5.3	4.1	1.2	2.4
— 2009	1.4	0.9	1.1	2.1	1.8	4.5	5.2	1.3	2.9

Notes: a: PPP means purchasing power parity. b: Data refer to 2005. c: Data refer to 2001. d: Data refer to 2008. e: Data refer to 2003. f: Data refer to most recent year available. g: Data refer to 1998.

Sources: Rows 1–10, 16, 17: World Bank 2011f; Rows 11, 15: World Bank 2011f and MHHDC staff computations; Rows 12, 13: World Bank 2011c. Row 14: World Bank 2011c and MHHDC staff computations. Row 18: World Bank 2011a. Row 19: World Bank 2011d.

9. Demographic Profile

	India	Pakistan	Bangladesh	Nepal	Sri Lanka	Bhutan	Maldives	South Asia (weighted average)	Developing countries
Total estimated population (million)									
— 2000	1,043	148	141	24	19	0.6	0.27	1,376T	4,920T
— 2009	1,198	181	162	29	20	0.7	0.31	1,592T	5,596T
Annual population growth rate (%)									
— 1990–2000	1.9	2.5	2.0	2.5	0.8	0.2	2.3	2.0	1.7
—2000–09	1.6	2.2	1.6	2.1	0.8	2.4	1.4	1.6	1.4
Population rural (million)									
— 2000	754	99	108	21.2	15.8	0.42	0.20	998T	2,952T
— 2009	842	116	118	24.0	17.3	0.46	0.19	1,118T	3,099T
Population urban (million)									
— 2000	288	49	33	3.3	3.0	0.14	0.08	377T	1,968T
— 2009	356	64	45	5.3	2.9	0.24	0.12	474T	2,497T
Growth rate of urban population (%)									
— 1990–2000	2.7	3.3	3.8	6.8	–0.8	4.7	3.0	2.9	3.2
— 2000–09	2.4	3.1	3.4	5.5	–0.3	5.8	5.4	2.6	2.7
Crude birth rate (per 1,000 live births)									
— 2000	26	33	27	33	18	28	22	27	23
— 2008	23	30	21	25	19	22	19	23	22
Crude death rate (per 1,000 live births)									
— 2000	9	8	8	9	6	9	6	8	9
— 2008	7	7	7	6	6	7	5	7	8
Total fertility rate									
— 2000	3.3	4.7	3.0	4.0	2.2	3.8	2.8	3.4	2.9
— 2008	2.7	4.0	2.3	2.9	2.3	2.6	2.0	2.8	2.7
Dependency ratio (dependents to working-age population)									
— 2000	64.70	81.60	67.20	80.00	49.20	81.00	76.40	66.85	62.60
— 2009	56.50	69.40	54.70	68.30	46.50	54.70	47.80	57.87	55.40
Total labour force (million)									
— 2000	385	42	63	10	8	0.18	0.09	508T	2,250T
— 2008	450	56	77	13	8	0.29	0.14	604T	2,586T
Male labour force (million)									
— 2000	280	35	39	6	5	0.12	0.06	365T	1,375T
— 2008	325	45	45	7	6	0.18	0.08	428T	1,570T
Female labour force (million)									
— 2000	105	6	24	4	3	0.06	0.03	143T	875T
— 2008	125	11	31	6	3	0.11	0.06	176T	1,016T
Annual growth in labour force (%)									
— 1990–2000	1.9	3.0	2.4	3.0	1.4	0.3	4.1	2.1	1.8
— 2000–08	2.0	3.8	2.5	3.1	0.8	5.8	5.9	2.2	1.8
Unemployment rate (%)									
— 1999–2000[a]	2.7	7.8	4.3	1.8	7.6	1.1	2.0	3.4	…
— 2005–09[a]	3.1	5.5	4.2	…	5.6	4.0	14.4	3.6	…

Notes: a: Data refer to most recent year available.

Sources: Rows 1–5: UNPD 2011 and MHHDC staff computations; Rows 6–9: World Bank 2011d; Rows 10–13: World Bank 2011d and MHHDC staff computations; Row 14: ADB 2011.

10. Profile of Food Security and Natural Resources

	India	Pakistan	Bangladesh	Nepal	Sri Lanka	Bhutan	Maldives	South Asia (weighted average)	Developing countries
Food production net per capita index (1999–2001=100)									
— 2000	98	101	102	100	101	92	103	99	…
— 2009	104	108	114	108	111	123	84	106	…
Food exports (% of merchandise exports)									
— 2000	13	11	8	10	21	13	54	12	10
— 2009	8	17	7	25	26	6	98	9	11
Food imports (% of merchandise imports)									
— 2000	5	14	16	13	15[a]	18[a]	24	7	8
— 2009	4	11	23[b]	15	16	15	16[c]	7	8
Cereal production (1,000 metric tonnes)									
— 2000	234,931	30,461	39,503	7,116	2,896	107	0.004	315,013T	…
— 2009	246,774	38,374	46,812	8,114	3,788	161	0.376	344,023T	…
Cereal imports (1,000 metric tonnes)									
— 2000	55	1,054	2,496	203	1,029	57	35	4,929T	…
— 2008	22	1,860	2,287	50	1,144	8	52	5,423T	…
Cereal exports (1,000 metric tonnes)									
— 2000	2,822	2,087	0.7	0.0	2.0	19.2	0.0	4,931T	…
— 2008	6,499	3,205	8.8	5.0	149	0.2	0.0	9,867T	…
Forest production (1,000 cubic meter)									
Roundwood (1,000 cubic meter)									
— 2000	296,141	33,560	28,459	14,023	6,583	4,355	13	383,133T	…
— 2009	331,737	32,483	27,641	13,815	5,894	5,040	15	416,626T	…
Fuelwood (1,000 cubic meter)									
— 2000	277,380	30,880	27,836	12,763	5,907	4,221	13	358,999T	…
— 2009	308,545	29,493	27,359	12,555	5,283	4,783	15	388,034T	…
Crop production index (1999–01 =100)									
— 2000	98	103	103	100	102	91	103	99	100
— 2009	116	125	130	135	115	171	96	119	123[c]
Land area (1,000 hectares)									
— 2000	297,319	77,088	13,017	14,335	6,271	4,008	30	412,068T	…
— 2008	297,319	77,088	13,017	14,335	6,271	3,839	30	411,899T	…
Land use									
Arable land (% of land area)									
— 2000	54.7	27.6	61.9	16.4	14.6	3.2	13.3	51.3	…
— 2008	53.2	26.4	60.7	16.4	19.9	3.3	13.3	49.8	…
Permanent cropped area (% of land area)									
— 2000	3.1	0.9	3.2	0.7	15.9	0.6	16.7	3.0	…
— 2008	3.8	1.1	6.1	0.8	15.1	0.7	13.3	3.8	…
Irrigated land (as % of cropland)									
— 2003–08[d]	31	73	62	28	…	…	7	39	…
Daily dietary consumption									
Daily dietary energy consumption (kcal/person/day)									
— 2000–02	2,280	2,270	2,170	2,260	2,360	…	2,550	2,268	2,570
— 2005–07	2,300	2,250	2,250	2,350	2,390	…	2,680	2,291	2,630
Intensity of food deprivation (kcal production against minimum daily requirement)									
— 2000–02	260	270	290	230	250	…	180	263	240
— 2005–07	260	280	290	190	250	…	80	264	242
Undernourished people									
number (millions)									
— 2000–02	200.6	36.1	42.3	4.6	3.9	…	0.0	287.5T	816.0T
— 2005–07	237.7	43.4	41.7	4.5	3.8	…	0.0	331.1T	835.2T
% of total population									
— 2000–02	19	24	29	18	20	…	8	21	17
— 2005–07	21	26	27	16	19	…	7	22	16

Notes: a: Data refer to 1999. b: Data refer to 2007. c: Data refer to 2008. d: Data refer to most recent year available.

Sources: Rows 1, 4, 5, 6, 7, 9, 10, 11: FAO 2011a; Rows 2, 3: World Bank 2011f; Row 8: FAO 2011a and World Bank 2011f; Row 12: FAO 2011b and World Bank 2011f; Row 13: FAO 2011b.

11. Energy and Environment

	India	Pakistan	Bangladesh	Nepal	Sri Lanka	Bhutan	Maldives	South Asia (weighted average)	Developing countries
Energy use per capita (kg of oil equivalent)									
— 2000	452	461	132	332	445	...	...	418	892
— 2008	545	499	175	340	443	...	...	497	1,157
Total electricity production (billion kwh)									
— 2000	562.2	68.1	15.8	1.7	7.0	...	...	654.8T	5,552.9T
— 2008	830.1	91.6	35.0	3.1	9.2	...	...	969.0T	9,174.7T
Motor vehicles per kilometer of road									
— 2007	3	8	...	...	11	...	...	4	...
The number of disaster-affected people (000)									
— 2000	100,425	0	2,853	51	775	1	...	104,105T	...
— 2008	4,267	20,398	877	13	239	0	...	25,795T	...
Economic losses from natural disasters (million US$)									
— 2000	1,496	0	500	6	3	0	...	2,005T	...
— 2008	2,149	9,518	0	0	105	0	...	11,772T	...

Sources: Rows 1, 2: World Bank 2011f; Row 3: World Bank 2010; Rows 4, 5: CRED 2011.

12. Governance

	India	Pakistan	Bangladesh	Nepal	Sri Lanka	Bhutan	Maldives	South Asia (weighted average)	Developing countries
Average annual rate of inflation (2000=100)									
— 2000	4.0	4.4	2.2	2.5	6.2	4.0	...	3.9	...
— 2009	10.9	13.7	5.4	11.6	3.5	4.4	4.0	10.6	...
Annual growth of food prices (1999–2001=100)									
— 2000	1.8	2.2	2.6	0.4[a]	4.5[b]	2.2[c]	−10.5	1.93	...
— 2009	7.5	23.7	7.2	16.7[a]	2.6[b]	9.0	1.5	9.42	...
Annual growth of money supply (%)									
— 2000	15.2	12.1	19.4	18.9	12.9	17.4	4.2	15.3	...
— 2009	18.0	14.8	20.3	29.4	18.7	29.7	12.5	18.1	...
Total revenue (% of GDP)									
— 2000	9.8	13.4	8.5	10.5	16.4	23.2	30.0	10.2	...
— 2009	9.7	14.5	11.3	14.0	14.6	22.7	50.6	10.6	...
Total expenditure (% of GDP)									
— 2000	15.5	18.9	14.5	16.3	25.0	42.2	37.3	15.9	...
— 2009	16.3	19.8	15.3	19.6	24.0	33.7	60.3	16.8	...
Budget deficit/surplus (% of GDP)									
— 2000	−5.7	−5.4	−4.5	−4.3	−9.3	−3.9	−4.4	−5.5	...
— 2009	−6.6	−5.1	−3.3	−1.9	−9.8	1.8	−6.7	−6.1	...
Tax revenue (% of GDP)									
— 2000	9.0	10.1	7.6[c]	8.7	14.5	10.3	13.8	9.0	10.9
— 2009	9.8	9.3	8.6	12.2	13.3[d]	9.1	14.1	9.7	14.0[d]
Tax revenue by type (%)									
Taxes on international trade									
— 2001	15.7	11.2	31.1	23.7	10.9	1.1	26.4	16.8	8.2[e]
— 2009	12.6	8.0	24.4	16.2	14.3[d]	1.0	30.1	13.3	6.9[d]
Taxes on income, profits and capital gains									
— 2001	26.7	21.0	11.5	16.1	14.5	13.8	2.1	24.2	16.1[e]
— 2009	46.6	25.2	19.3	14.5	18.4[d]	15.9	4.1	40.4	21.1[d]
Taxes on goods and services									
— 2001	30.1	34.8	24.8	31.4	57.0	6.3	12.8	30.5	33.1[e]
— 2009	23.0	31.8	28.8	34.8	44.6[d]	10.4	10.0	25.0	35.8[d]
Other taxes									
— 2001	0.2	5.6	4.5	2.3	3.5	1.0	0.5	1.3	2.1[e]
— 2009	0.1	0.4	3.4	5.1	7.9[d]	0.1	0.4	0.6	1.9[d]
Public expenditure per capita									
Public expenditure per capita on defence (US$)									
— 2000	14.1	20.8	4.5	2.1	43.9	...	...	13.9	...
— 2009	31.5	27.8	6.2	6.6	73.1	...	...	28.4	...
Public expenditure per capita on debt Servicing (US$)									
— 2000	10.7	20.7	5.4	4.2	42.1	11.9	72.8	11.5	68.6
— 2009	14.0	20.2	5.9	6.0	69.8	108.3	223.6	14.5	94.8
Public expenditure per capita on education (US$)									
— 2000	20.0	9.8	8.0	6.7	26.1[f]	44.4	76.6[f]	17.5	44.7
— 2006–09[g]	26.4	25.6	11.9	19.9	22.4	87.1	332.9	24.8	82.8
Public expenditure per capita on health (US$)									
— 2000	5.7	3.4	3.7	2.8	15.7	40.6	93.4	5.4	28.3
— 2009	16.3	8.2	5.9	8.8	37.0	82.5	247.2	14.5	84.6
Imports of goods and services (% of GDP)									
— 2000	14.2	14.7	19.2	32.4	49.6	51.3	71.6	15.6	25.5
— 2009	24.0	20.4	26.6	37.4	27.9	48.3	94.2	24.2	26.4

Continued

	India	Pakistan	Bangladesh	Nepal	Sri Lanka	Bhutan	Maldives	South Asia (weighted average)	Developing countries
Net inflow of FDI (million US$)									
— 2000	3,584.2	308.0	280.4	−0.5	172.9	2.5ᶜ	...	13.1T	148,612.9T
— 2009	34,577.2	2,387.0	674.3	38.2	404.0	36.4	...	112.3T	359,401.4T
Total external debt (% of GDP)									
— 2000	21.8	44.3	33.0	52.2	55.7	47.6	33.0	26.6	36.2
— 2009	17.3	33.2	26.7	29.4	41.0	59.7	53.0	20.0	21.3
Total debt service (% of GDP)									
— 2000	2.4	3.9	1.6	1.9	4.8	1.6	3.2	2.6	5.9
— 2009	1.2	2.1	1.1	1.4	3.4	5.9	4.7	1.3	3.2

Notes: a: Data for urban areas only. b: Data for capital city. c: Data refer to 2001. d: Data refer to 2008. e: Data refer to 2003. f: Data refer to 1998. g: Data refer to most recent year available.

Sources: Rows 1, 3, 7, 8, 10, 11: World Bank 2011f; Row 2: ADB 2010; Rows 4, 6: ADB 2011; Row 9: World Bank 2011a, d, f and MHHDC staff computations. Rows 12, 13: World Bank 2011c and MHHDC staff computations.

KEY TO INDICATORS

Indicator	Indicator table
A, B, C	
Armed forces personnel	
number	7
% of total labour force	7
Birth rate, crude	9
Births attended by trained health staff	6
Birthweight, low	6
Budget, public sector, as % of GDP	
deficit/surplus	12
expenditure, total	12
revenue, total	12
Cereal,	
exports	10
imports	10
production	10
Contraceptive prevalence rate	3
Crop production index	10
Children,	
one-year-olds fully immunized,	10
against DPT	3
against measles	3,6
against polio	6
against tuberculosis	6
in the labour force	6
mortality rate, infant	1, 6
mortality rate, under-five	4, 6
not in primary school	2
reaching grade 5, (%)	2
D	
Dietary energy consumption,	
daily, kcal per person	10
intensity of food deprivation	10
Death rate, crude	9
Debt external,	
total	8
% of GDP	12
Debt servicing,	
% of exports	8
% of GDP	8, 12
per capita expenditure	12
Defence expenditure,	
annual increase (%)	7
% of central govt.	7
% of GDP	7
per capita	7, 12
total	7
Dependency ratio	9
Disaster, natural	
affected people	11
economic losses	11
E	
Economic activity rate, female as % of male	5
Education expenditure, public	
% of GDP	2, 8
per capita	12
Electricity production	11
Energy use, per capita	11

Indicator	Indicator table
Enrolment,	
combined 1st, 2nd and 3rd level, gross ratio,	
female	5
total	1, 2
primary level, gross (%),	
female	5
total	2
primary level, net (%),	
female	5
total	2
secondary level (%),	
gross	2
net	2
technical and vocational (%)	2
Exports, % of GDP	8
F	
FDI, net inflow	12
Fertility rate, total	9
Food,	
exports, % of merchandise exports	10
imports, % of merchandise imports	10
production, net per capita index	10
prices, average annual growth	12
Forest production,	
fuel wood	10
round wood	10
Fuel, consumption	11
G	
GDP,	
sectoral composition, value added %,	
agriculture	8
industry	8
services	8
growth rate	1
per capita growth	8
per capita, PPP US$	1,8
total	8
Gender Inequality Index	1, 5
Global militarization index	
index	7
rank	7
GNI per capita	8
Gross capital formation	8
Gross domestic savings	8
H, I, J	
Health expenditure, public	
% of GDP	3, 8
per capita	12
HIV/AIDS, affected	
population, total	3
adult population (as % age 15–49)	3, 4
Human Development Index	1
Illiterate,	
adults,	
% of adult population	4
number	4

Indicator	Indicator table	Indicator	Indicator table
female,		under-five,	
% of adult (female) population	4	% of total	6
number	4	number	6
Immunization, one-year-olds fully immunized,		under 18,	
against DPT	3	% of total	6
against measles	3, 6	number	6
against polio	6	urban,	
against tuberculosis	6	annual average growth rate	9
Import,		number	9
arms	7	Poverty, income	
goods and services	12	population below 1.25 $ a day	4, 8
Income share: ratio of top 20% to bottom 20%	8	population below national poverty line,	
Inflation, average annual rate	12	rural	8
		urban	8
K, L		total	4
Labour force,		Professional and technical workers, female	5
annual growth rate	9	Pupil teacher, ratio	2
child	6	Researchers	
female	9	R&D expenditures	2
male	9		
total	9	**S**	
Land,		Sanitation, population	
area	10	with access	3
irrigated, % of cropland	10	without access,	
Land use,		number	4
arable (% of land area)	10	percentage	4
permanent cropped area (% of land area)	10	School life expectancy,	
Life expectancy at birth,		primary to secondary	2
female	5	primary to tertiary	2
total	1		
Literacy rate, adult		**T, U, V**	
female	1, 5	Tax revenue,	
female as % of male	5	by	
male	2	goods and services	12
youth	2	income, profits and capital gain	12
total	1, 2	international trade	12
		other taxes	
M, N, O		% of GDP	8, 12
Malnourished, weight for age (children under-five)	4	Trade, % of GDP	8
Money supply, average annual growth	12	Undernourishment,	
Mortality rate,		number	10
infant	1, 6	% of total population	10
maternal	3	Unemployment rate,	
under-five	4, 6	female	5
Motor vehicle, per km of road	11	total	59
Official development assistance received, net			
% of GDP	8	**W, X, Y, Z**	
total	8	Water, population using improved	
		with access	3
P, Q, R		without access,	
Parliament, seats held by women	5	number	4
Physicians, per 1,000 people	3	percentage	4
Population,		Weapons, number of heavy	7
annual growth rate	1, 9		
female,			
% of male	5		
number	5		
rural	9		
total, estimated	1, 9		